CONSUMER AND OPINION RESEARCH

Consumer
and
Opinion Research

THE QUESTIONNAIRE TECHNIQUE

ALBERT B. BLANKENSHIP, Ph.D.

Director of Market Research
N. W. Ayer & Son, Inc.

HARPER & BROTHERS PUBLISHERS

NEW YORK AND LONDON

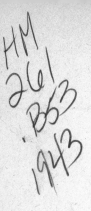
CONSUMER AND OPINION RESEARCH

To
My Wife

Contents

Preface

wwwwwwwwwwwwwwwwwwwwwwwwwwwwwwwwwwwwwwwwwwwwwwwwwwwwwww

DURING the past few years there has been an increasing emphasis upon questionnaire surveys of various publics. The opinion polls have inquired on subjects ranging from attitudes towards management of the war to acceptance of birth control. Less known to the public are the commercial surveys, although these outnumber the publicized polls.

Both commercial and opinion surveys use the same basic technique—the questionnaire. Criticism of opinion polls has been offered both by popular writers and technicians in the research field. Criticism of commercial polls and their techniques has largely been limited to those within the field. Instructors in sociology, psychology, marketing, advertising, political science and statistics have been interested in both of these developments.

The entry of our country into war has sharply increased the importance of both commercial and opinion surveys. Our national government has entered the survey field in order to have public guidance for some of its decisions. Since the questionnaire survey has become more important, there seems a need for critical summary and discussion of the techniques employed.

The present volume is intended to meet this need. It should therefore have its uses in college classes. It is not intended as an exhaustive analysis, but rather as a running narrative, the more complete elements of which can be filled in by supplementary reference. At the same time it is hoped that the volume will prove to be a convenient reference for practitioners in the survey field. It should help the business man to obtain a clearer concept of the steps in conducting a survey.

The emphasis throughout is upon techniques. The book concentrates discussion on the "formalized" sort of questionnaire, where a specific set of questions is used.

Many individuals have contributed directly and indirectly to the publication of this volume. Those whose work is quoted are acknowledged by stating the reference. Mr. J. M. Wallace and Mr. W. B. Ricketts, both of N. W. Ayer & Son, gave many hours of time in critical reading of portions of the manuscript. Lieutenant-Commander John G. Jenkins, U.S.N.R., gave many valuable suggestions. Drs. Paul F. Lazarsfeld, Director of the Office of Radio Research, Columbia University; Sydney Roslow, Director of the Pulse of New York; and Lucien Warner, Office of War Information, gave unstintingly of their time to make suggestions on the manuscript. Mr. Harry H. Field, Director of the National Opinion Research Center, made many useful suggestions. Mrs. Marion Walker, my sister, was kind enough to read proof.

In many places throughout the book there are discussions of studies without any description of the source. Most of these were conducted by the staff of N. W. Ayer & Son, and the writer is indebted to this organization for permission to use such examples. Naturally, however, the writer alone is responsible for any errors or arguments in the volume.

Albert B. Blankenship

N. W. Ayer & Son, Inc., Philadelphia

CONSUMER AND OPINION RESEARCH

CHAPTER 1

Introduction

vvvvvvvvvvvvvvvvvvvvvvvvvvvvvvvvvvvvvvvvvvvvvvvvvvvvvvvvvvvvvvvvvvvvvvvvvvvvvvvv

THIS country is engaged in a total war. The prime thought rightly is for the fight, but winning the fight alone will not insure victory. We must not only defeat the Axis nations, but retain an essentially democratic government and a functioning economic system.

Public opinion[1] will play an important role in both of these victory aspects. The tool for discovering the status of public opinion is the questionnaire technique.

Use of public opinion poll results by our national government demonstrates that this country is still being run by and for the people. Industries and manufacturers are making use of the consumer questioning process to keep pace with changing markets and conditions.

1. *Opinion polls in wartime.* The opinion poll has taken on increased importance during this time of war. Legislators are guided in part by polling results. Before our entry into the war, some 75 per cent of our Congressmen were influenced by results of opinion surveys (15)[2]. Our public officials are now more interested in opinion polling results than ever. A government office conducts periodic opinion surveys, reporting results to the President. Apparently both the legislative and executive branches of our government are influenced, to some extent, by questionnaire survey results.

The present conflict has been termed, among other things, a "battle of propaganda." Each belligerent prepares propaganda

[1] "Public opinion" is broadly defined here as any public reaction obtained to questionnaire studies, whether the inquiries refer to opinion, knowledge or behavior.

[2] Parenthetical numbers refer to sources listed at the end of each chapter.

designed for maintenance of home morale and destruction of enemy morale. The opinion survey can determine whether or not propaganda has changed attitudes. Questionnaires can also be designed to measure morale.

The questionnaire survey can determine how many are reached by a particular propaganda operation. There are questionnaire techniques for checking the size of a radio audience or the number of people reading a particular portion of editorial or advertising matter in publications.

2. *Commercial surveys in war-time.* The commercial survey is useful in helping a producer remain in business in these difficult times, or making possible the planning of postwar production and distribution.

Government orders are exerting a tremendous influence in changing the characteristics of many products. In the furniture field manufacturers may no longer use such items as steel springs, kapok, or rubber filler. Consumer preference surveys can help such companies to devise substitutes containing real appeal.

The war is changing product containers. Tin cans and fancy containers are disappearing from the market. A company which must change its container will be on safer ground if it considers consumer desire as well as government requirement. An unattractive container can cause a drop in sales. A consumer survey can be designed to show the relative appeal of a number of different containers.

Scarcity of goods and difficulties of transportation are also causing container and product changes. Where a product must be changed, the questionnaire procedure in many cases may help to tell whether production should be suspended for the duration, or whether a substitute should be offered. Placing a new item on the market and co-ordinating distribution with a sales campaign is an expensive process; a well designed consumer questionnaire will frequently provide a speedy basis for decision as to whether or not a campaign will be fruitful.

War can break down a nation's economic structure if, at the conclusion of the fighting, the war material producers are not able to adapt their production to consumer needs. There should be little reason for this to happen at the end of the present conflict. American ingenuity, through the survey technique, has provided a means for determining not only what the people will want and buy, but how much they will be willing to pay for it. Equipped with such knowledge, the manufacturer will be in a better position to make a change-over to profitable consumer production.

In Great Britain, experience has shown (20) that a wartime material shortage sometimes causes retailers to buy raw materials, package them, and offer them in competition with branded goods. The survey is a quick and relatively inexpensive means of continually checking the movement of branded goods, and will tell the manufacturer of such an occurrence.

The survey enables the manufacturer to adjust also to the changing consumer market. A *Fortune* analysis (24) suggests that the war is aiding union-protected workers and farmers, in particular. In the past these groups were given relatively little marketing consideration. For adaptation to this changing market and its requirements, the survey is a simple approach.

Purchasing habits are changing due to rationing. Shopping trips to central business areas are decreasing because of the increased demand upon public carriers. A fast method of checking upon shifts of this nature is continuous research. Surveys will also tell the manufacturer about new habits of consumers in relation to conservation of materials, and will therefore provide him with additional clues on the marketing of his goods.

Advertising appeals are shifting. The manufacturer is not so interested in creating a market as he is in keeping his name before the public. At least one research organization has made a comprehensive study of what the consumer wants to be told in advertising, and more of this sort of information will be gathered as the war goes on. By adjusting advertising to the war situation, the advertiser will win greater readership, and therefore will register his company name even if he cannot sell goods.

The very effectiveness of advertising media is undergoing a change. One of the radio-audience measuring organizations (14, 25) has found that newscasts obtain a marked increase in 1942 over 1941, so that newscasts presumably are now a better buy than they were in 1941.

Since some of the leading periodicals have changed their purchase price (and some the nature of their contents), it may be that the character of their circulation has changed. Such possibilities require careful checking before the advertiser can reach any conclusions. The survey is useful here because it is inexpensive, yet reliable.

ORIGIN AND DEVELOPMENT OF QUESTIONNAIRE SURVEYS

The survey technique has been used by business for the past twenty years. Persons with scientific background have been common in the field since 1930. Let's trace the antecedents of the present-day questionnaire study.

1. *Journalism.* Newspapers conducted some of the earliest questionnaire researches in this country. In 1824 the *Harrisburg Pennsylvanian* took a straw vote to measure Presidential sentiment (5, p. 35). A month later a southern newspaper canvassed political meetings in North Carolina to measure relative strength of the Presidential possibilities. By the turn of the century straw-votes were a more common affair. Such papers as *The New York Herald* polled voters in an effort to measure candidate sentiment.[3]

By the twenties, straw-votes were the vogue for many publications. The *Literary Digest* canvassed opinion about both candidates and issues. Straw-votes had become so popular by 1928 that there were some 85 such efforts to measure sentiment for the various Presidential nominees (22).

Most of these straw-votes were conducted by mailing ballots to any list of names the publication could obtain. Many of the studies were inaccurate. Causes for distortion in mail surveys will be discussed in later chapters.

2. *Psychology.* The technique of the questionnaire was adapted by those in the intelligence-testing movement during the early twentieth century. In the First World War there was the first use of the scientific questionnaire on a large scale. Our Army used a printed intelligence test which could be administered to a group, and is now using a similar sort of test for purposes of personnel

[3] A detailed history of straw-votes can be found in (22).

classification. Simultaneously questionnaire technique was adapted for measurement of personality characteristics. Professor L. L. Thurstone devised the first attitude scale in the late twenties.[4]

3. *Commercial research.* The earliest known research concerning markets was performed by N. W. Ayer & Son in 1879 (11). The Ayer management was soliciting a threshing machine account, and was told to make up a list of newspapers in which the manufacturer could run advertisements. The Ayer management decided that it needed crop statistics to prepare this list. The firm wired state officials and informed publishers throughout the country. It obtained a fairly complete record of crop statistics. Along with this, data on circulation and rates of appropriate newspapers throughout the areas were assembled.

This is a far cry from the questionnaire study, but it was the gathering of information about a market. Since the questionnaire procedure is one of the specialized techniques of market analysts, there is no question that this first market research was one of the antecedents of the present-day questionnaire study.

Although a few organizations had commercial research staffs by the time of the First World War (3, 10), no real impetus in this movement occurred until after the war. The excess of production capacity and a shrinkage of markets at that time forced a shift of executive attention from production to marketing. New markets and new appeals had to be found, and the marketing research specialist began to come into his own.

Market research studies before the twenties were largely the analysis of market statistics on such facts as the number of persons in a given area who had telephones. This was a census type of operation as distinguished from what we now call the questionnaire approach.

Psychologists and commercial research experts had got together a few years previously in order to pool some of their training and

[4] Although the attitude scale is roughly similar to the opinion poll of today, it does differ in certain important respects. The attitude scale contains a number of statements all bearing on the same general issue, and the respondent is asked to indicate his degree of feeling about each one. In addition, the attitude scale, though useful with groups, was devised primarily for individual application. Where groups are used, they are generally college students, rather than the entire population.

experience. As early as 1913 psychologists were having "juries' of respondents rank advertisements in their "order of merit," and this technique was quickly adopted by those in the advertising field (23). This is one of the earliest known examples of the commercial use of the questionnaire approach. Although copy testing, as it is known, has a separate history, it is so closely related to the usual questionnaire procedure that many organizations now in the commercial or opinion survey field also use their same personnel in copy testing.

4. *Modern surveys.* By the early 1930's the presence of scientifically trained surveyors was common in the field. Close attention was being paid to such problems as the phrasing of questions and obtaining a sample of respondents who would be similar in their characteristics to the population they were intended to represent. By 1934 one organization was conducting careful studies on brand-buying behavior (*18*). Two years later a number of organizations were in the presidential poll field, and some of these groups conducted commercial surveys as well.

The Scope of Surveys

The political candidate poll and the social issue poll are well known to the American public, but it is not so commonly realized that the survey approach is utilized to an even greater extent by American business. Numerical superiority belongs to business, as this list of major types of surveys shows:

1. *The political and social issue poll.* This is the sort of survey which inquires whether you are for or against prohibition, whether or not you favor price control, etc.
2. *The candidate poll.* This type of survey measures sentiment on candidates, and is the usual type of pre-election poll, such as the Gallup presidential poll.
3. *Copy testing.* Most copy tests are designed to determine, either before or after an advertisement has been published, what its relative efficiency is. For example, before an advertisement is run, it may be exhibited, along with others, to a group of consumers who may rank the advertisements, or simply select the one they believe best.
   After an advertisement is run, a survey can be made to determine the number of people seeing and reading the copy. Though there are many

other questionnaire procedures sometimes used in copy testing, they will not be outlined here.

4. *Evaluation of advertising appeals.* Questionnaires may be designed to measure motives of consumers in purchasing. Once such motives have been uncovered, use of associated advertising appeals is relatively simple.

5. *Media measurement.* This is a broad heading, and covers many different kinds of questionnaire surveys. There are services which measure the size of audience listening to individual radio programs. Most of the better-known publications conduct their own research on the group they reach, so that they can describe their audience to actual and potential advertisers.

6. *Product research.* By the questionnaire procedure it is frequently possible to determine whether or not a new item will have a market, and what the market will be willing to pay for it. There are many specific applications of this technique. If a change in a product is being considered, a consumer survey may aid in determining whether or not it has consumer approval. Even such an apparently minor item as a packaging change can affect consumer sales, and a survey may aid the manufacturer in advance in making his decision.

7. *Movement of branded goods and causes for shifts.* The Psychological Barometer of the Psychological Corporation (*18*) is a continuous series of consumer studies inquiring about the brand of various commodities last purchased by the respondent. By the use of these results, a company can determine its relative position in the market, and can obtain a quick measurement of shifts that might not be reflected for months in sales figures.

A survey of this sort can also measure what brands were bought previously by the respondent, and why a shift, if any, was made. A manufacturer whose sales are dropping is thus able to measure any consumer reason for the drop-off.

8. *Testing of sales methods.* The survey may be used to learn dealers' methods of selling a product. One recent survey made among consumers showed that their fuel dealers had not "sold" them on the idea that the coal stoker is a clean, convenient, and economical method of heating (*7*). Of course with present transportation difficulties and government restrictions, there is no selling of oil burners.

Recently there has been some interest in the "point of purchase" survey, in which the behavior of clerk and customer are observed, with the observer asking appropriate questions of each following the sale. One recent application of this technique provided evaluation of consumer appeal for each of two proposed names for an aspirin product. When consumers asked the clerk for aspirin, they were asked whether they preferred brand X or brand Y, both of which were the identical product.

A record of the frequency with which each name was selected provided the manufacturer with an indication of the relative appeal of the names.

9. *Public relations studies.* The opinion sort of survey is useful to measure public reaction toward a particular company or industry, its practices and products. Since the object of any public relations program is to make attitudes more favorable toward the interested organization, polls have a definite part to play here. A measurement of opinion before, during, and after the program will provide some indication of the program's success.

There are other specific uses of the questionnaire procedure; this list is informative rather than exhaustive. A natural question at this point is: Who conducts these surveys? Since there can be such a range of purposes of surveys, are the types of survey conductors just as diverse?

TYPES OF ORGANIZATIONS CONDUCTING SURVEYS

The answer to this last question is "yes"; there are persons with all sorts of backgrounds in the survey field. As an approach to this subject, a brief review of the types of organizations which conduct surveys will be helpful.

1. *Public opinion survey agencies.* The American Institute of Public Opinion, of which Dr. George Gallup is director, is best-known among this group. This organization conducts periodic surveys of opinion on both issues and candidates and releases its results to subscribing newspapers.

2. *Commercial research organizations.* There are a number of such organizations, and the quality and nature of their work varies considerably. Some of these firms are wholly competent to take a vague problem, to state it adequately, to prepare a sound questionnaire, to obtain a cross-section of respondents, and to write a good report which answers the problems raised.

3. *Advertising agencies.* Many large advertising agencies have their own research organizations which can perform a survey from start to finish. Although these were originally set up for the purpose of performing research in line with advertising problems, many of them will now undertake almost any sort of investigation as an aid to the client, whether it be a public relations study, a marketing investigation, or something else.

The smaller agencies, plus a few of the larger ones, have one or two men competent in research who, when necessity arises, can engage a commercial research organization to undertake a study.

4. *Publishing firms.* Publishers of periodicals have set up their own research staffs. The work that this personnel performs may be of various sorts. Surveys for advertisers and prospective advertisers may be conducted as a service, even though unrelated to publishing. Frequent studies among readers are conducted to define better to advertisers and agencies the groups that they reach (in terms of sex, age, income level, locality, and the like). Some of the publications do "editorial research," in which they make an effort, by questioning a sample of their readers, to find out what portions of the publication are read and, among those read, which are liked and disliked.

To indicate the extent to which research is offered as a service by publishers: The *New York World-Telegram* has a continuing block-by-block analysis, in terms of income level of families, of the whole of New York City.

5. *Manufacturers.* Some of the larger manufacturers also have their own commercial research departments in order to keep in touch with consumer developments and ideas.

General Motors Corporation, for example, has spent thousands of dollars keeping abreast of what consumers want in the way of automobiles. Although this work has been curtailed for the duration of the war, it is interesting to learn that the company believes customer research to be as important as engineering research in the designing of automobiles. Naturally the company does not expect the public to design cars, but if the company can find out which of two possibilities is preferred, it then has some idea of what design to use.

Such organizations as Procter & Gamble, Lever Brothers, Eastman Kodak, and General Electric have also been active along the lines of commercial research.

6. *Public relations firms.* At least one public relations firm has experimented with its own research division. Since the survey is such a natural part of public relations activities, it seems safe to say that in the future the large public relations firms will probably have such personnel within their organizations.

7. *Trade associations.* Trade organizations have entered the survey field. There are frequent problems within an industry which the survey can aid in answering. The Magazine Marketing Service, for instance, is an organization set up by a number of magazine publishers. It is engaged in research which will establish the "marketing pattern" of magazines. This group intends to find out to what sort of persons magazines as a group go. They will learn the relationship, for instance, between the number of magazines read and the income level of the family.

The usual trade organization does not have a complete research organization. Ordinarily it has a research man or two who determines the problem and perhaps develops the specific survey procedure. A survey organization is called in to handle the matter of making calls and summarizing the report.

8. *The federal government.* For several years the Bureau of Agricultural Economics, in the Department of Agriculture, has been conducting opinion surveys to determine how well its farm policies were received. Recently another government agency is conducting opinion polls which are reported to the President.

9. *Endowed organizations.* A relatively new development in the survey field is the appearance of endowed organizations which perform survey activities. Dr. Paul Lazarsfeld is Director of the Office of Radio Research, Columbia University, a Rockefeller-endowed organization, which conducts noncommercial surveys on radio listening habits and public opinion. The National Opinion Research Center, located at the University of Denver, is another foundation-sponsored organization. This group has been endowed by the Field Foundation and has as its functions:

"1. to establish the first non-profit, noncommercial organization to measure public opinion in the United States. . . .

2. to make available to legislators, government departments, academicians, and non-profit organizations a staff of experts in the science of public opinion measurement, and a highly trained nation-wide corps of interviewers.

3. to analyze and review the results of surveys made by other polling organizations.

4. to create at the University of Denver a research center to discover, test, and perfect new methods, techniques and devices for ascertaining the status of public opinion.

5. to provide at the University of Denver a graduate department devoted to the study of the new science of public opinion measurement" (19).

This organization has an opportunity to make notable progress in the field of survey techniques, as well as to aid nonprofit organizations and others in conducting opinion polls. Already the Center is co-operating with government agencies in the measurement of public opinion.

10. *Colleges and universities.* A few colleges and universities have departments that conduct occasional surveys. These are generally non-profit surveys, conducted either for pure research purposes or for the edification of students who are learning the problems and techniques.

11. *Private individuals.* At least one Congressman has been "polling" his constituents on issues of national importance by sending them post-

cards on which to check their feelings. There are professors of marketing, psychology, advertising, sociology, political science, and business administration who have, on occasion, undertaken surveys of their own, either for commercial or for pure research purposes.

This discussion naturally leads back again to the question of who conducts surveys—what sort of people are active in the field.

UNDER WHAT DISCIPLINE DO SURVEYS BELONG?

Discussion shows many varieties of surveys, many types of organizations active in the field. There are almost as many types of persons in the work. Gallup (of the American Institute of Public Opinion) and Link (Psychological Corporation) are psychologists. Robinson (Opinion Research Corporation) and Stouffer (conducting questionnaire studies for the War Department) received their training in sociology. There are others in the field from statistics, market research, advertising, journalism, political science, and economics. Which of all these disciplines can call the survey its own?

No categorical answer to this question can be given. Claims and contributions of each field must be considered.

1. *Journalism*. The historical advantage lies with the journalists, who began straw balloting over a century ago. But straw ballots have not survived, and there are now few journalists active in the field. Periodicals which now publish survey results depend on experts from other fields, whether inside or outside of their organizations.

Journalists have a distinct contribution to make. The journalist is trained to work close to the public. Thus he is not only able to aid in setting the problem (by defining what the public can and will answer), but he should have such a broad social consciousness from his experience that he will be able to frame issues which are of vital social import.

The journalist will be of value in preparing the report. This is one of the most difficult portions of the technique. There is distinctly a place for the journalist in the survey field.

2. *Psychology*. A psychologist was one of the first to work with

a scientific questionnaire; psychology also has some claim to priority in the field. But there is more than this to its claim.

Psychology may be regarded as the study of behavior. The survey technique measures and explains behavior. Many surveys are designed to uncover motivating influences, and motivation research is commonly accepted as a field of psychological study. In many university psychology departments there are courses which cover the survey technique. At one university a doctorate in psychology can actually be earned with market research as a specialty.

Psychologists have a contribution to make in questionnaire development, but this is a small portion of the value they have in survey work.

The psychologist's traditional background has been to study individual behavior. In surveys, therefore, the psychologist tends to be on the lookout for all sorts of factors which may have any relation to the individual's reply—his income level, his political affiliation, his occupation, his age. It is important to learn the relation of such factors as these to replies in order to make deductions; thorough conclusions cannot be drawn without this extraction process.

The psychologist is the only one in the survey field who has been trained in the experimental laboratory. He knows how important it is to control all factors except the one variable whose influence is being measured. Since survey results can be influenced by such factors as the nature and number of the respondents interviewed, the wording and sequence of the questions asked, and the way in which interviewing is conducted, it is clear that poor control of one or more of these and other factors could distort the results obtained. Laboratory training makes these necessary factors of control obvious to the psychologist. His training in experimental techniques will make him strive continuously to improve the survey procedures.

3. *Political science.* The political scientist has contributions to make, particularly in the case of the opinion poll. He is invaluable in the setting of political issues and in the interpretation of results obtained with these issues. Political scientists were among the first

to indicate some of the sampling problems in polls. They indicated, for instance, that the idea of one farmer in upstate New York is more important politically than the opinion of one New York City resident. Why? Because among farmers a greater proportion of persons cast votes. In a sample of respondents interviewed on a pre-election poll the proportion of interviews must be made in accordance with voting population rather than with total or adult population.

The political scientist has some little priority in the polling field. In the middle twenties one of the earliest papers on scientific poll work was produced jointly by a political scientist and a psychologist. More recently a number of political scientists have been active in the measurement of attitudes.

4. *Sociology*. Sociology is the study of group behavior. Since surveys are usually made with groups which are defined in some terms of social units, it seems clear that this is a field for the sociologist.

The "case history" approach is applicable in questionnaire research. The sociologist, studying individual cases, delves into the background of the individual, probes deeply for information related to the problem. It will be shown later that the survey researcher uses a similar approach in making "conversational interviews" at the time he is attempting to clarify the assigned problem. A survey may be composed of these intensive interviews, which provide opportunity for the uncovering of explanations relating to motivation and behavior.

5. *Economics*. Economists have a role to play in survey work, especially in commercial studies. The business survey frequently concerns studies of markets—buying habits or some other phase of the distributive process. The economist will understand how to interpret survey findings in the light of current economic facts. He will be aware of sources of economic data which bear upon the problem of the questionnaire study.

The economist will also be of value in the contribution he can make in obtaining a cross-section of the public. He is acquainted with sources of statistical data regarding purchasing power and incomes; and he will be able to describe the type of respondents

that should be secured for a survey. He can do more than this—
he is adept at telling just how many families in a survey should
fall within each economic classification, and he will be able to
describe concomitant sampling data—ownership of telephones,
automobiles, refrigerators—that are a part of this.

6. *Market research.* Some of the earliest scientific questionnaire
work came from market research men—men who began describing
markets in terms of available statistical data such as the Census.
Since these men were some of the first in the survey field, they
have obtained comprehensive experience in the questionnaire
technique. Universities offering courses in market research now
include the questionnaire approach as one of the methods of collecting information.

Not only is the market researcher fully competent to obtain
market data before a survey is undertaken, but he is also experienced and trained in all aspects of the procedure—from statement
of the problem to the writing of the report. His contribution to
the technique is present in all phases of the work.

7. *Advertising.* Advertising has value as a background for the
survey man. A good understanding of advertising—its purposes
and techniques—aids the research man, especially when he is confronted with problems concerning advertising and promotion. The
survey researcher with an advertising background will be able to
see just how his questionnaire study will fit into the advertising
scheme—its purposes and values. Because of his broad background
in advertising, he will be aware of other means by which he can
accumulate data required on his particular problem. It is important for the researcher to realize that there frequently are other and
better means than a questionnaire survey for obtaining certain
information.

8. *Statistics.* The surveyor cannot get along without a knowledge of statistics. The statistician has developed the information
essential for knowing how many and what kind of people to question on a particular survey.

The field of statistics has developed the necessary tools for treatment of results. The statistician has indicated methods of determining whether the survey measures what it intended to measure, and

whether it would tend to give the same results if repeated. Since all questionnaire work is designed to collect and summarize data, exactly the process in which statisticians engage, there is no question as to the importance of statistics in the work.

Summary. In a technique so young an argument as to whose field this new survey work is may be expected. The questionnaire procedure is so dependent upon many different disciplines, the technique has grown simultaneously from many fields, and survey work has so many ramifications for government, business, and the public.

It is interesting to observe what happens to a man with specialist training who enters the survey field. The psychologist, for example, normally enters the position not as a psychologist, but rather as a research man. He becomes a practitioner of all phases of the survey research; if he limited himself to psychology as he had learned it, he could not perform the job.

A similar thing happens when a person with any specialized background enters this work; although he makes use of that background, he finds himself (within the bounds of his work) becoming many other things—a statistician, a political scientist, and a journalist. He is confronted with problems which are not only psychological, but sociological, marketing, advertising.

All of the mentioned disciplines have something to offer the new procedure. If a broad training could be secured by a man before he entered the survey field, he would immediately be that much more valuable. When the new survey technique has matured somewhat, men trained broadly probably will appear. Their training may include such diverse but related fields as engineering and English. When men with such a background do appear, progress in the survey field should be more rapid.

References

(1) ADVERTISING RESEARCH FOUNDATION. *Copy Testing*. New York: Ronald, 1939.

*(2) AMERICAN MARKETING ASSOCIATION. *The Technique of Marketing Research*. New York: McGraw-Hill, 1937. See especially pages 3-12.

 * Starred references are those suggested for additional information or details on various topics discussed in each chapter.

*(3) BROWN, L. O. *Market Research and Analysis*. New York: Ronald, 1937. Chapters 1, 2, 3 and 4.

(4) CHICAGO ROUND TABLE DISCUSSION. *Election and Results*. November 6, 1941.

*(5) GALLUP, GEORGE, AND RAE, S. F. *The Pulse of Democracy*. New York: Simon and Schuster, 1940. Chapters 1, 2 and 3.

(6) HARTWELL, DICKSON. "Business Asks the Public How It May Serve Best," *Nation's Business*, May, 1940. Pages 26-28.

(7) HARTWELL, DICKSON. "Domestic Sales Still Open for Intensive Effort, Survey of Household Fuel Users Indicates," *Coal Age*, April, 1940.

(8) HARTWELL, DICKSON. "John Q. Public Answers Nineteen Questions on Coal," *Coal Age*, July, 1939.

(9) HARTWELL, DICKSON. "What the Public Thinks of Food Manufacturers," *Food Industries*, June, 1940.

*(10) HOVDE, H. T. "Recent Trends in the Development of Market Research," *American Marketing Journal*, 1936, 3, 3-19.

(11) HOWER, R. M. *A History of an Advertising Agency*. Cambridge: Harvard Press, 1939.

(12) KAROL, J. J. "Pre-testing New Radio Programs," *Market Research*, 1938, 8, No. 3, 7-10.

*(13) KATZ, DANIEL. "Psychological Tasks in the Measurement of Public Opinion," *Journal of Consulting Psychology*, 1942, 6, 59-65.

(14) LEHMAN, A. W. *War Listening Since Pearl Harbor*. New York: Cooperative Analysis of Broadcasting, 1942.

(15) LEWIS, G. F. "The Congressmen Look at the Polls," *Public Opinion Quarterly*, 1940, 4, 229-231.

(16) LIFE's continuing study of magazine audiences. 1938, 1939, 1940, 1941.

(17) LINK, H. C. *The New Psychology of Selling and Advertising*. New York: MacMillan, 1934.

(18) LINK, H. C., AND LORGE, IRVING. "The Psychological Sales Barometer," *Harvard Business Review*, 1935, 14, 193-204.

(19) NATIONAL OPINION RESEARCH CENTER. Untitled pamphlet on purposes, sponsors, directors, etc. 1941.

(20) NEILSEN, A. C. *Your Marketing in the Days Ahead*. New York: A. C. Neilsen Co., 1942.

(21) REILLY, W. J. *Marketing Investigations*. New York: Ronald, 1929. Chapter 1.

*(22) ROBINSON, C. S. *Straw Votes*. New York: Columbia University, 1932.

(23) STRONG, E. K. "Psychological Methods as Applied to Advertising," *Journal of Educational Psychology*, 1913, 4, 393-404.

(24) UNSIGNED. "The Lost $40 Billion," *Fortune*, August, 1942, 75-79.

(25) UNSIGNED. *Radio listening*: Second quarter, 1942. New York: Cooperative Analysis of Broadcasting, 1942.

CHAPTER 2

General Technique of Conducting Surveys

∿∿

THE basic principle of the survey is that the reactions of a group of persons similar in their characteristics to the entire population will approximate reactions of the entire population. The process of deciding the issues, framing the questions, and interviewing the sample is complicated. The surveyor cannot simply sit at the desk, write the questions, and then question a few people seen on the street corner or in the drugstore—the *Literary Digest* showed some of the dangers.

Before 1936, the *Digest* postcard vote was considered an accurate indicator of public opinion. When it mispredicted the 1936 presidential winner, its flaws became apparent to the layman although they were already clear to the professional.

In that same year Dr. George Gallup, originator of the American Institute of Public Opinion polls, predicted the re-election of Roosevelt. When his poll was correct, the facts highlighted the distinctions between the *Digest* and Gallup methods. Gallup had not actually developed a new technique; he had merely dramatized the procedures which a number of survey agencies had already been using for solution of business problems.

The general outline of techniques used by the "scientific" survey agencies is essentially similar. As with any investigative procedure, the purpose of the study must first be determined. The next logical step is to decide upon the broad outlines of the method of collecting the information. Selecting the respondents to be approached is another problem, and finally the questionnaire must be written and tested to make sure that the procedure is sound. The questionnaire is then utilized to collect the desired information from respondents. Collected material must be summarized. Interpretation of the material follows, and then comes a report of the entire study and its implications.

Although each step will be subsequently discussed in detail, a brief outline of each is given here to illustrate the entire process.

STATING THE PROBLEM

The nature of the problem must be thoroughly grasped before a method of attack can be planned. A baking concern informed a research agency that it wished to increase sales of the bakery. Other than this the client could not state the problem. The research organization had the task of specifying the objectives in research terms so that a procedure for the study could be planned.

This is a common situation; it is only when the executive has been trained in research that he can tell the research personnel precisely what is expected of the survey. The research staff must therefore specify the problem—translate it into research terms.

There are three parts to this process: (1) situation analysis, (2) informal investigation, and (3) statement of objectives.

1. *Situation analysis.* Situation analysis is the process of obtaining sufficient background information about the general problem, the client, and the industry to proceed sensibly. The intensity of this analysis depends upon the general purpose of the investigation. A survey designed to measure consumer acceptance of a new product would not require the detailed situation analysis indicated for a thoroughgoing consumer study of attitudes toward an industry, and reasons for those attitudes.

2. *Informal investigation.* The informal investigation follows. This is an exploration of the subject. During the course of the informal investigation there are conversations with consumers or voters, depending upon the particular survey. Intensive interviewing, without any formalized list of questions, is carried on by experienced investigators. The extent of this step varies with the scope of the survey.

3. *Statement of objectives.* Situation analysis and informal investigation make it possible to restate the original, broad objectives in concrete and research terms. This restatement usually makes

it clear what sort of respondents should be obtained on the survey and what method of collecting the data may be used. It also provides material for development of a concrete list of questions.

METHOD OF COLLECTING THE DATA

Complete understanding of the nature of the problem enables the researcher to begin more detailed planning of the study. A basic problem is the method of collecting people's reactions—whether telephone interviewing, mail questionnaire, or personal interviewing.

1. *The telephone method.* In this method field workers telephone respondents, getting reactions to various questions. This is quick and inexpensive. It is particularly useful where the respondents are hard to see personally.

The method has disadvantages. It is impossible to obtain a cross-section of the entire population. The point has already been made that the basic assumption on any survey is that the representative group of respondents will be similar to the entire population from which the sample has been selected. Telephone owners are not similar to the entire population.

Party lines, found in small towns and rural areas, are almost impossible to use. In rural telephoning the toll charges tend to be expensive. Wartime restrictions of telephoning are another drawback, even if only temporary.

The number and scope of questions asked during the telephone call are limited. There are other disadvantages as well.

2. *The mail questionnaire.* In the case of a mail survey in which a high proportion of replies is received, the cost per reply will be low. The potential inexpensiveness of the study is one of its biggest attractions.

The mail questionnaire is useful with geographically scattered respondents. It might be prohibitive to obtain a scattered sample of rural housewives by any procedure but the mail questionnaire.

In any other procedure there is always a potential danger of bias in the results owing to the investigator. The mail questionnaire eliminates this possibility.

The procedure has disadvantages. It is difficult to obtain a representative mailing list. It is even more difficult to get a representative group of recipients to mail back the replies. Usually those most interested will reply.

3. *The personal interview.* In this method a field worker personally talks to each respondent. This procedure permits rigid control of the sample of respondents.

A questionnaire of wide scope can be used. The questionnaire can be long. The questioner can "probe" into the reactions of the respondent, obtaining full and detailed answers where necessary.

Personal interviewing is expensive. There is potential danger of the interviewer's biasing the results. Despite these and other disadvantages the personal interview method is generally conceded to be best of the three procedures, though there may be exceptions.

DEVELOPMENT OF THE QUESTIONNAIRE

The first draft of the questions is usually a result of "conversations" held during the setting of the problem. Issues are phrased as nearly as possible in terms respondents use. Even so, it is difficult to predict how well a particular question will work in practice. Though some principles can be set for drafting of questions, final selection of question-wording is always a problem requiring testing of phrasings on a number of respondents. To illustrate care required on question-wording, look at the results of one study (2) which asked about propaganda and false news stories received from England and France (before the fall of France) and Germany. It might be assumed that for all practical purposes *propaganda* and *false news stories* have the same connotation in such a setting. The results show otherwise. Alternative phrasings were:

(A) From which countries are we now getting more propaganda: England and France, or Germany?

(B) From which countries are we now getting more false news stories: England and France, or Germany?

	A	B
England and France	23.0%	10.1%
Germany	28.2	33.3
Same	30.1	38.6
Don't Know	18.7	18.0

Results indicate not only that the question-wording must carry the precise shade of meaning intended, but that the question will have to be tried out with a number of people before it is used extensively, to insure that the intended meaning is what the respondents interpret from the phraseology.

Chapter 5 shows that the answers secured are always a function of the form of the question. Chapter 6 shows how the sequence of the questions is fully as important as their form.

Occasionally the accuracy demanded of the investigation will require a preliminary large-scale study. The procedure and advantages of such a step will be outlined in Chapter 7, which discusses the process of testing the questionnaire.

SELECTING THE RESPONDENTS

This is a step closely allied to the method of collecting the data in two ways: (1) the nature of the sample, and (2) the number of questionees.

1. *The nature of the sample.* It has been indicated that the sample must be representative; the problem here is to define the population which the sample is to represent. The sample may be *random* (in which every person in the population has an equal chance to be interviewed) or *controlled* (in which the surveyor defines the sample to be obtained in terms of such factors as age and sex, and then assigns the proper proportion of calls within each classification). The controlled method is preferable in most studies utilizing the personal interview; there are many pitfalls in the path of the investigator when the random method is applied. He may make his calls within a restricted area. He is likely to work within his own age and standard-of-living group. He may call only upon neighbors. Even when told to interview in every eighth residence, he may see that the eighth home appears very pretentious, and therefore go next door.

If the worker is told how many persons to interview in each age, sex, and standard-of-living group, there will be little opportunity for the sample to be biased.

2. *The size of the sample.* Owing merely to the number of

respondents questioned, there will always be a "chance error" on any survey. No survey figure may ever be interpreted as 100 per cent accurate, since the questioning of the entire population from which the sample was selected could be expected to change the results to some extent.

Although sample size cannot reduce any sampling bias, the accuracy of any percentage figure is directly proportionate to the square root of the size of the sample. To double accuracy on a survey the sample size must be quadrupled.

In determining the desirable number of respondents on a survey, the necessary accuracy of results will be the first consideration. Other minor considerations are outlined in Chapter 9.

PREPARING AND DISTRIBUTING MATERIALS

The procedure used in preparing and distributing the materials for the investigation is somewhat different for the mail questionnaire from that for the personal and telephone interview.

1. *The personal and telephone interview.* In both approaches consideration must be given to preparation and distribution of the questionnaire, field workers' instructions, assignment of calls, and the timing of the study.

Method of duplicating the questionnaire depends largely upon the number of blanks required. Typing is possible with a small number of questionnaires. For a larger number, use of a stencil may be considered. If the number of questionnaires required is well up in the thousands, unit-cost may permit a typesetting or photo-offset process.

Prime consideration in format of the questionnaire is ease of the interviewing process. Any feature making the investigator's job simpler is advisable. Indentation of certain questions, condensation of the physical length of the questionnaire (where this can be accomplished without reducing its content), and inclusion of simple instructions on the face of the questionnaire can all help.

The instruction sheet should tell the investigator the purpose of the investigation; whom, when, and where to interview; what introduction to use to obtain co-operation; how to obtain and record sampling information (such as sex, age, and standard of living); how he is to be paid; and how to ask specific questions.

Distribution of blanks is largely a mechanical problem, since at the planning stage the description of the necessary sample will have been sufficiently detailed to make an assignment to each field worker.

The study must be timed so that reactions are representative. Holiday interviewing is undesirable; it is difficult to find a representative group of persons at home, and it is also possible that over holidays people will tend to be more favorable than at other periods. Another aspect of timing is the day of the week and the hour of the day that the investigator can best approach his particular group. This varies with the nature of the sample; it is always easier to find women at home than men.

2. *The mail questionnaire.* Since there is no field worker with the mail questionnaire, there will be no instruction sheet. There will be a covering letter requesting co-operation. The questionnaire must be clear. Physical appearance of the questionnaire must be attractive and interesting to arouse interest of the recipient. Any instructions must be placed right on the questionnaire itself or in the covering letter.

The letter must be adapted to the person to whom it is addressed. A survey among housewives will require a different approach from one used with executives. Judicious preparation of a letter can increase the proportion of returns on a mail survey. There are other techniques for increasing replies—a premium, a duplicate copy of the questionnaire, or a personally typed covering letter.

Distribution of the mailing will differ in accordance with the requirements of the individual survey. In any case there must be provision for checking the proportion of returns from each area to determine whether the return was representative of the mailing on a geographic basis. On some mail questionnaires it is also possible and desirable to obtain additional sampling information such as age and sex, as a further indication of the representativeness of the sample.

Collecting the Information

The mail questionnaire requires no field worker; both the personal and the telephone methods do. In these cases the process of collecting information becomes important; the field worker can bias the replies. Field-work quality can be improved by good selection of field force, having the field workers acquainted with certain principles of interviewing, and careful training and supervision.

1. *Interviewer bias.* Interviewer bias can influence the results obtained owing to preconceptions on the part of the field worker or to poor work throughout.

2. *Principles of interviewing.* If the investigator is instructed to make a few trial calls before beginning an assignment, this will be of some aid. Importance of careful adherence to instruction should be emphasized. Proper timing of calls upon respondents will help. He must understand that his returns must be identical with his assigned sample. Where a formal questionnaire is used, questions must always be asked word-for-word as they appear on the blank. A favorable impression must be made upon the questionee. The field worker must remain neutral throughout the questioning process; he is merely to repeat, not to interpret questions when they are misunderstood. He should record only adequate replies. Finally, he must always be sure that he has recorded all of the required information before completing any call.

3. *Selection of field force.* Although each interviewing job is likely to be unique, it still appears that there are common elements in all field work. Thus it is possible to list a few requirements for investigators: good appearance and manners, intelligence, health, and honesty.

4. *Careful training and supervision.* Potentiality of the field force can be properly developed through training and supervision. Proper field management guarantees high-quality interviewing.

Summarizing the Results

There are several steps in the summarizing of results: the editing of replies, their classification, planning tabulations, examining the data, and preparation of tables.

1. *Questionnaire editing.* Careful editing of the returned questionnaires eliminates errors in the data and prepares the data for tabulation. There are a number of things to look for in editing. Returns should be examined by area and investigator. This sometimes reveals concentration of substandard work (or even dishonest work) which might otherwise be missed.

Incorrect answers should be discarded. In a case in which one answer by a respondent is inconsistent with another he has made, the inconsistency should be eliminated as a source of error. Where possible, through clues on the questionnaire, incomplete answers should be filled in. Sometimes an answer to a subsequent question reveals that a previous answer should be modified.

Numerical answers should be converted to similar units so that the tabulator will not have too difficult a task. To save the tabulator additional trouble, and to insure standard interpretations, the editor should also indicate, in free-comment questions, into what category of answer a particular reply belongs.

2. *Classification of replies.* Classification of replies is the basis for the entire summary work, so the problem needs careful consideration. A classification must be articulate—carefully constructed so that it will hold together and be meaningful. This can be accomplished by first defining only a few groups of responses, and then subdividing these as additional ramifications come to light. Classifications must be psychologically adequate—they must represent the best possible scheme for classification of the replies. This means there will be no overlapping of categories, and no cases which do not fit into the classification scheme.

Classification must be logically correct. It cannot include items put into the same category on different bases. The basis for differentiation must be constant throughout. A classification of coffee brands cannot include those in cans and those in drip grind, because these are different bases for classifying.

The classification must also be psychologically pertinent—it must be meaningful in terms of behavior. This point is explained in Chapter 12.

The meaning of each reply must be carefully considered. The reply "Don't know" can mean several things, depending upon the particular question asked. Other replies should be given detailed consideration for meaning.

3. *Planning the tabulations.* In planning tabulations it is important to consider the purpose of the investigation, possible cross-tabulations of questions, speed with which results are required, order of question summary, and the problem of hand-versus machine-tabulation. This last question requires especially careful consideration, plus a working knowledge of the two methods and their advantages and disadvantages. Ultimate choice of the method will depend upon the nature of the particular study. By and large, the machine method is used when there is a large number of cross-tabulations.

4. *Examining the data.* Data should be examined carefully for relevancy of the data to the purposes of the investigation, goodness of the sample, reliability of the results, and validity of the results. Some indication has been given as to what is meant by goodness of the sample. Reliability means consistency of the survey results; Chapter 14 discusses this as well as the problem of validity—the extent to which the survey measures what it intends to measure.

5. *Preparation of tables.* Tables must be prepared with thought of how each aids in answering purposes of the investigation. There are problems in computation of percentages: direction in which to run per cents, selection of the base for the computation, and deciding the detail of percentage calculation. These are discussed in Chapter 12.

PREPARATION OF THE REPORT

The nature of the report varies with the type of audience for whom it is intended. It must be designed so that it will be read. The report consists of conclusions and recommendations, as well as detailed tables and discussion of procedure.

1. *Drawing of conclusions.* First step in the drawing of conclusions is consideration of the facts. Relationships among data are the key for the drawing of conclusions. The process of fractionation will be illustrated in Chapter 13.

From fractionation of data test conclusions can be set up. The test conclusion itself must be subjected to a number of tests.

In one study (2) this question was asked: *Do you think that advertising is less truthful today than it was a year or two ago?* Some 56 per cent replied "No." The casual observer might be ready to conclude that the public believes advertising more truthful than formerly. The results show nothing of the kind. This 56 per cent did not say they thought advertising to be more truthful; they merely said that they didn't believe it was less truthful. This is not just quibbling over terms, for at the time the question was asked another was asked of a comparable sample of respondents: *Do you think that advertising is more truthful today than it was a year ago?* If this question means just the reverse of the preceding one, 56 per cent should be expected to reply "Yes." Actually the proportion was only 47. Here are the results to the two questions:

	Less truthful?	More truthful?
Yes	24.7%	46.7%
No	56.5	31.2
Don't Know	18.8	22.1

Some 24.7 per cent have replied that they think advertising less truthful. An additional 46.7 per cent think it is more truthful. On the average, 20.4 per cent tell us that they don't know. This leaves a remainder of some 8.3 per cent who must believe that advertising is neither more nor less truthful than it was a year ago. This seems to be the only conclusion on beliefs possible from the data.

2. *Making recommendations.* Recommendations are actions suggested from the findings. They must meet several standards in order to be acceptable. These standards are discussed in Chapter 13.

But Is It a Science?

Discussion has shown that the survey must be carefully conducted, with a great deal of developmental testing. With such detailed work and all the controls required, the question arises whether the technique of questionnaire surveys may be classed as a science.

What is a "science"? No two workers seem to agree on a definition, though in common practice anything carefully carried on in an effort to collect sound and reliable data is regarded as scientific, while guesswork and armchair thinking are regarded as the opposite. Physics and chemistry are looked on as sciences largely because their measurements can be so precise. A science is usually considered to be a technique subject to a sufficient number of rigid controls to provide a basis for generalization of principles in the field.

On the basis of these criteria, is the conducting of a questionnaire survey then a science? An effort is made to collect sound and reliable data. But this sort of measurement cannot ever be as precise as that in the physics and chemistry laboratories. It is true that rigid controls are applied all the way through the procedure.

The method of collecting the information is controlled, the sample of respondents is usually rigidly controlled, the questionnaire is carefully devised and tested so that it will work properly, and results are analyzed as objectively as possible. Yet with all of these rigid controls, procedural details are subject to individual judgment. The field is still so young that details of procedure vary from one organization to another. There are even minor differences of opinion within a single organization.

In addition, since every investigation is so specific, requiring such individual application of methodology, it seems useless to pretend that the procedure may be classed as a science.

On the other hand, the methods used are the application of scientific steps. Sampling control is possible largely because of the work of mathematicians, and mathematics is as exact as any field. Questionnaire work, developed chiefly through the industry of psychologists, shows that the work of other scientists is used in the survey procedure. Discussion of the origins of survey work and the contributions of various fields to the procedure, outlined in Chapter 1, shows additional ways in which science aids the survey procedure. The entire exploratory investigation is an effort to anchor more firmly the purposes of the study, so that this is a step in the scientific direction.

Instead of defining the field as a science, it is more reasonable to describe it as the application of scientific principles.

REFERENCES

*(1) BROWN, L. O. *Market Research and Analysis*. New York: Ronald, 1937. Chapter 5.

(2) ROSLOW, SYDNEY, WULFECK, W. H., AND CORBY, P. G. "Consumer and Opinion Research: Experimental Studies on the Form of the Question," *Journal of Applied Psychology*, 1940, 24, 334-346.

CHAPTER 3

Statement of the Problem

~~~~~~

STATEMENT of the problem before the survey begins protects the results from being so ambiguous or broad in scope that analysis is impossible. Statement of the problem aids in determining the method of collecting the survey material, in defining the type of respondents required, in providing a basis for working up a questionnaire, and in suggesting methods for analysis of results. In other words, it gives a unified view of the study by providing a direction in which to channelize work on the particular investigation.

The objectives of a research, as stated by the individual who wants or needs the survey, may be different from the objectives as restated by a research man. The general problem is sharpened and brought into focus for a research attack. A vague assignment is translated into a concrete objective. If the problem is well verbalized, and makes use of the general background of information related to the problem, then translation of the problem into procedure should flow naturally from the process.

On complex investigations there may be four steps in this statement of the problem: (1) situation analysis, (2) an informal investigation, (3) statement of the objectives of the study, and (4) planning of the study in broad outline.

SITUATION ANALYSIS

1. *What it is.* Situation analysis is the securing of pertinent background information. In one study undertaken for an airplane manufacturer it was necessary for the research staff to know the major plane manufacturers and names and purposes of the more

common models before planning how to ask the public about their knowledge of such facts.

The nature of situation analysis varies with the nature of the survey. Where a merchant wants to know public thought and action about his store, his goods, and his policies, dozens of background items about the store must be explored, so that it is possible to focus upon the issues which would constitute the questionnaire. A "once over lightly" situation analysis may suffice for a simple problem. An advertiser wanted to know the size of his radio audience. Since the show was broadcast weekly, in only one town, situation analysis requirements were satisfied by obtaining full details about the broadcast.

2. *Examples*. In one study there was the problem of obtaining listener reaction to a radio broadcast. Details of the broadcast—the station, the day, hour, age on air, and a typical script—were obtained. A previous station study gave listener reaction to this and other shows. A questionnaire was developed from this information, and from talking with some listeners. Some questions asked respondents to compare the program with other programs on the same station to which they listened.

Later it was learned that the show was a station-owned feature broadcast six days a week, the sponsor changing each day. It was too late to get comparisons of the particular advertiser's show with the same show on other days. Since each advertiser could modify the show to some extent, this might have been a better comparison than some of those obtained. One small slip-up in the situation analysis can decrease the value of a study.

Situation analysis may change the concept of the problem. An advertiser sought concrete evidence that his program was definitely contributing to the sale of his product—an expensive luxury. The agency appreciated the difficulty of "proving" that a particular campaign sells goods, and in addition it had the broader point of view that the program was really designed to build up prestige and good will for the client. Discussions with the client revealed his interest in measuring listener reaction, so the problem was reformulated.

3. *Check-list of possible background information to obtain.*

Since full lists are available elsewhere (1, 2), only an abbreviated list is given here.

Check-List of Possible Information

Products (the entire line of goods, the uses to which consumers put these goods, product quality, packaging, price, production methods, seasonal sales variation, secular trends of sales . . . .)

Industry and Company (history of industry, competitive sales trends, competitive sales policies and activities, competitive products . . . .)

Present Market (description of portion of public who purchase item—in terms of location, sex, age . . . .)

Channels of Distribution (method of distributive organization, locations of wholesalers and retailers, methods of selling, wholesaler-retailer relations, wholesale and retail profit margins . . . .)

Nature of Sales Organization (structure and policies, salesman's work, sales and advertising coordination . . . .)

Advertising and Sales Promotion (media used, appeals used, seasonal variations in efforts and their causes . . . .)

This check-list was developed for business questionnaire studies. A similar list cannot be developed for the public opinion study, since the nature of the background information is likely to vary so greatly. A research organization which wanted to obtain reactions to the proposed draft act first had to learn provisions of the bill.

Sources of information for situation analysis are varied. In one study there was the specific problem of finding out how many towels the hotel guest liked to find in the bathroom. Exploration convinced the research staff that the more towels in the bathroom, the more the guest tended to use! This observation provided a new assumption—that guests preferred all the towels they could get—so the specific problem was rephrased.

At one time New Jersey was planning to conduct a referendum on the question of horse racing and pari-mutuel betting. Only through observation of the bill was it learned that a voter had to vote either for or against both of the issues simultaneously. This modified the nature of the opinion survey which preceded the vote, since one question had to cover both issues.

Interviews with the staff of the sponsor's organization aid in clarifying the problem. On the hotel guest survey, first talks with the sponsor indicated his interest in *all* aspects of preferences regarding bathroom linen. As an extended list of possible questions developed, the interested person focused his attention on a limited number of points, and thus restricted the study's scope.

Records are another source of background data. Only records will reveal sales figures, sometimes essential before the research problem can be stated. Reference to trade publications and literary works may provide useful material. "Yearbook" issues of trade publications, for instance, sometimes provide summarized and up-to-date information on the particular subject which cannot be obtained from other sources.

THE INFORMAL INVESTIGATION

1. *What it is*. Informal investigation, usually the next step, consists of preliminary questioning of a number of respondents similar in nature to the final sample of people believed to be required. Intensive interviewing, usually without an outline of issues to be covered, is carried on by skilled investigators. From these conversations it is usually possible to define more accurately the nature of the problem.

Extent of the informal investigation varies with the nature of the particular survey. A comprehensive survey, designed to be nation-wide in scope or intended to cover a number of different issues, requires thorough and extensive informal interviewing.

2. *Example*. The original problem on one study was to develop copy appeals which would be effective in advertising a new commodity—the automatic electric blanket. Here is an exploratory informal conversation on the subject:

I just bought my blanket two weeks ago. I saw the advertisement for it in the Post. Of course I had heard about the use of these blankets in hospitals, but that was the first time I realized that they were on the general market. The ad itself sold me the blanket—I like the way the ad read. I thought the blanket would be a marvelous thing.

As soon as the ad appeared, I knew that I wanted one of the blankets, so I went to Strawbridge's, Gimbel's, and Wanamaker's. When I couldn't get it at any of those places I wired the company, so you know how sold I was on it.

The reason I wanted the blanket and like it so much is that in this cold and damp house I used to get aches. If I had enough covers to keep me warm, their weight kept me awake. Naturally when I saw the ad for the blanket, I knew it would be perfect for my needs.

There are other advantages besides those I just told you. We used to use three blankets, and it was a tough job to make the bed. Now with the one it's a simple matter.

I've been using the blanket regularly since we got it three weeks ago. It's probably too early in the winter to judge, but on the few cold nights we've had the window has been wide open and we're still warm.

I'm so sold on the blanket that I've been talking it up to all my friends. I know this is safe because I have a friend in New York who has had one for two or three years, and it's still working well.

How was this conversation useful in setting the problem? The first paragraph identified the source of knowledge about the blanket, and suggested a question to cover this point in the questionnaire to be developed.

The second paragraph told about the method of purchase. It cast light on the interest intensity; the buyer made four efforts to purchase the blanket before she was successful. Both of these leads were followed up at the time the problem was further specified.

Additional paragraphs provided further clues about the intensity specific advantages it offered. The fourth paragraph suggested that of interest, and showed that the blanket was bought for highly at least one additional advantage of the blanket was learned from using it. It showed that *appeals* and *advantages* of the blanket were distinct.

A number of conversations made it possible to develop a specific list of issues covered by the original objective, and to broaden this objective as well. In addition to copy appeals, the study was not designed to find out place of purchase, how the blanket was heard of, and how intensely the person felt about the blanket.

The informal conversations did more. Since they showed that place of purchase had no relationship to attitudes about the product, it was possible to simplify the method of obtaining names of persons to be interviewed.

One research organization was assigned the task of finding out whether the hours of a department store's business could be changed. Informal interviews with a cross-section of purchasers of the store showed that certain types of people preferred evening hours while other types preferred daylight hours. The problem became the question of what sort of customer the store wanted to cultivate. This implied a study of the buying behavior and influence of each of the groups.

3. *Who should make this informal investigation?* The informal investigation is a difficult process, requiring investigator imagination. The field worker must be sensitive to casual remarks which may suggest a probing approach, interested in developing the new channels of thought which may be suggested by a respondent. One writer (2) suggests that he must have the following qualities:

1. He must be able to interest people in a subject and get them to talk freely.
2. He must possess ingenuity and imagination.
3. He must be able to evaluate the information obtained and to interpret statements to bring out their true significance.
4. He must be able to uncover the motives behind the habits and attitudes which are found.
5. He must be able to report accurately the information obtained from an informal conversation.
6. He must have an adequate knowledge of the field.

This list of qualifications makes it fairly clear that the interviewing should be handled by the individual in charge of the research project. He is likely to have most interest and experience, and will have obtained the required background information. Others should co-operate so that an assortment of views may be obtained.

Different types of persons may be needed for informal interviewing. The well-dressed and affluent field worker secures better co-operation from the higher social and income groups. The chapter on interviewing cites other illustrations.

Statement of Objectives

1. *What it is.* Before situation analysis and informal investigation have been undertaken, the problem has been stated only in broad terms. In the automatic electric blanket study the original assignment was to develop copy appeals. Situation analysis and

exploratory interviewing made it possible to restate the specific research objectives in the following way:

To find out: (a) who bought the blanket, (b) where it was bought, (c) how it was heard of, (d) why it was bought (its appeal), (e) who uses the blanket, (f) its advantages and disadvantages in use, and (g) intensity of feeling about the blanket by the user.

With this specific list of objectives it was possible to decide the issues to be included; the list of purposes was almost identical with the issues. It permitted description of the sample of respondents required (in terms of purchase and use). There was an indication that people were so interested in the subject that a mail questionnaire might be used. (The return on the final mailing was 75 per cent!)

The difference between the ultimate and immediate objectives of a study must be understood. If the ultimate or broad objective—determination of copy appeals—was all required to plan the procedure of the investigation, the resulting study would not have been so valuable as it turned out to be.

2. *How to do it.* The example above shows that the defining of objectives is a natural outgrowth of previous steps in the investigation. Up to this point the work has been somewhat general, but now it is being localized, focused on particular objectives.

After situation analysis and intensive interviewing, specific objectives can usually be set down readily. Initial tentative ideas will be subject to review and revision at this time. Writing out the objectives will help to clarify the hazy points, and definite reference points will be established for the whole future operation.

PLANNING THE STUDY[1]

Careful preliminary work and statement of objectives greatly simplifies planning of the entire procedure. This section of the chapter shows specific ways in which the preliminary work contributes to the planning of the procedure.

1. *The sample.* Exploratory work sometimes modifies the con-

[1] This section is a further development of some of the ideas presented in the second chapter, except that in this case the emphasis is on the relationship between statement of objectives and planning.

cept of the nature of respondents to be interviewed. An advertising agency was asked to measure consumer acceptance of a particular coffee brand in a given city. Exploratory work showed clearly that buyers of different brands had different habits, and that some of these differences might be important for the coffee manufacturer. The final statement of objectives, therefore, included the comparison of habits and preferences of users of other brands with those of users of the particular brand. Statement of objectives then made it clear that a cross-section of housewives (rather than of users of the particular brand) was required.

In the case of a survey on aeronautics, the surveying organization was confronted with the problem of deciding where the calls were to be distributed. A national sample would mean that every state would be represented, and proper proportions of rural and urban calls. In some cases the field workers would have had to travel hundreds of miles before making each call. From the standpoint of cost and complications, decision was against such a survey. In this case the sponsors were really in search of urban opinion, so rural calls were eliminated. Concentration of calls within a limited number of scattered cities made it possible to answer such problems as the extent of differences between men and women, between persons of various age groups, between persons of various standards of living, between large and small cities, and, to some extent, between sections of the country. The exploratory work convinced the research staff that differences within one city were likely to be greater than those between cities, and this was the assumption upon which the final decision as to distribution of sample was based. With thorough knowledge of the problem from situation analysis and exploratory interviewing it was possible to state a hitherto puzzling objective and to settle the sample problem simultaneously.

2. *The method of collecting the data.* Statement of objectives also indicates what method of obtaining interviews to use—personal, mail, or telephone. One manufacturer had just placed a new product on the market. His general objective was to find out how well the purchasers of the product liked it. Exploratory interviews showed that the specific objectives were reasonably simple

and relatively few. Although a questionnaire had not yet been drafted, it appeared that there would be few questions and that most could be answered in a few words. People who had been approached were interested. Talks with retailers indicated willingness to supply purchasers' names for a small fee. It was then possible to state objectives tersely and to show at the same time that most of these persons, practically all of whom were in the higher-income brackets, could be reached by telephone.

3. *The questionnaire.* When the specific objectives of a study have been outlined, the issues in the questionnaire will be a natural outgrowth. On page 37 were listed the specific objectives developed for a survey among automatic electric blanket purchasers. The questionnaire used, shown on page 40, illustrates how questions grew naturally from these objectives. "Who bought the blanket?" will be answered by queries 4, or 8 and 9. "Where it was bought" is covered by inquiry 5. Number 6 covers the subject of how it was heard of. Question 7 answers the objective of determining the appeal of the article. Question 3 tells characteristics of the user of the blanket, and questions 1b and 2 inquire about advantages and disadvantages in use. Space provided for comments is an effort to measure the last objective— the intensity of feeling.

Clarity of the relationship between objectives and questions in this case oversimplifies the procedure of phrasing the questions. Phrasing is difficult, and must be preceded by clear statement of issues to be included. There are several rules to be followed in determination of issues: (a) People must know enough about the questions asked to give reliable and meaningful replies (4, 5); (b) people must have such convictions on the subject, or show such consistent behavior about which they are questioned, that there is real stability to their answers (5); (c) the questions must have real significance in light of the study's purposes (5).

The last point has been emphasized in the present chapter. The first point raises the question of validity: Do the questions measure what they intend to measure? The second problem is one of stability of reply: Do respondents give answers from time to time that are consistent? These problems will be dealt with later.

Shown on the reverse side is the name under which General Electric Automatic Blanket is registered. If there are any errors, please make the necessary changes.

1. Have you used the blanket as yet?   Yes ☐   No ☐
   a. If Yes, do you like it?   Yes ☐   No ☐
   b. What do you like best about it?

   ....

   ....

2. Have you any criticisms of the blanket?   Yes ☐   No ☐
   a. If Yes, please list

   ....

   ....

   ....

3. What is your first preference in blanket color? ....
   a. What color is your Automatic Blanket? ....

4. Will you check your approximate age
   Under 20 ☐   21 to 30 ☐   31 to 40 ☐   41 to 50 ☐   Over 50 ☐

IF *YOU PURCHASED* THE BLANKET, PLEASE ANSWER THESE QUESTIONS: (5, 6, 7)

IF *YOU DID NOT* PURCHASE THE BLANKET PLEASE ANSWER THESE QUESTIONS: (8, 9)

5. Where did you first look for the blanket?
   Electric light and power Co. ☐
   Hardware store ☐
   Furniture store ☐
   Electric appliance store ☐
   Department store ☐
   Direct from G. E. ☐
   Other (describe) ....

   Were you able to get it there?
   Yes ☐   No ☐
   If No, where did you buy it?
   Electric light and power Co. ☐
   Hardware store ☐
   Furniture store ☐
   Electric appliance store ☐
   Department store ☐
   Direct from G. E. ☐
   Other (describe) ....

6. How did you first learn about the blanket?
   Advertising ☐ (Publication.......)
   Read Article ☐ (Publication......)
   Store ☐ (Kind.................)
   Friend ☐
   Doctor ☐

7. What particular feature of the blanket attracted you? ....

   ....

8. Who bought the blanket (check which)?
   Husband ☐   Wife ☐
   Son ☐   Daughter ☐
   Father ☐   Mother ☐
   Brother ☐   Sister ☐
   Other male relative or friend ☐   Other female relative or friend ☐

9. Will you check the approximate age of the purchaser here.

   Under 20 ☐   21 to 30 ☐
   31 to 40 ☐   41 to 50 ☐
   Over 50 ☐

Once issues have been outlined, intensive interviewing will aid in phrasing questions in terms used by respondents. Level of vocabulary to be used will be indicated by the exploratory work.

4. *The analysis.* The planning portion of the survey may seem an early stage at which to begin thinking about analysis of results. This sort of thinking is necessary in connection with purposes of the study. The competent researcher must start to plan what summaries are to be made for the purposes of the investigation. In a coffee survey, a specific purpose was to learn importance of the drip grind, since the sponsor of the study did not have that grind. Not only were questions drawn up with this purpose in mind, but relationships of one question to another were considered for the aid they might give. Here are two questions asked:

1. What method of coffee-making do you use?
2. What brand do you buy regularly?

Methods of coffee-making used by customers of the sponsor did not differ significantly from the methods used by purchasers of all other brands combined. This fact, along with other data from the survey, made it possible to conclude that a drip grind was not an important consideration for the coffee concern in that market during that time.

Analysis of results should be planned at the time at which objectives have been listed and the questionnaire outlined. It is the only way to make sure that the analysis will tie in closely with purposes of the study; if this planning of the analysis is left until questionnaires are collected, it is all too possible to overlook important relationships between questions, or to neglect some breakdown of results in terms of characteristics of respondents.

Since planning and carrying out of survey studies is a broad subject, and since there are so many details to be observed under each step, remaining chapters will take up various phases of the operations.

References

*(1) AMERICAN MARKETING ASSOCIATION. *The Technique of Marketing Research.* New York: McGraw-Hill, 1937. Chapters 1 and 2.

*(2) BROWN, L. O. *Market Research and Analysis.* New York: Ronald, 1937. Chapter 8.

*(3) COUTANT, F. R., AND DOUBMAN, J. R. *Simplified Market Research.* Philadelphia: Walther, 1935. Chapters 2 and 3.

(4) GALLUP, GEORGE, AND RAE, S. F. *The Pulse of Democracy.* New York: Simon and Schuster, 1940. Chapter 7.

(5) KATZ, DANIEL, "Three Criteria: Knowledge, Conviction and Significance," *Public Opinion Quarterly,* 1940, 4, 277-284.

(6) REILLY, W. J. *Marketing Investigations.* New York: Ronald, 1929. Chapter 1.

CHAPTER 4

The Method of Collecting the Data

A PRINCIPAL decision to be made following the statement of the problem concerns the basic methodology to be used in securing the information: mail, telephone, or personal call.

THE MAIL INTERVIEW

The mail questionnaire, usually accompanied by a letter requesting co-operation, is sent to a mailing list of names. These names may come from voters' lists, telephone or city directories, automobile registrants, credit listings, tax lists, corporation lists, organization mailing lists (clubs, societies, etc.), or magazine subscribers. In one study designed to secure responses from farm wives representing the better-class farm market, names of women readers of a farm publication were secured geographically in accordance with farm population in the 1940 Census.

There are a few mailing-list dealers and addressing companies who will supply names of persons in various income groups, various occupational groups. The client may have a file of customer names. In one study it was possible to mail questionnaires to 1000 persons who had recently sent in warranty cards upon purchase of the particular product. This group naturally was highly interested in the investigation, so that it was not surprising that over 70 per cent replies resulted from only one mailing.

The particular method used can influence the extent of co-operation obtained, and the type of mailing list and the nature of the problem may be expected to influence the rate of return and the completeness of individual reply to the questionnaire. The way in which the covering letter is written will affect the proportion of replies. If it is an interesting letter, providing good reasons for response, rate of return will probably be higher than normal. The letter must always be written from the recipient's point of view rather than from that of the research organization.

Weaver (18) shows how a clever approach can stimulate the proportion of replies on a mail questionnaire. Mere inclusion of a duplicate copy of the blank increases returns. In another experiment conducted by Weaver returns were increased threefold by stating that no reply was desired!

1. *Advantages of the mail questionnaire.* The most commonly claimed advantage for the mail questionnaire is its economy. The argument runs that all you have to do is to print and mail out the questionnaire.

This argument of economy does not stand up too well. Since returns commonly do not exceed 15 per cent, the cost of each returned mail questionnaire may be higher than for an equivalent personal interview. The purchase expense of a mailing list may be high. Clerical cost of getting out the questionnaires may be high, and if a premium is offered, still another cost is added.

The mail questionnaire can be of value where a wide distribution of respondents is required. The technique is flexible; it permits a wide distribution of respondents at relatively small cost compared to the personal approach. On the survey of the better-class farm wives, it would have been ten times as expensive to have interviewed personally the 1000 women required, scattered throughout the nation. The tire and gasoline situation would have been an additional drawback. In cases similar to this it is practically impossible to use any but the mail technique.

The mail questionnaire is also of advantage in approaching persons who are scattered throughout sections within a particular area. One organization maintains a list of consumers who have recently built new homes. In any one town there are few of these homes located close together except in developments. It is literally impossible to use any but the mail approach here.

The mail approach is frequently used by publications that wish to make inexpensive surveys of their readers. It is a relatively simple matter to include a copy of the questionnaire in the issue of the publication, and thus avoid the expense of a separate mailing. If the questionnaire is especially well designed, returns will be particularly high. Naturally there are a number of dangers in such an approach as this. Those reached by the questionnaire may or may not be typical of the readers of the publication. Those who reply may tend to be those particularly interested in the subject of the questionnaire.

One great advantage of the mail questionnaire is that it eliminates any possible interviewer bias. (This problem of fieldworker bias will be discussed later.) The individual will not be rushed in deciding what his answers will be. Theoretically he will have just as long as he wishes to think about the queries.

The usual mail questionnaire does not require the respondent to identify himself. Since the questionnaire is anonymous, it is frequently possible to inquire about subjects which would be more difficult to handle in a personal interview. One large advertising agency has, for several years, conducted a series of surveys about slide fasteners for men's trousers. This sort of subject would be difficult to handle in a personal interview.

The mail questionnaire may be used to reach groups that can be approached by no other procedure. Several years ago a study was being made of the backgrounds of a number of the most important American business executives. Two investigators (16) were able to get replies from over half of the executives to whom they sent their questionnaires. It seems doubtful that such a proportion of replies could have been obtained by use of any other method. It is usually a real problem to get past the assistants and secretary of a top executive.

2. *Disadvantages of the mail questionnaire.* The mail questionnaire, where used, commonly presents drawbacks. Its greatest deficiency is the lack of assurance that a representative group of persons will reply. Seldom are the replies received from a group which is representative of the entire mailing. Suchman and McCandless (15) made two studies concerning this problem. Their first investigation was a measure of listening versus non-listening to a child-training program. The questionnaire was mailed to 600 women selected at random from a telephone directory. After the

first set of returns had diminished to practically nothing, a second mailing was made to those who had not replied. Finally a third effort was made to reach by telephone those who still had not answered. If the survey had stopped with the original returns, the proportion of the sample who knew of the program would have been greatly overestimated.

In their second study these same workers mailed a questionnaire to a random sample of 900 listeners from a list of 10,000 subscribers to the Masterwork Bulletin, radio program listing of a New York radio station. The identical series of questions was sent out three times, the second and third waves being directed to those who still had not replied to previous questionnaires. A fourth effort to reach the remaining listeners in the sample was made by means of a final and shortened mail questionnaire. The first response to the mailing indicated a much higher level of interest and experience than actually existed among the 900 listeners.

In a different type of survey, Stanton (14) shows the same sort of factor to be potent. He sent a mail questionnaire to teachers, asking whether or not they had a classroom radio. On the original wave of questionnaires, 33 per cent indicated that they had classroom radios, while on the follow-up wave only 24 per cent reported classroom radios. Obviously those who owned radios were the ones who tended to reply to the first mailing.

This factor of interest and experience seems to motivate persons to reply to a questionnaire "within their field" regardless of the subject matter. Rollins (11) sent a questionnaire to 750 readers of a publication, asking their reactions toward commercial flying. A second wave of the same questionnaires was sent to those not replying to the first. Comparison of results from the two waves showed that the first returns overestimated the proportion of those who had flown—17 per cent of the first wave, but only 7 per cent of the second wave. The factor of interest and experience in the topic as a motivating factor to answer mail questionnaires seems well substantiated by all of these independently obtained results.

The mail questionnaire can be dangerous unless the investigator is aware of its limitations. Difficulty in securing replies from a representative group of those to whom the questionnaire was mailed has been shown. Another difficulty in obtaining a cross-section with the mail procedure is illustrated by the *Literary Digest* disaster. Here the mailing list itself was not representative of the population which the survey intended to study.

Salisbury (12) lists a number of dangers in the mail survey. One is that the answers submitted are likely to be brief and superficial. While the subject matter covered in the questionnaire is limited, there doesn't seem to be any real reason why a cleverly designed series of questionnaires submitted by mail should obtain superficial replies. One of the real dangers is that the questionnaire may be answered by someone other than the person to whom it is addressed. In one survey it was learned that an enterprising secretary, rather than bother her boss with a mail questionnaire, had filled out the blank herself, even though she knew nothing about the subject.

A few of the common practices in the mail survey add further dangers to its use. The majority of the mail questionnaires we have seen make no effort to hide the name of the sponsor. The name of the sponsor provided on a letterhead or elsewhere might cause those who feel most strongly about the concern to reply. Where the name of the respondent is requested (except so as to send him a premium for reply) persons might fear that an answer would subject them to a sales campaign, or that they were divulging some highly personal information.

THE TELEPHONE INTERVIEW

The two major radio-audience measurement services obtain a random sample of telephone subscribers' names. In other cases names of persons are obtained from other lists, and these are then approached over the telephone.

This method is not particularly complex. Field workers merely sit at telephones, dial numbers, and ask their questions of the respondents. The list of questions must be short and to the point, since it is too simple for the respondent to break off whenever he feels the urge.

1. *Advantages of the telephone interview*. Field investigators commonly report difficulty in securing personal interviews with persons of the top-income groups. It is difficult to get past the maid or the butler who answers the door, and sometimes the person even insists that you arrange an appointment! If the correct individual himself can be approached without any intermediary, there is less chance that the interview will not be completed. This is why the telephone interview is often used when the highest-income groups are being canvassed.

Recently the manufacturer of a food product wanted to determine how each dealer in New York City was moving his product. It would have been expensive to have sent one investigator to each store merely to ask a single question. Instead, the manufacturer had one of his clerks telephone each outlet to inquire how many of his items had been sold there during the past week. No difficulties were encountered, and there were no problems of securing a cross-section, since each dealer was approached. Where the group to be interviewed is a selected one, such as known purchasers of a product, the telephone interview is useful.

A special advantage of the telephone interview is the rapidity of field work. Expense is likely to be considerably less, in terms of cost per completed interview, than either the mail or the personal interview methods.

If facts, rather than opinions, are desired, the telephone approach has particular value. It is a simple matter to telephone a large number of individuals during a given hour of the day, and to determine whether they are listening to the radio, and if so, to what program and station. It takes but a few moments for the inquiries, and the questions are all factual affairs which the respondent can answer with a minimum of thought.

Another advantage of the telephone method is that a random selection of telephone subscribers is so easily made. Depending upon how many total interviews are required, every 50th, 100th, or 500th name may be selected in numerical order from the directory. Such a method of selection is practically certain to insure that no one locality, no one racial or religious group will dominate the sample of respondents obtained on the survey. The technique aids in selecting a sample of respondents typical of telephone owners within the community.

2. *Disadvantages of the telephone method.* It is impossible to obtain a cross-section of the general population by the telephone method. Only the upper-income groups, in general, can be reached through the telephone. Some 55 per cent of the families (and the lower half in terms of income) are immediately eliminated from the sample because of lack of telephones. Chappell (4) argues that this biased selection may not be too important in the commercial or radio-audience survey, since the groups that are best prospects for advertised goods are probably those in the upper-income brackets. Chappell proceeds to show that in a small-scale study he conducted, very few differences actually existed in listening habits between those who did and those who did not have telephones in their homes.

Contrary evidence is presented by Link and Corby (8), who, in a listening-habit survey conducted in Buffalo, found major differences in the relative popularity of programs between telephone and non-telephone owners. The Pulse of New York (9), a syndicated radio-audience service under the direction of Dr. Sydney Roslow, presents detailed evidence to show that telephone and non-telephone homes have different listening habits. This service asks respondents by personal interview to what programs they listened, and in this case the results for seven programs are shown for those who do and do not have telephones:

	% of Telephone Homes Listening	% of Non-Telephone Homes Listening
Romance of Helen Trent	2.6	6.6
Trans Radio News	11.5	4.5
Road of Life	1.3	5.7
Make-Believe Ballroom	3.4	8.7
Yours Sincerely	3.1	1.5
Gambling's Musical Clock	4.7	.8
Breakfast Symphony	2.1	0.0

The evidence should make one cautious about using the telephone method for an over-all sampling procedure.

It might be thought that the representativeness of the sample secured over the telephone could readily be checked by comparing its characteristics with those of the population at large. For instance, if it were known that 25 per cent of the population of a given locality owned automobiles, it could be determined what proportion of those interviewed owned automobiles. The argument would then run that other characteristics, such as the size of family, age, etc., could also be secured in the telephone interview, and the distribution of replies could then be compared with the distribution of the same characteristics within the general population. The difficulty is that it is almost impossible to secure such information during the telephone interview. This sort of question can be asked only after the confidence of the individual has been obtained. Real rapport between the interviewer and his subject is possible only through personal contact. This sort of information cannot be obtained over the telephone; it has been tried, and it just doesn't work!

The telephone interview is difficult to use in either rural or small-town areas. In the first place, it is hard for the interviewer to get to the place from which to make the calls; few organizations have any need of a permanent investigator located in a small town, so it would be necessary to send someone there. In addition, telephone ownership among such groups is low, so that it would be even more difficult than in the city to obtain a cross-section. For rural calls the telephone charges mount up alarmingly. Anyone who has made use of a rural party line knows, in addition, that when the telephone rings, others on the line listen in. The implication would be that the investigator could make only one call on each party line; otherwise he would be taking a chance that others who answered would be "prepared" for the call.

Any telephone interview will necessarily have to be limited in time and scope, just as in the case of the mail questionnaire. Involved questions cannot be asked; this sort of question requires a personal interview. The respondent may become confused by such a query over the telephone. He may require a little more time to give his answer. Only short-answer questions may be asked successfully by telephone; no comment or discussion questions can be included. One great difficulty is that the interviewer has little opportunity to evaluate the responses of the individual. Observation by the investigators is sometimes one of the most valuable concomitants of the personal interview approach, yet all of this is lost when the telephone interview is used.

Perhaps this discussion has overemphasized the dangers of the telephone method. The researcher should be sure that the method is of less value than some other approach before he discards it. In some situations it may be more applicable than any other procedure.

THE PERSONAL INTERVIEW

Where the personal interview is used, the field worker talks to his respondents personally, recording his answers as their conversation progresses. Details of this method will be discussed throughout the remainder of this volume.

1. *Advantages of the personal interview.* Chief advantage of the personal interview is that it permits rigid control of the sample of respondents. Since such control is the very basis for modern survey work (see Chapter 8), it is not surprising that it is one of the most common methods used today in survey research. Practically any desired distribution of characteristics of respondents can be obtained with the personal interview. It is virtually impossible to set too many controls of this nature. Ordinarily about five or six variables are controlled. This is accomplished by telling each field investigator how many interviews with persons of each classification (income, sex, age, etc.) he is to obtain. By proper assignment of quotas to each field worker, the investigating organization can see that the total distribution of desired characteristics will be in accordance with predetermined figures.

The personal interview approach permits the use of questionnaires of wider scope than in the case of mail or telephone interviews. Complicated questions can be included. The skilled investigator can "probe" into the reasons underlying a superficial answer. The very fact that the personal approach is being used will permit a longer questionnaire. Whatever the length, the fact that there is a skilled field worker means that he will be able to secure co-operation from some people who would not bother to answer a mail questionnaire. The same factor makes it possible to ask comment or discussion questions, impossible with the mail or telephone method.

2. *Disadvantages of the personal interview.* The personal call is usually expensive. But the expense per question may sometimes be less than with either mail or telephone methods. When the cost per return of the mail method is computed, and is divided by the total number of questions, it is likely to be larger than the cost per question of the longer questionnaire utilized in the personal approach.

Except with an unusually competent field worker there is a tendency for the respondent to be quick in his answering. This "hurry-up" means that answers are likely to be given without time for reflection that the mail questionnaire supposedly permits. Of course there are no objective data to show that people spend more time in answering mail questionnaires; this is simply an assumption. Even if we assume that they do spend more time on mail questionnaires, this factor should not be important in behavior questions, but only in opinion and "reason why" questions, where it may require a little time to give the real answer. Where a most thoughtful answer is required, the mail questionnaire just isn't the way to get it; in such a case the use of an especially competent field worker is necessary.

With the addition of a field worker to the study, many potential sources of error are present. The investigator may select the wrong sort of respondents, causing an error in the cross-section. He may interview only those who are most co-operative, that in itself biasing in the cross-section. The interviewer may also cause bias in the responses. One study (2) showed that interviewers' attitudes were correlated with the results they obtained on a public opinion survey. Bias may creep in through an emphasis on particular words in the question, by risreading the question. . . . In fairness to the personal interview method it must be pointed out that proper selection and training of field investigators can eliminate much bias.

The personal interview method is generally superior to either the telephone or the mail approach. It is the only method by which the sample of respondents may be adequately controlled. In special cases there may be particular circumstances which make the mail or the telephone method a superior one for the study. The generalization holds in spite of these exceptions.

COMBINATION METHODS

Occasionally a combination of methods is the most desirable technique to follow. In one study on magazine readership it was necessary to interview New York City readers. It was relatively easy to approach most of the readers. But when field workers attempted to obtain interviews with residents of Park Avenue and West End Avenue, they found it practically impossible to get into the apartment houses past the doormen. Maids and butlers presented an additional problem. Finally these persons were telephoned. On a telephone call, the maid or butler usually asked no more than the name of the caller, and then brought the correct respondent to the wire. Once this had been accomplished, there was no difficulty in getting the person to answer the short series of questions.

The telephone method could not have been used with the entire series of respondents; some were in lower-income brackets and could not afford telephones. The only way to reach this group was through personal interview.

There are other situations in which combination methods may be used. One application of the combination method is to ask for co-operation by one approach and to conduct the interview using another method. On one study with construction men, a postcard was sent asking for co-operation. Personal interviews were concluded in over 90 per cent of the cases. More recently one survey technician wrote letters to executives asking for their co-operation in a telephone interview. He obtained co-operation—for a fifteen-minute conversation!

One of the greatest advantages of the usual combination method is that results can be compared as gathered by two or more techniques. This sort of comparison will provide further facts about the merits and demerits of each method.

The only generalization warranted by present information is that usually the personal interview method is superior to any other.

REFERENCES

*(1) AMERICAN MARKETING ASSOCIATION. *The Technique of Marketing Research.* New York: McGraw-Hill, 1937. Chapter 2.

(2) BLANKENSHIP, A. B. "The Effect of the Interviewer Upon the Response in a Public Opinion Poll," *Journal of Consulting Psychology,* 1940, 4, 134-136.

*(3) BROWN, L. O. *Market Research and Analysis.* New York: Ronald, 1937. Chapters 4 and 8.

(4) CHAPPELL, M. N. *How Adequate is the Telephone Sample for Obtaining Radio Program Ratings?* New York: C. E. Hooper, 1941.

(5) GALLUP, GEORGE, AND RAE, S. F. *The Pulse of Democracy.* New York: Simon and Schuster, 1940. Chapter 6.

(6) KAROL, J. J. "Measuring Radio Audiences," *Public Opinion Quarterly,* 1937, 1, 92-96.

(7) LAZARSFELD, P. F. "The Use of Mail Questionnaires to Ascertain the Popularity of Network Stations in Family Listening Surveys," *Journal of Applied Psychology,* 1940, 24, 802-816.

(8) LINK, H. C., AND CORBY, P. G. "Studies in Radio Effectiveness," *Journal of Applied Psychology,* 1940, 24, 749-758.

(9) PULSE OF NEW YORK. The 100% *Yardstick for the Measurement of the Radio Audience.* New York: Pulse of New York, 1941.

(10) REILLY, W. J. *Marketing Investigations.* New York: Ronald, 1929. Chapters 11, 12, 13, and 14.

(11) ROLLINS, MALCOLM. "The Practical Use of Repeated Questionnaire Waves," *Journal of Applied Psychology,* 1940, 24, 770-772.

*(12) SALISBURY, PHILLIP. "Eighteen Elements of Danger in Making Mail Surveys," *Sales Management,* 1938, 42, No. 4, 28-29.

(13) SCHWERIN, HORACE. "Copy Pre-testing," *Printer's Ink,* November 1, 1940, 67-68.

(14) STANTON, F. N. "Problems of Sampling in Market Research," *Journal of Consulting Psychology,* 1941, 5, 154-163.

(15) SUCHMAN, E. A., AND McCANDLESS, BOYD. "Who Answers Questionnaires?" *Journal of Applied Psychology,* 1940, 24, 758-769.

(16) TAUSSIG, F. W., AND JOSLYN, C. S. *American Business Leaders.* New York: Macmillan, 1932.

(17) UNSIGNED. "Non-telephone Homes Listen More," *Business Week,* October 21, 1939, 24.

(18) WEAVER, H. G. "Consumer Questionnaire Technique," *American Marketing Journal,* 1934, 1, 115-118.

CHAPTER 5

Preliminary Phrasing of the Questions

> Most people will frankly admit that they can't direct a dance
> orchestra—that they wouldn't know how to operate for
> appendicitis—but almost everyone seems to feel that he (or
> she) can work up an effective questionnaire.
> —BRUCE BARTON

∿∿

BEFORE the 1940 presidential election, one organization worded
two questions:

Do you think George Washington was right in refusing to be a candidate
for a third term as President?

Do you think the tradition against a third term is a safeguard against
one-man rule and Fascism?[1]

It would be surprising if the survey group had not found the public
opposed to a third term *as expressed by these propositions*.

Though care has been given to defining the problem and planning the method of collecting the data, this alone does not carry
the implication that a good set of questions will result.

Probably no final set of "principles" for wording will ever be
written. The circumstances and purposes of each study are unique.
The manner in which the respondents are to be approached, which
differs in every survey, will influence the phrasings used. The type
of interviewer and the sort of respondent to be approached will be
factors which influence the phrasings. There are still some general
guiding "rules" which should be useful.

Before these are discussed, it may be in order to outline the
general *types* of questions commonly used on surveys: (a) the
yes-no question, (b) the *multiple-choice* (or check-list) question,

---

[1] Quoted from Robinson (*18*).

(c) *assignment of weights to alternatives,* and (d) the *free-response* query.

The *yes-no* type is common today; only a simple affirmative or negative statement is obtained from the person replying. The question *Is the present government helping business?* requires only an affirmative or negative reply (or a possible "Don't know," "Both," or "Neither" response). This sort of question makes summary of replies simple, but permits no qualitative answer (in terms of degree).

Where a measure of intensity of feeling is desirable, the multiple-choice form may be useful. In this case the government and business question could be worded:

Is the present government:
  a. Helping business a great deal
  b. Helping business a little
  c. Hurting business a little
  d. Hurting business a great deal?

The problem of intensity of feeling may also be approached by a ranking question. On a radio study the call letters of the listener's favorite radio station were obtained (9); Station XYZ was selected by 75 per cent of respondents. Many of those replying had indicated a second, third, and fourth choice as well. When the average rank for each station was computed, Station XYZ dropped to second. In this case, if the surveyor had wanted to find out which station was preferred by a majority of respondents, no weighting was necessary. If highest average preference rating was the purpose, then the weighting method should have been used.

In some cases it may be preferable to allow those replying complete freedom in the replies they give—to make replies in their own words without suggestion from the investigator. This is the *free-response* question. For example, *Whom would you like to see as our next President?* would fall under such a heading. No answers are suggested to the respondent, who is free to make any reply, going into long detail if necessary. This sort of question is less likely to bias response, since it suggests no particular reply; and it receives fuller responses than any of the *short-answer* questions.

This fullness of reply makes it almost essential to use the free-response question in the first form of a questionnaire. This form of question will insure that all possibilities of reply and elaboration are at hand before the final drafting of questions takes place. This kind of question is generally used only with studies restricted in number of calls. With a large number of respondents, it presents great difficulty in summary—a great variety and volume of replies.

There are with all question forms a few general rules that are helpful in proper phrasing. Any question asked must obtain replies which can be summarized in meaningful fashion. Usually the queries must permit a simple reply; otherwise a chaotic mass of involved responses will be obtained. Carrying this principle to extremes, however, will result in loss of valuable information.

1. *The introduction and opening questions must create rapport with the respondent.* Following this principle will aid in securing a good sample of respondents and will also help to get real opinions and honest reactions.

Chapter 8 shows the importance of securing a cross-section of respondents. To obtain such a cross-section, co-operation from the majority of the prospective respondents approached is necessary. Both the introduction used and the way the introductory questions are asked will either aid or hinder co-operation. Rapport is necessary to secure real opinions and reactions.

Surveys as popularly known as the *Fortune* and Gallup polls will encounter little difficulty in securing co-operation once their names have been mentioned. Other organizations have a sizable problem on their hands in developing a simple introductory statement which will gain the confidence of prospective respondents. Most organizations do not use their names at all in introducing the questioning, but simply state, "We are making a little study in this neighborhood. I would like to ask you a few questions, such as . . ."

This approach is usually effective in producing the proper frame of mind. The first few questions must then be simple, and must arouse interest, so that the respondent will want to continue with the questions.

2. *The questions must not be ambiguous.* Each question should be phrased in such a way that its meaning is clear. Ambiguity

can take several forms: (a) The question may be susceptible to different interpretations by various respondents; (b) the wording may be difficult; (c) the words may not be understood.

Examples of lack of clarity because of possibility of multiple interpretation are easy to find. One writer (*14*) cites this question, from a cosmetic study, as ambiguous: *What kinds of powder do you use?* The word *kinds* can be taken to refer to brands, form of powder (loose or compact), or color.

In one study a question was asked: *Is the electric utility in your community privately or publicly owned?* (*17*) The particular company was not owned by the government, yet many replied that it was. It was discovered that this reply had been given because the public owned the shares. The word *publicly* could probably have been used satisfactorily in reference to other issues. Ambiguity of any word is probably dependent on the context of the questionnaire, subject matter, and the particular group of respondents with whom it is used.

A general "catch-all" *why* question can also be ambiguous. Lazarsfeld (*1*) has emphasized the necessity of asking a specifying *why* question. If the question *Why did you change to this dentifrice?* be used, non-comparable answers will result, because people will interpret the question in different ways. Some will give replies in terms of attributes of the product ("It cleans teeth better"), some will tell of advertising influences ("I saw it advertised in the newspaper"), while others will mention their own personal tendencies ("I like to economize, and this brand was cheaper"). In such a case many people are influenced by more than one factor, but will tend to answer in terms of only one. A general *why* question is therefore dangerous to use; more specific questions dealing with various aspects of behavior must be utilized. If the surveyor wants to discover the immediate reasons for brand change he may say, *What made you start using this brand?* If it is the qualities of the product which are being evaluated, he may ask, *What are the advantages of the dentifrice you use?*

Frequently questions may be interpreted either literally or figuratively. The surveyor should make the question specific enough so that the one desired interpretation is general. In the question

Is commercial air-travel safe? the person who takes the question literally would have to reply "no," since no form of travel is absolutely safe. If the respondent were interpreting the query figuratively, he would reply "Yes," since commercial air-travel is comparably as safe as any other form of transportation.

Wording of the question may be so difficult or involved that its meaning is not clear. Negative phrasings are not as easily understood as positive. One study (24) measured sentiment on sixteen propositions. After having subjects vote on these questions as worded in a clear, positive manner, a revote was taken in which negative phrasings were used. Negative phrasings caused a high degree of confusion among respondents. The implication is clear: Phrasings have a better chance of being understood when expressed positively.

Ambiguity may occur because the level of vocabulary is too high. Words used in the questions should be understood by a majority of the respondents; otherwise there will be too many "Don't know" replies received merely because those replying do not understand the query. On a recent study the question *Would you prefer to have radio programs with or without the commercials?* was included. Among the more highly cultured groups, the question worked satisfactorily. When the same question was asked among the lower groups, the word *commercials* had no meaning to them. Other words may be equally difficult for some respondents.

The role of vocabulary need not warrant serious consideration if only the highest cultural group is to be interviewed.

3. *The question must be phrased in psychologically concrete and specific terms.* Each question must be related to specific experiences of the individual. The question *How many razor blades do you use in a year?* isn't close to the person's experience—it involves considerable computation and thought on his part. The question *How often do you change your blade?* places the individual in a familiar situation, and he will be able to answer without involved reasoning.

One study (20) was designed to find out the approximate annual beer consumption per individual. The question *How much beer do you consume in a year?* would be difficult to answer because

35

☑ *Check items that are most important from your standpoint*

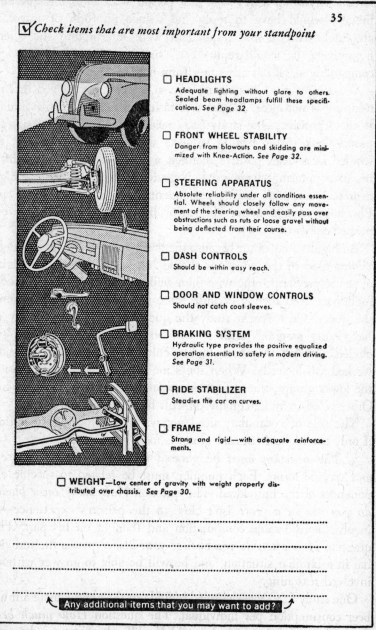

☐ **HEADLIGHTS**
Adequate lighting without glare to others. Sealed beam headlamps fulfill these specifications. *See Page 32*

☐ **FRONT WHEEL STABILITY**
Danger from blowouts and skidding are minimized with Knee-Action. *See Page 32.*

☐ **STEERING APPARATUS**
Absolute reliability under all conditions essential. Wheels should closely follow any movement of the steering wheel and easily pass over obstructions such as ruts or loose gravel without being deflected from their course.

☐ **DASH CONTROLS**
Should be within easy reach.

☐ **DOOR AND WINDOW CONTROLS**
Should not catch coat sleeves.

☐ **BRAKING SYSTEM**
Hydraulic type provides the positive equalized operation essential to safety in modern driving. *See Page 31.*

☐ **RIDE STABILIZER**
Steadies the car on curves.

☐ **FRAME**
Strong and rigid—with adequate reinforcements.

☐ **WEIGHT**—Low center of gravity with weight properly distributed over chassis. *See Page 30.*

....

....

....

....

↖ Any additional items that you may want to add? ↗

Reproduced by permission of General Motors Corporation

of memory and the computation involved. Instead, two questions were asked:

How much beer did you buy on the last purchase?
When, how long ago, did you last buy beer?

By asking these questions at various seasons of the year, a true picture of the annual consumption could be obtained.

Too direct a question may lead to inaccuracy if the directness is contrary to the respondent's experiences (either in thought or in action). A person could not be asked a direct question on the food value of milk. Such an attitude could be secured by inquiring, *Which do you consider more nourishing: a glass of milk, ½ pound of potatoes, 2 eggs, or ½ pound of string beans?* (1) Since all of the alternatives are approximately equal in their nutritive value, the individual chooses on the basis of belief rather than knowledge.

General Motors Corporation, during peacetime, makes frequent surveys among automobile owners to determine their opinions on the various features of cars. These questionnaires, a page of which is reproduced here, carry the principle of providing a means of expressing thought to the utmost. Rather than ask a motorist to describe his preferred style of car, the questionnaires present several alternative possibilities in picture form, and the respondent merely checks his selection.

On another study it was necessary to find out what size of diamond the public preferred for certain uses. It was known that consumers in general could not define a given stone as one, two, or three carats—such knowledge was simply not within the scope of their experience. Each respondent was shown five stones of definite size and asked to make his selection. In this way the issue was not confused; it was known precisely what size stone was preferred. There was no need to depend upon respondents' inaccurate knowledge of carat size.

4. *Wherever possible, questions should refer to objective behavior.* This is closely related to the preceding point—it is additional effort to relate phraseology to experience of the respondent, to get at specificities instead of depending upon broad (and some-

times invalid) generalizations by those who reply. It would be possible to find out the proportion of people who like and dislike advertisements on the radio. More valuable would be a behavior question asked on a study: *Would you be willing to pay a license fee to eliminate radio advertising?* Asking even about possible behavior is an improvement over asking a broad attitude question.

A behavior question results in material which can be checked against actual behavior as an indication of survey accuracy. The behavior question is the only sort which has a great deal of practical significance. Any commercial survey is directly or ultimately aimed at measurement of past, present, and future behavior.

The behavior question also has more meaning in opinion polls. It would not have meant much to learn the results to the question *Do you like or dislike Germany?* It meant a great deal more to find out on April 19, 1941, that 17 per cent of the public were in favor of sending part of the army to Europe to aid the British, that 24 per cent wanted us to send part of the air force with American pilots to aid the British, and that 27 per cent wanted us to send American-manned warships to help.

This behavior sort of question also comes closer to the actual experiences of respondents than does any hypothetical question. Hence it is more sound than the pure "opinion" type of inquiry.

5. *The intensity of phrasing will influence the replies.* Use of a modifying word or phrase can so extend or limit the meaning of the proposal that the replies will be influenced. During the depression one research organization asked a question in two different forms (12):

Are you willing to have an increase in prices with the hope that it will bring back prosperity?

Are you willing to have a reasonable increase in prices with the hope that it will bring back prosperity?

The second form of the question, different only in that the word *reasonable* had been inserted as a limiting adjective, caused 11 per cent more persons to give affirmative answers to the proposal.

Another experiment (8) provides an example of two similar questions worded differently enough to produce entirely different results:

Is the service at Blank's reasonably good?
Is the service at Blank's all you could expect?

The latter form of the question implied that an affirmative answer would indicate close to perfection in Blank's service, while the former phrasing was more moderate. As a result, the first phrasing produced a 60 per cent affirmative reply, while only 20 per cent agreed with the latter statement.

Another change in the point of reference is illustrated by the pair of inquiries:

About how many cans or bottles (of beer) do you and your family drink at home during the winter (per week)?

How many cans or bottles of beer did you and your family use in the past week at home?

These two questions were asked of comparable groups of beer drinkers, at a two-month interval. To the first query 21.3 per cent replied that they averaged less than one can or bottle, while 28.1 per cent of those answering the latter question gave this reply. It would be expected that in any particular week a large proportion of beer users would not buy beer, even though on the average some of these consumed better than this figure.

A nation-wide survey recently asked this question: *Do you happen to pay any taxes?* Some 25 per cent of the public was not aware of the payment of indirect taxes. Another survey organization believed that this distribution of answers might be due to the fact that many people interpreted the question as referring only to direct taxes. This agency consequently asked the question of comparable samples of respondents in two forms:

Do you happen to pay any taxes?
Do you happen to pay any taxes, either direct or indirect?

The latter phrasing, which called attention to the two kinds of tax, caused an additional 5 per cent of those interviewed to reply that they paid taxes in one form or another.

In two studies, a month apart, these questions were asked of comparable samples of respondents:

Which of these companies do you think well of generally, which not so well?

Do you think favorably or unfavorably of the following companies?

In each case the names of companies were then read to the respondent, and reactions were secured. In the case of the five companies included in both questions, the proportion of respondents favorable was greater in the former question. Apparently the term *well* was interpreted as being milder than *favorably*, and thus secured a higher proportion of affirmative response by shifting the point of reference.

6. *The questions must be worded so that they will not damage the pride of the respondent.* The entire background of the public being approached must be carefully considered in the phrasing of questions. A question which damages the pride of the respondent will not be answered frankly, if at all. To find out what proportion of the public had read *Gone with the Wind* a direct question could not be asked, for practically everyone would claim that he had read it. To circumvent this factor of pride, the question was phrased, *Do you intend to read "Gone with the Wind?"* This approach (*17*) flattered everybody. Those who had never read the book and never would read it were still given a chance to say that they intended to read it, while those who had already read it commented to that effect. By this means an accurate measure of readership was secured.

7. *The questions must be nonemotional and unbiased.* One of the most frequent criticisms against surveys is that the form of the question is frequently so biased that a particular response is suggested to those approached. This would make the results more a reflection of question-wording than of popular sentiment on the issue. Spingarn (*21*), for example, criticizes a question in a publicized poll which was worded, *In your opinion which will do more to get us out of the depression—increased government expense for relief and public works, or helping business by reducing taxes?* The words *helping business* imply that not to reduce taxes would have the effect of hurting business. Thus a favorable reply to the second alternative is suggested by phraseology alone. Such apparently innocuous phrases do occasionally enter into poll questions and affect the result. Studenski (*22*) shows experimentally that in the question *To increase prosperity should government spending be decreased, let alone, or increased?* the term *govern-*

ment spending has an unfavorable connotation and will secure, merely because of the term itself, a large number of "decreased" answers. Again, in the question *To increase prosperity should taxes be lowered, let alone, or raised?* it has been pointed out (22) that taxes are not levied to increase prosperity. Increased taxation and increased personal property are generally assumed to be inversely related, so the results of such a question could be closely predicted merely from knowledge of the question form.

Experimental studies have shown that many types of words may have a prejudicial influence, thus when used in questions may secure responses which are not representative of popular feeling. One investigation (15) showed that propositions not grouped under any labels secured more approval from college students than the same propositions grouped under the heading of *communism*. *Radicalism* and *fascism* showed similar effects. Different results might have been obtained if the sample had been taken from the general population, but the experiment is at least indicative of danger words.

There is considerable work being performed upon this field of emotionally colored words and their possible influence. *Public Opinion Quarterly*, one of the journals active in the survey field, is co-operating with one of the research organizations to determine experimentally some of these danger words and the type of issue on which they are most likely to occur. Professor D. A. Hartmann, of New York University, is conducting a continuous study to develop a list of similar nature. The Institute for Propaganda Analysis has provided a list of such words that should be avoided.[2]

Names of political figures can also influence results to issue questions. One poll asked a question in two forms: (3)

Do you approve of having Thanksgiving a week earlier this year?

Do you approve of President Roosevelt's idea of having Thanksgiving a week earlier this year?

The second wording, attributing the idea to Roosevelt, caused an additional 5 per cent of respondents to approve! Yet Cantril (4) reports these results with two questions:

[2] These include such examples of "name-calling" as *demagogue, dictator, muckraker, alien, economic royalist,* and *Tory.*

Do you approve of Sumner Welles' visit to European capitals?

Do you approve of President Roosevelt's sending Sumner Welles to visit European capitals?

Disapprovals increased 6 per cent on the second phrasing, and this difference reiterates a point made previously. The influence of a word or phrase is not "absolute," but depends upon such factors as the nature of the sample, the context of surrounding questions, and the time of the study.

The name of Hitler is another magic word for the American public. Cantril (4) reports results of two questions asked before our entry into the war:

Do you think the United States should do more than it is now to help England and France?

Do you think the United States should do more than it is now doing to help England and France in their fight against Hitler?

The word *Hitler* caused an additional 9 per cent to reply in favor of helping England and France.

Even a verb may have an unfavorable connotation and therefore influence the replies. It has been demonstrated (*19*) that if a question be phrased *Do you think the United States should do everything in its power to promote world peace?* the *yes* vote is overwhelming. If the same question be reworded *Do you think the United States should become involved in a plan to promote world peace?* the affirmative replies are considerably reduced because of the use of the word *involved*. It has also been shown experimentally (*22*) that use of the word *force* may cause suggestion when placed in the question *Should every worker be forced to join a union?* This question would seem to imply that the behavior of workers would be controlled without regard for their own desires.

8. *If a check-list is used, its influence must be carefully considered.* A check-list (a list of possible replies) may be used either for the respondent's benefit or merely to aid field workers in the recording of replies. This discussion concerns the respondent check-list.

A check-list is valuable in memory questions because it can aid in the stimulation of recall. Experience with check-list questions reveals that the proportion of replies within each category tends to be substantially higher than with a corresponding free-response query. When it is a question about ideas (rather than memory), then the check-list query stimulates imagination. What the check-list question does is to suggest replies, and the respondent merely makes a selection, rather than thinking of his own response(s). The form of the respondent check-list question may seriously influence the survey results. The order of alternatives can influence returns. In one experimental study (13) the first item in the answer list (the order was counterbalanced so that equal average position resulted for each alternative) was checked by 2 to 3 per cent more of the respondents than when it was later in the list. In another study the proportion of respondents who liked a particular radio program was being measured. Persons were asked to compare this show with four other programs. All were counterbalanced to insure equal average position in the question. Results of the study showed that listing a program first resulted in an average of 2.3 per cent of the respondents naming a program simply because of position.

The number of degrees offered in alternatives may also affect the proportion of replies to each possibility. Gallup (5) reports that in a series of choices running from one extreme to the other there is a tendency for respondents to avoid the extremes and to select a middle position. Ghiselli (7) reports, from experimental study, that a four-point scale using "very" and "fairly" as steps in describing *yes* and *no* responses gave results different from a straight *yes-no* question. A greater proportion of subjects was willing to select a point in the scale than was willing to answer *yes* or *no*. In addition, the total proportion of replies on either side of the neutral point varied between the two question forms.

Completeness of the check-list is an additional factor determining the responses that will be obtained. Jenkins (9) used a check-list which developed through a free-response trial. The check-list and free-response gave roughly similar results. When the first five most frequently checked items were deleted from the list, even though space was provided for additional answers, these five were entirely displaced in terms of frequency of response. Item one dropped from 52 to 14 per cent, item two from 41 to 8 per cent, item three from 33 to 7 per cent, item four from 3 to 6 per cent, and item five from 28 to 2 per cent. Simultaneously other items increased in frequency of mention, one from 20 to 79 per cent.

The check-list has the advantage of eliminating what one investigator calls the "tacit presupposition." Lazarsfeld (*1*) has pointed out that in answering many questions the respondents assume certain limitations. When school children were asked what they most desired in life—income, reputation, etc. were the most frequent answers. When a check-list including *great intelligence* was presented, all checked it, even though none had given this response in the free-answer query. The assumption was that one either had or lacked great intelligence, so that there was little point in listing it. The check-list, of course, can be designed to eliminate such assumptions.

In using a check-list, it is essential that answers provided for the respondent be comparable. This would seem a reasonable requirement to meet, and the logic underlying it is so simple as to require no explanation. Nevertheless some survey agencies still err in this respect. Consider this question used on one poll:

Do you think:
    WPA should be continued by the Federal government on the same scale as it is now
    WPA should be continued by the Federal government, but on a smaller, more restricted scale
    All relief, including work relief, should be handled by the states only
    All relief should again become the responsibility of private charity?

The first two possibilities are identical in kind, differing only in degree. The latter two possibilities differ in kind, are not necessarily related to the first two alternatives. WPA is not the same as all relief, including work relief. Moreover, the possibility of local (city or county) relief is not offered, and hence the check-list is incomplete.

A complete and unbiased check-list, containing comparable items, is a useful tool in survey work. A properly developed check-list can be accurate. One organization asked two questions in a gasoline survey (20):

What do you think are the most important qualities about a gasoline? (free response)
Which of the following qualities of a gasoline do you regard as important? (check-list)

Although many more answers were given in the case of the second question, there was a high degree of agreement between the order of items on the two questions.[3]

This chapter indicates that phrasing the question is one of the most difficult parts of the entire survey technique. By no means are all wording problems at present even clearly recognized, but the chapter should aid in pointing out some of the difficulties encountered in the phrasing of issues. Pre-testing, discussed in Chapter 7, will aid the investigator in checking the quality of this phrasing.

REFERENCES

*(1) AMERICAN MARKETING ASSOCIATION. *The Technique of Marketing Research*. New York: McGraw-Hill, 1937. Chapters 3 and 4.

(2) BENSON, E. G. "Three Words," *Public Opinion Quarterly*, 1940, 4, 130-134.

(3) BLANKENSHIP, A. B. "The Influence of the Question Form upon the Response in a Public Opinion Poll," *Psychological Record*, 1940, 3, 345-424.

(4) CANTRIL, HADLEY. "Experiments in the Wording of Questions," *Public Opinion Quarterly*, 1940, 4, 330-332.

(5) GALLUP, GEORGE. "Question Wording in Public Opinion Polls," *Sociometry*, 1941, 4, 259-268.

(6) GALLUP, GEORGE, AND RAE, S. F. *The Pulse of Democracy*. New York: Simon and Schuster, 1940. Chapter 7.

(7) GHISELLI, E. E. "All or None Versus Graded Response Questionnaire," *Journal of Applied Psychology*, 1939, 23, 405-413.

(8) HOUSER, J. D. "Measurement of the Vital Products of Business," *Journal of Marketing*, 1938, 2, 181-189.

(9) JENKINS, J. G. *Psychology in Business and Industry*. New York: Wiley, 1935. Chapter 15.

[3] Statistically this relationship is indicated by a rank-order correlation of .93.

(10) JENKINS, J. G. "The Questionnaire as a Research Instrument," *Transactions of the New York Academy of Science*, Series II, 2, No. 5, 1940.

(11) KATZ, DANIEL. "Three Criteria: Knowledge, Conviction and Significance," *Public Opinion Quarterly*, 1940, 4, 277-284.

(12) LINK, H. C. "How Many Interviews Are Necessary for Results of a Certain Accuracy?" *Journal of Applied Psychology*, 1937, 21, 1-17.

(13) MATHEWS, C. O. "The Effect of the Order of Printed Response Words on an Interest Questionnaire," *Journal of Educational Psychology*, 1929, 20, 128-134.

(14) POFFENBERGER, A. T. *Psychology in Advertising*. New York: McGraw-Hill, 1932. Chapter 7.

(15) RASKIN, E., AND COOK, S. W. "A Further Investigation of the Measurement of an Attitude Toward Fascism," *Journal of Social Psychology*, 1938, 9, 201-206.

(16) REILLY, W. J. *Marketing Investigations*. New York: Ronald, 1929. Chapter 15.

(17) ROBINSON, C. S. "The New Science of Public Opinion Measurement and Its Implications for Business," *Harvard Business School Alumni Bulletin*, July, 1939, 3-8.

(18) ROBINSON, D. E. "In Agency Research, Results May Be Better if These Pet Don'ts Are Heeded," *Printers' Ink*, March 15, 1940, 61.

(19) ROPER, ELMO. "Wording Questions for the Polls," *Public Opinion Quarterly*, 1940, 4, 129-130.

(20) ROSLOW, SYDNEY, AND BLANKENSHIP, A. B. "Phrasing the Question in Consumer Research," *Journal of Applied Psychology*, 1939, 23, 612-622.

(21) SPINGARN, J. H. "These Public Opinion Polls," *Harper's*, December, 1938, 178, 97-104.

(22) STUDENSKI, PAUL. "How Polls Can Mislead," *Harper's*, December, 1939, 180, 80-83.

(23) THORNDIKE, E. L. *A Teacher's Word Book of Twenty Thousand Words*. New York: Teachers College, 1932.

(24) WEMBRIDGE, E. R., AND MEANS, E. R. "Voting on the Double Negative," *Journal of Applied Psychology*, 1918, 2, 156-163.

(25) WHITE, PERCIVAL. *Marketing Research Technique*. New York: Harper, 1931. Chapter 14.

CHAPTER 6

Preliminary Assembly of the Questionnaire

~~~~~~

READ the following paragraph just once, and see if you come out with the correct answer.

The Western Limited started from Philadelphia with five passengers in the club car. At Overbrook three of these got off, and four more got on. Then at Paoli four got off, and two more came on. The train stopped for a moment at Downingtown, where no one got off, but two people boarded the train. At Parkesburg three persons got off. At Christiana three got off, and one got on. When the train arrived in Lancaster, two more got on, and one got off. How many stops did the train make?

You are an exception if you got the answer to this on the first reading. Your thinking was misdirected. Your chain of thought was set up along other channels.

The respondent's thoughts must be set up in such channels that unbiased, considered, and meaningful replies will result. The problem in the assembly of the questionnaire is to list a set of questions which is not too long, and arranged in an order which makes sense to the respondent. If the questionnaire is too long, thoughts of the respondent may be lost. If the arrangement of the questions is poor, the person answering is forced to skip around with his thoughts, and the replies obtained are not likely to be meaningful.

LENGTH OF THE QUESTIONNAIRE

How long can the questionnaire be? This is a problem which the most highly trained survey technician cannot answer arbitrarily. The queries should be carefully scrutinized, so that any which do not contribute to the purposes of the study may be eliminated. Usual procedure is to make the interview form as short as possible, retaining only the questions which bear directly upon the problem under study.

Feasible length of the questionnaire depends upon several factors. In general, the personal interview permits the asking of more questions than does either the mail or the telephone approach. An interesting questionnaire may be longer than a dull one.

Locale of the questioning influences the length of the questionnaire. Persons approached on street corners may be willing to spend less time answering questions than those who are approached in their homes. On the other hand, people waiting for trolleys or trains are frequently glad for something which will help them pass the time.

The type of person interviewed will also influence the questionnaire length. By and large, it is more difficult to get persons of high economic level to talk with an investigator for twenty minutes than it is to obtain co-operation for the same period of time from a person of medium income.

Length of the questionnaire can be set only after trial interviews. In policy some of the survey organizations attempt to limit their list of questions to some fifteen minutes' conversation where the personal approach is used. Other groups contend that length is no problem for a competent investigator. Probably the truth is somewhere between these extremes.

Naturally the mail questionnaire commonly does not include as many questions as the personal approach (about eight or ten simple questions is the usual limit), and the telephone interview is generally limited to five minutes or less.

It is the respondent who sets the length. The maximal length of time during which it is possible to keep the respondent actively interested (and hence in the proper frame of mind for answering questions) dictates the length of the questionnaire.

Respondent interest, however important, is not sufficient. Thoughts of the person replying must be directed into proper channels in order for replies to be significant. Sequence of the questions is the key to this problem.

Sequence of Questions

The trial interviewing, outlined in Chapter 7, determines the degree of success achieved in the arrangement of questions in the series.

Although the arrangement must always be subjected to test, and will depend upon the nature of the particular series of questions, a few general principles of order may be listed.

1. *The opening question must create rapport.* The list of questions, as mentioned in Chapter 5, should always be carefully considered from the standpoint of interest. Those which seem to have greatest appeal should be tried at the start of the questionnaire. Some issue of much general interest at the particular period of the study may be available, but the introductory question should not be one of the really vital issues of the study.

The first question of the interview is at a disadvantage. It is acting as an "ice breaker," designed to secure the co-operation of respondents. A large proportion of those answering will not yet be in the proper mood for answering, so will at the start be unprepared for almost any question that might be asked. The introductory question can be expected to produce a greater proportion of "don't know" answers than when it is asked farther along in the questionnaire. According to one report (5), 3 per cent more respondents replied "Don't know" when the identical question was asked first than when it was asked later on during the period of questioning.

2. *The first few questions must be simple.* Some survey organizations make it a point never to ask any but straight *yes-no* questions at the start. This sort of query appears simpler to the respondent than one which calls for a reply in his own words.

If a difficult question is asked at the beginning, a large proportion of respondents reply "Don't know," and others refuse to continue with the questions. This question was used as the first in one series: *What do you consider the outstanding business and secretarial school for women?*

It was a difficult question. There was also a belief on the part of those interviewed that the field worker was attempting to sell a business course. The question did not meet either of the two discussed criteria, so it is not surprising that some 50 per cent of those who did reply said "Don't know." Interviewers also reported difficulty in persuading interviewees to continue with the remaining questions.

3. *The first few questions must be ones on which respondents can and will express themselves.* The person who has difficulty answering the first few questions may feel that doubt is being thrown upon his intelligence. If he does continue, he may give false or facetious replies to bolster his ego. The first few questions should never reflect upon the respondent's ego or pride. If they do, there may be no opportunity to set up the interviewee's thoughts in the desired channels.

In many surveys, as Chapter 8 shows, it is necessary to ask persons ownership of automobiles, telephones, radios. Possession of such items is used as an indication of economic status. Such questions can seldom be asked at the start of the questioning. Those who did not own cars might not be willing at that point to make the admission. Those who did own might be annoyed at the impertinence of the inquiry. Only after rapport has been established can such questions be asked.

One study of attitudes toward picketing contained several necessarily involved questions. These could not be used at the start of the questionnaire. Since this was in 1940, the first question asked was: *Do you favor a third term for President Roosevelt?* This was an issue on which almost everyone held an opinion, and usually a strong one. It tended to make the respondent "open up," to continue the series of questions, in fact to welcome additional questions. Yet it had no real purpose other than to establish rapport; its results were not used in summary.

One organization conducted a study in which people were asked a number of questions relating to their attitudes, knowledge, and action they had taken in regard to various aspects of aviation. By trying out various approaches, it was soon discovered that a simple question, *Have you ever been up in an airplane?* worked well as an opener. This was a question on which respondents could and did express themselves. It also met the other suggested standards for opening questions since it was simple and since it helped to establish rapport by creating interest.

4. *Any personal question should be placed well in the body of the questionnaire.* Some questions may require as a prelude the building up of the respondent's confidence. In one study about workers' feelings toward their fellow workmen and supervisors (9), it was clearly essential to gain the confidence of the interviewee before such questions could be asked. The purpose of the questioning had to be disguised, and the particular subject of interest had to be introduced gradually. The first few questions concerned the government and its effect on business. Following questions concerned subjects such as employment conditions in general, the interviewee's own neighborhood, his friends, and finally himself. From these questions there was no difficulty in asking:

How regular has your work been in the past year?
How long have you worked for your present employer?
Do you intend to stay with him in the future?

5. *Questions which may reflect upon the respondent's intelligence must be placed well in the body of the questionnaire.* Occasionally it is necessary to ask questions which reflect upon the intelligence of the respondent. One study reported (5) included questions similar to these:

What cold remedy have you seen or heard advertising:
(a) Actually kills a cold in a day?
(b) Sells over 53 million packages a year?

Only a small proportion of the public can give answers to questions like these, except where the advertising has been unusually effective. If too many questions of this nature are included, the respondent may either refuse to continue or continue with false or facetious replies.

If this sort of query must be asked, it should be saved for the last portion of the questioning. Then, not only will there be a better chance of securing co-operation of the person being interviewed, but even if the interview is terminated, it will not be too serious. Previously answered questions will still be of value.

6. *Questions with little respondent interest must be placed well*

in the body of the series. The query of little interest should be surrounded by questions of higher interest value. On one survey this question had to be included: *Do you think that married women should be permitted to work in tax-supported jobs if the husband is earning $200 a month?* Since this question lacks interest value, it should be well along in the questions, and surrounded with other queries that are more interesting. If city dwellers were asked: *Do you approve of the farm policy of the national government* not only would the subject have little interest for them, but the chances would be that the majority of respondents would not know of the farm policy of the national government. This type of question too would have to be well along in the interview.

7. *Questions should be arranged psychologically.* What general sequence should be used in the arrangement of questions? In the case listed on page 75, where personal questions were asked successfully of workers, a succession of related questions led the respondent's thoughts naturally to the subject in which the investigators were interested.

Right along this line is the process of questioning about motives. Until recently, many of those in the survey field looked askance at any question designed to uncover motives. Lazarsfeld (1), through his emphasis on a series of questions to measure motives, has shown fairly conclusively that motives can be measured by the questionnaire procedure. Through his work, those in the survey field have learned not to ask a single question about motives, but to ask a series of related questions which delve into various aspects of motivation.

Whether motives, opinions, or actions are being measured, one question should lead to the next, so that a train of thought is established. The arrangement cannot be made at the desk; it is a problem calling for field work. It is only by talking with people that you can learn about thought processes. To obtain responses without setting up this chain of thought is of little value.

Lazarsfeld calls one application of this sort of process "interviewing on the time line" (1). He illustrates the technique by saying that if we want to find out what a person did at 8 P.M. yesterday, we should first ask him when he left his office, for he is sure to remember that. We can then ask what he did next, what following that, until the 8 p.m. hour is reached.

This concept might be broadened and termed "the psychological line." It can be applied to all sorts of questions, whether memory or opinion. It is possible to interview along the line of thought. By and large it is also possible not to break that chain of thought.

In most questionnaires this process can be followed without too much difficulty. One study (1) was concerned with determining why people went to motion pictures, how they selected their company, and the factors that influenced the choice of the particular picture they went to see. Preliminary analysis revealed that a different approach had to be used for those who went especially to see a given picture, and for those who went for general entertainment rather than for the particular feature.

Among those who reported dominant interest in the picture, questions were first asked as to how they had selected the film. These were followed with inquiries about how they selected their company, and why they chose this particular time for attending. Among those who sought general entertainment, the logical beginning was why they had decided to go to the movies, how they selected their company, and finally, how they happened to choose this particular picture. In other words the recall process was aided by asking questions in the same sequence in which the individual had experienced his decisions.

The importance of following some chain of thought in the questioning process can scarcely be emphasized too greatly. Once a train of thought has been established, breaking that sequence can lead to poor results. Where questions must be turned into different channels, it is possible to do this gradually, so that the respondent turns to the new thoughts gradually, with a minimum of effort. A series of intervening questions can generally be inserted to change the trend of thinking.

A totally unrelated question, suddenly asked, is not desirable. The individual is not prepared to give an answer on a subject entirely different from previous discussion. One organization has asked a series of social attitude questions in questionnaires which contained only similar questions and in questionnaires in which the surrounding questions concerned buying behavior. An average of from 7 to 13 per cent more indecision answers resulted when the questions appeared in the buying context (5). This finding illustrates that a change from one subject to another produces more "don't know" replies than is true when related issues precede the same question.

8. *The sequence of questions can, under certain circumstances, bias the replies to some of the later questions.* A particular question can secure biased replies because of preceding questions. In the case of memory questions this bias takes the form of clues, or some other form of memory stimulation. In the case of opinion questions, it may be due to forcing respondents' thoughts into specific rather than general channels, or to the fact that arguments or ideas are presented about the proposition before the issue itself is presented.

a. *Bias in memory questions.* Brock (6) tells of a questionnaire which opened with a question about car ownership. Those who admitted possession were questioned about their gasoline and oil purchasing. These queries were followed by a question about a local news broadcast, and the product advertised on the program. Because of the order of the questions, seven of ten respondents tried to guess the name of an automobile or gasoline company as sponsor of the show. The order of the questions turned the thinking of the respondents toward these two types of business, thus biasing replies to the last question. The inquiries on broadcast and sponsor should have preceded the other queries in order to eliminate such bias.

Another survey was made for a company which was introducing its product in a town by means of an extensive sampling campaign supplemented by newspaper and radio advertising. Following the close of this campaign, a questionnaire study was conducted in the locality to determine the effectiveness of the promotion. Among the questions were these subjects (these are not the phrasings used):

The advertising media in which any of this *commodity* (not brand) advertising was seen or heard.

Whether or not the respondent had received a sample of this particular commodity.

(Among those who had heard advertisements of the particular *brand*) A description of the forms of radio advertising heard.

In one questionnaire form the order of the queries was just as outlined. In the other form these same issues were included, but the details of the radio advertising were obtained before the sampling question was asked.

Those asked first about the sample apparently began to think in terms of the particular brand, and were able to mention more details about the radio advertising than those asked about the details before any other clue had been given as to who was making the study. In the first group identification of all four radio advertisements averaged 6 per cent higher than in the second group.

It is sometimes undesirable to eliminate bias resulting from question order. A study (1) was being conducted among readers of a technical publication. Hobbies and technical interests were covered by the first few questions, and this question followed: *Did you ever buy anything following up an advertisement in X magazine?* Practically all advertising influences mentioned by respondents concerned the buying of technical tools and materials. More common commodities were seldom mentioned. In order to get respondents thinking about these general commodities as well, specific questions relating to food, garments, and other commodities were included. When these questions, as well as those on hobbies and technical interests, preceded the advertising question, thoughts of respondents were so directed that all types of products were given in answer to the advertising inquiry.

b. *Bias in attitude questions.* In one case the attitude of women toward advertising was being investigated (1). In some of the questionnaires, queries about dresses preceded those on attitudes toward advertising, while in other forms the advertising questions were first. Results showed that attitudes toward advertising were more favorable when the dress questions preceded. It was learned that the order of the questions tended to make women think in terms of dress advertising, toward which they were favorable. When the advertising question preceded, it became apparent that women were thinking in broader terms—about many forms of advertising.

In a questionnaire concerned largely with beer consumption (9), three specific queries about the use of beer opened the questionnaire. These questions had the effect of making the respondent think in terms of local brews. The fourth question was: *What brand of beer do you consider to be best?* This produced answers largely in terms of local beers. At a later point in the questioning, after the thoughts of interviewees had been turned to nationally known brands, this question was asked: *What do you consider the very best brand of beer in the country?* With this question the names of many more nationally known brands were given.

Another case in which it is not desirable to eliminate the influence of order is provided by a situation where it is necessary to place the respondent's thoughts in channels which make him maintain a critical attitude toward the vital issues of the study. In a recent study conducted with two questionnaire forms (*10*), two questions were varied in order—one pertaining to the payment of a license fee in order to eliminate radio advertising, the other an estimate of time consumed by radio commercials. When the fee question preceded, a shorter time was estimated for the commercials. With this same order, respondents were more favorable in general toward radio advertising. The investigators concluded that the fee question tended to make individuals consider more seriously the implications of eliminating radio advertising, and as a result softened their general attitude toward it.

References

*(1) AMERICAN MARKETING ASSOCIATION. *The Technique of Marketing Research*. New York: McGraw-Hill, 1937. Chapter 3.

(2) BLANKENSHIP, A. B. "The Influence of the Question Form Upon the Response in a Public Opinion Poll," *Psychological Record*, 1940, 3, 345-424.

(3) BLANKENSHIP, A. B. "Psychological Problems in the Measurement of Consumer Preferences," *Journal of Marketing*, 1942, 6, No. 4, Part 2, 66-75.

(4) BLANKENSHIP, A. B. "These Opinion Polls Again!" *Sociometry*, 1942, 5, 89-101.

(5) BLANKENSHIP, A. B., AND ROSLOW, SYDNEY. "The Effect of Context and Point of Reference Upon Responses to Questions." Unpublished manuscript, 1939.

(6) BROCK, SPENCER. "Mechanism of Research," *Printer's Ink*, May 25, 1939, 21-23.

(7) LINK, H. C. *The New Psychology of Selling and Advertising.* New York: Macmillan, 1934. Chapter 3.

(8) REILLY, W. J. *Marketing Investigations.* New York: Ronald, 1929. Chapter 15.

(9) ROSLOW, SYDNEY, AND BLANKENSHIP, A. B. "Phrasing the Question in Consumer Research," *Journal of Applied Psychology*, 1939, 23, 612-622.

(10) SAYRE, JEANETTE. "A Comparison of Three Indices of Attitude Towards Radio Advertising," *Journal of Applied Psychology*, 1939, 23, 23-33.

CHAPTER 7

Testing the Questionnaire

> The technique of pretesting is in a rather nebulous state so
> far. A more exact system would be a very helpful contri-
> bution. . . . It is something that should come in time.
> —*The Technique of Marketing Research*

~~~~~~

THOUGH no "exact system" has been developed since the time of
this statement, at least some progress has been made.

Knowledge of principles of phrasing and sequence do not insure
an effective questionnaire. The problems arising on any study are
unique. The subject matter of the questionnaire is likely to be
different from all of its predecessors, and the time element has
changed. Especially in these days it is true that the rapidly changing international situation may be expected to cause individuals'
reactions to change almost from day to day.

In other words, humans are dynamic rather than static. Because
of this fact, no questionnaire, regardless of how carefully it is
planned, may be assumed to work well until some trial has been
given it under field conditions. A limited number of trial interviews may provide rough checks upon the quality of wording of
the questions, their scope and sequence, the length of the questionnaire, instructions to field workers, plans for tabulation, and
the final cost of the survey. In some cases a preliminary study
preceding the possible "final" study may be desirable for more
accurate answers to such problems.

THE PRE-TEST

1. *The method.* The pre-test is the first step in the testing of
any survey procedure. Interviewers talk with a number of persons,

using the drafted form of the questionnaire. Calls may be made with ten persons or with several hundred, depending upon the dictates of the particular study. The test may (and probably will) reveal a need for additional testing. When the pre-test indicates that a question should be rephrased, the revised wording itself will require additional testing.

Especially difficult questionnaires sometimes require as many as ten or fifteen revisions before the final form is evolved. Time available for the study may be short, and in this case testing is necessarily limited. Accuracy required on the final survey may not be great; if only a rough indication of facts will be required, there is little point in spending a great deal of time and money on testing. Previous experience of the survey director sometimes shortens the period of testing, particularly if he has conducted studies of a similar nature. Some of his colleagues in the survey field may have related investigations available, thus shortening his period of trial and error.

First testing should always be carried on with the personal interview procedure, even when the final study is planned with the use of mail or telephone approach. Generally speaking, favorable or unfavorable reactions of respondents to the questionnaire as a whole are difficult to detect when the questionnaire is a mail or telephone inquiry. Free comments cannot be obtained from the usual mail or telephone series of questions. False or facetious answers cannot be controlled except by the personal approach.

Where the mail or the telephone approach is to be used on the final survey, the personal interview pre-test should be followed by another pre-test which makes use of the particular method of contact planned finally. If a mail survey is to be used, a sample of the persons on the mailing list will provide an accurate measure of the nature and proportion of responses which may be expected on the final mailing. In the case of the telephone approach, the subsequent telephone pre-test will answer problems which the personal interview cannot, such as length, and scope of information.

Since the usual pre-test uses the personal call, most of the discussion here concerns that form of test. Chapter 8 shows that the personal interview makes it reasonably simple to obtain the kind of respondents needed for the study. It is possible to question respondents who are generally similar in characteristics to the final group of persons with whom interviews are to be obtained. If women are to be interviewed about their bread-buying, then only women should be interviewed on the pre-test. Pre-test findings based on a group different from that within which the final study is to be conducted may not hold for a different sort of sample.

2. *The results.* Principal purpose of the pre-test is to check upon the quality of survey technique: method of collecting the data, phrasing and sequence of questions, length of the questionnaire, subject matter, adequacy of instructions. Finally, it provides a method for estimating final costs of the study.

a. *Checking the method of collecting data.* One procedure required ten minutes of conversation with each of a number of private school teachers. The pre-test workers went around to private schools and received permission to interview teachers. Permission was easy to obtain, but there was difficulty in finding a time at which teachers could and would talk. No more than one interview could be obtained during a recess period. Lunch-time was no better; most of the teachers in these particular schools seemed to go out for lunch. Directly following the end of the schoolday it was possible to talk to one teacher, but by the end of that one interview the rest of the faculty had left for parts unknown. Final solution was to use a mail questionnaire.

b. *Testing question-phrasing.* An outcome of the pre-test is an improvement in the question-phrasing. Testing will provide clues as to the clarity of questions, their bias (if any), the quality of the check-list (if any).

One question used on the first form of a questionnaire was: *Do you think well, or not-so-well of the following industries? (The name of each industry in the list was read, with the query:) Well, or not-so-well?*

Many of those interviewed on the pre-test replied, "How can I answer such a question? Are you referring to the way they treat their labor, their contributions to the war effort, the products they make, or what?" So the question was rephrased: *As far as the industries themselves are concerned, and the way they are run, do you think well or not-so-well of the following?* No further difficulties were encountered with this question.

In the same study a question on the first test was phrased: *Would a government-owned food industry in this country result in higher or lower food prices for: milk and dairy goods, fish, meat, etc.? (Each food was asked about separately.)* Respondents tended to give the same reply to each item, and generally remarked, "Oh, I feel the same about all of those products. If the government would raise (lower) prices for one food, it would do so for all." The interviewees had a generalized attitude on how government ownership would affect food prices; they did not believe that such a scheme would have different effects upon various foods. The question was reworded: *Would a government-owned food industry in this country result in higher or lower food prices?*

Pre-testing is valuable for the aid it provides in securing proper vocabulary level of words in questions. In one test a question was asked: *Do you think that present government expenditures are too high, too low, or about the right amount?* The test revealed that the word *expenditures* was not understood by many of the respondents, so the question was rephrased: *Do you think that the government is, at present, spending too much, too little, or about the right amount?* This phrasing worked satisfactorily.

The pre-test provides the only means by which an adequate check-list can be obtained. Only by asking free-response questions in pre-tests can such a list be developed. In the case of the gasoline question mentioned in Chapter 5, the phrasing on the pre-test had to be *What qualities of a gasoline do you regard as important?* After a sufficient number of answers had been tabulated, a check-list for respondents was developed. The list included practically all items mentioned, including such points as pick-up, quick-starting, and mileage. The good check-list must have a complete and comparable list of items. The order of items offered in the trial interviewing must be varied to measure any possible position effect.

c. *Testing sequence influences.* The first few questions must arouse respondent interest and co-operation. They must be simple, and questions on which respondents can and will express themselves. Any personal question must be well along in the series; so must questions which may reflect upon the intelligence of the interviewee and those with little respondent interest. Chapter 6 pointed out that the key to arrangement of questions was that they should follow the line of thought. The pre-test, if well designed, will give answers as to how well these points of sequence have been met.

Sequence must be observed closely in order to make sure that it provides no basis for answer bias. Particularly where general questions follow a few specific inquiries, interviewers must watch carefully to make sure that the general questions are not answered in terms of the preceding specific questions. As a rule it is better to proceed from general to specific questions than the reverse.

In a survey about alarm clocks (6), two questions were to be included:

> What improvements do you think can be made in alarm clocks?
> How does the tick of a clock affect you at night?

The improvement question had to be placed prior to the tick question; otherwise too many persons would have responded in terms of the loud ticking at night when the improvement question was asked.

d. *Determining feasible length of questionnaire.* Co-operation, of course, is the big factor here, but not the only one. The field workers must observe at what point, even with continued co-operation, the person tends to become bored and unresponsive. Answers past that point are likely to be worthless. Respondent interest must remain at the highest possible level in order for answers to be valid. Only close observation of interviewers determines the degree to which this interest is maintained.

Length can be seriously influenced by the sequence of questions. In one questionnaire concerned largely with attitudes and knowledge about advertising, a number of questions similar to the following were included: *What brand of cigarette advertises: Something new has been added?* This sort of question can seriously reflect, from the respondent's point of view, upon his intelligence. The first pre-test of the questionnaire in which a number of these questions was to be included showed that the interviewee apparently lost interest after two or three of these questions had been asked. In a subsequent form of the questionnaire all such questions were left for the end. This way it was possible to maintain the highest interest of the respondent until the last few moments of questioning. Since it was known that interest level would be low on these questions in any case, the questionnaire was then adjudged a success.

e. *Suggestions for additional subject matter*. The good test interviewer will carefully record all spontaneous remarks which arise during the course of testing. In many cases these comments provide a basis for important additional questions.

In one case a questionnaire concerned with the influence of advertising in a particular publication was being tested (1). One respondent ventured the comment that he had looked in the publication for the advertisement of a particular product and had been unable to find it. This comment gave rise to the question *Did you ever look in this magazine for an advertisement which was not there?* This turned out to be an important issue. Other important issues frequently turn up in pre-tests.

Free-comment questions are those which usually secure the wide variety of answers which may turn out to be so valuable during the course of the testing. In one test a question was included as to how flour should be packaged (1). One respondent's reply, "Make it in biscuits," actually revolutionized one aspect of the flour industry. A new product was born with the innovation of the ready-to-bake biscuit mix.

f. *Suggestions for elimination of questions*. Testing the questionnaire may reveal that answers to certain questions are practically identical. On one test these two questions were asked:

Is the price of meat high, low or about right?
In comparison with the price of other foods, is the price of meat high, low or about right?

Even though other questions separated these two in the interviewing, practically all who responded "low" to the first question made the same reply to the second. However, some of those who replied

"Don't know" to the first were able to make up their minds and give a definite response by the time the field worker got to the second query. Probably the fact that the second question provided a basis for comparison was the reason for part of this. Since the second question appeared somewhat superior in its anchoring of replies, the former was eliminated from the series of queries.

g. *Checking adequacy of field workers' instructions.* Testing aids in developing instructions to the point where detailed suggestions may be made by the survey agency to those who will conduct the interviewing on the subsequent study. Tentative instructions given the field force for testing may not work out in practice, and will, in any case, require some modification in line with pre-test experience. On a bread-buying study the question was asked: *What brand of bread is advertised as having a high vitamin content?* Interviewers were instructed that if a specific brand of bread was named in reply, they were to ask, *Have you ever bought any?*

All of the pre-test canvassers reported a similar experience. Some of the women who couldn't name the brand still spontaneously remarked that they had bought some of the bread. Nor was this mere imagination on their parts. When the field workers asked them, *Which of these brands was it?* the majority of them were able to select the correct brand name. The original questionnaire was not obtaining an accurate measure of the proportion of women who had tried "vitamin bread," and had to be revised.

h. *Estimating the probable cost of the subsequent survey.* The test workers report on their total interviewing time, and average time required to complete each call can be computed. Total field-work cost can then be closely estimated. Cost of preparation and distribution of materials, supervision, tabulating, and report preparation can be added. Frequently without a pre-test it is impossible to make any sort of approximation as to costs, since field work is likely to be the greatest variable, and one of the major expenses of any questionnaire study.

3. *The interviewers.* The entire procedure has indicated that the test workers must be among the best available. They must be intelligent; much is left to their judgment. A good tester, for instance, will vary phrasing or sequence without being told if he

feels that it might make an improvement. He must record each comment made by a respondent regardless of how far afield from questionnaire issues that remark may appear. The pre-tester must have simple explanations of questions ready if respondents demand these.

Test workers must be critical. They must be ready to criticize every question, and sequence of the inquiries. They must be able to evaluate critically the responses of their questionees at the time of the conversation, to make sure that the question is eliciting the general type of reply for which it was designed. Trial workers must be able to tell the supervisor in precisely what ways instructions for field workers must be modified or extended.

Who ought to make these calls—what sort of worker should he be?

If the survey technician makes his own calls, work will probably be of high quality. This field work on his part will enable him to understand field problems which he would otherwise not appreciate. It is just as possible that the technician may be biased as to the quality of his own questionnaire.

A check by the survey director, supplemented by the work of qualified test workers, seems to be the best procedure. The more workers used for this testing, the better the indications that the procedure will work with a wide variety of interviewees, and the greater number of criticisms of procedure. The greater the number and variety of respondents, the more indication that it will work with a cross-section.

4. *Example of a pre-test.* An outlined example of a pre-test for one study will provide an indication of the general procedure and findings. This was a marketing investigation among farm people. Since it was made during wartime, and since the interviews were to be distributed all over the country, one of the original decisions was to make the study by mail. The series of questions, all concerning the same product, asked about the place of purchase, frequency of purchase, purchaser, seasonal influences upon use of the item, and an inventory of the types and quantities of the items owned.

Work was started with personal calls upon twenty farm people. These calls showed that detailed inventory questions couldn't be asked, especially since it was to be a mail questionnaire (with its accompanying shortness and simplicity).

It was also apparent that in the question *About how many times per year is*——*bought?* the word *times* had to be italicized; otherwise respondents tended to report the *number* of items purchased annually. Other questions were:

What was the name of the store where_____was purchased?
What kind of store is that?

The variety of answers obtained to the *kind of store* question made it imperative to provide a list of store "types" for the respondent to check.

Another question was: *About how long ago was the last purchase made? (please say how many)*____*weeks ago*____*months ago*. Two things were clear from use of this question. The words *How long ago* had to be substituted in place of *how many*, since a number of people were again reporting the number of items purchased. It was also learned that *years ago* had to be included as an alternative, since a few respondents hadn't purchased any of these items for several years.

Although this "final" study was to be made by mail, the first test was by personal interview. There was an effort made to simulate some of the conditions of the mail questionnaire. The investigator handed each respondent the questionnaire, and asked each one to fill it out himself. Meanwhile the field worker looked on, asked questions, and answered others.

The personal pre-test was followed by a sample mailing as the second portion of the testing procedure. Although it was felt that the changes made as a result of the personal pre-test were all desirable ones, there had to be a test under actual conditions of the "final" survey to insure the entire procedure would work well. In addition the very changes indicated by the first test had to be subjected to some testing. For that reason a random sampling of 150 names was taken from the mailing list, so that each geographic area was covered in its proper proportion.

Returns indicated several interesting facts. In addition to making it possible to predict the proportion of returns to be expected on the subsequent mailing, they suggested a few further modifications of the questionnaire. Some respondents were still confused, giving answers of *how many* instead of *how long ago*. It was decided that to overcome this and similar errors in replies, the order of questions would have to be made more logical and flowing to the respondent, so that there would be little reason for him to become confused. The questionnaire was revised so that the order of items covered now went from frequency of purchase to recency of purchase, who made the last purchase, the place this purchase was made, the kinds and number of items owned, and seasons in which each item owned is used. In addition such important words as *how many times* were capitalized. Little confusion resulted in the final mailing, and the proportion of returns was within 2 per cent of the figure predicted from the test mailing.

In some studies thorough pre-testing will be all that is required to develop the procedure to be used in the subsequent survey. In other studies a "test-tube" survey may be used as a preparation and/or test of the necessity of a wider-scale study. The following section discusses the test-tube study and its application to survey procedure.

THE TEST-TUBE STUDY

The test-tube study may be designed to answer one or both of two questions: (a) Is a further survey desirable; and (b) what refinements in procedure are desirable for this larger study?

Sometimes it is known that the final survey must be very accurate; in such cases the test-tube study is a natural step following the testing. In other cases there is a question as to whether the proposed large-scale survey is indicated; the test-tube study can also answer that question.

1 *The method.* The test-tube study is a limited survey carried out under field conditions which may be expected to operate in any larger survey. The usual pre-test at most involves a few hundred calls; the test-tube study may obtain several thousand respondents. The test-tube survey can be carried on only after the pre-test has revealed the extent of its information. The test-tube study is limited

in terms of the number of people who are interviewed, as compared with the final study. This limitation is usually handled by conducting the survey in only a few of the many localities contemplated for the final study. The usual type of worker, rather than the high type required for the pre-test, will make the calls.

2 *The results.* Results of the test-tube study will show whether a further study is desirable. It will give information on technique: the nature of the sample required, the quality of question phrasing and sequence, suggestions for additions and eliminations of questions, testing of instructions to field workers, practice in preparation of tables, and a measure of such points as the internal consistency of the results.

a. *Is a further study desirable?* Most frequent use of the test-tube study is to provide an indication of what any subsequent research might show. Survey agencies sometimes suggest a limited investigation to determine whether the proposed large-scale study will be worth the required investment.

In some studies the most important issues show sentiment so overwhelmingly in one direction that a further study would not be expected to change the results to any substantial degree. In this case it would be pointless to spend further time and money. Where sentiment is evenly divided on important issues, only further interviews will sometimes reveal the accurate division of reaction.

In this last sort of situation it is not unusual to find that a study regarded as "final" is only preliminary. On pre-election polls, if sentiment for candidates in a particular community is very close (in the neighborhood of 50-50), it is only by further field work that the statistical reliability of the results can be raised to the point where an accurate measure of sentiment can be obtained. One of the values of the test-tube study is therefore an indication of the required size of the sample on the subsequent survey. Chapters on sampling will explain what factors must be taken into consideration in planning the size of sample.[1]

If this basic question of whether a further study is desirable is

[1] Actually, an *indication of sample size* could be listed as one of the results of the test-tube study. Since this factor is so closely related to the question of whether a further study is desirable, the discussion of sample size is regarded here as a part of the larger problem of a further investigation.

answered affirmatively, then there are many other outcomes of the test-tube study. Most of these additional results are concerned with problems of technique. Although the pre-testing gave rough answers to problems of technique (such as wording), the test-tube study can be designed so as to give a far more accurate indication to specific technique questions.

b. *Defining the nature of the sample.* In some cases it is only by means of the test-tube study that the type of respondents required on the final survey can be defined. This definition usually takes the form of *limiting* the group of persons to be approached on the ultimate research, hence is important not only from a definition point of view, but also for financial reasons.

One test-tube study was conducted among both farmers and urbanites. Since there were no differences apparent in reactions to the particular issues, the farmer group, more expensive to interview, was eliminated from the sample on the subsequent research.

The test-tube study is also useful in defining a general cross-section of a given community. One organization uses this method continously to define the nature of the cross-section.

This group goes into a particular community and calls upon every 10th or 50th home, depending upon the size of the community. Such a procedure practically insures that a "typical" group of respondents will be obtained. On this preliminary study they secure from each family figures on family composition, income, occupation, etc. Field workers inquire whether the family would be willing to answer further questions if the worker were to return, and what days and hours the persons would most likely be at home. The organization can then compile statistics for the particular community, and can set up a group of families they can go back to to obtain a group of respondents who will be similar in characteristics to the entire group.

The chapter on the nature of the sample will describe sources of information on sex, age, family occupation, etc. But the particular organization which conducts these extensive preliminary surveys for gathering such information recognizes that with the large population shifts occurring in these days such statistics quickly get out of date.

c. *Testing question-phrasing.* A requirement of high accuracy on the final study may indicate that question suggestions from pre-testing must be supplemented with further testing of phraseology. The pre-test will show what wordings are promising, but at best this result will be an approximation. The test-tube study can be set up to measure accurately what results will be obtained with varying question-phrasings.

Five or six proposed wordings can be placed on different questionnaire forms identical except for this question variation. Interviewers who make the calls then use the questionnaire forms in serial fashion. This method insures a comparable sample of persons with each form. Each field worker will have made the same number of calls with each form. Any differences in reply to the question variations should then be due to wording variations rather than other factors.

After the results have been summarized for the variant phrasings, there is still the problem of deciding which form is superior. Ordinarily there is no objective criterion of behavior against which to check the accuracy of each form. The next best method of evaluating the forms begins with a comparison of their answers in order of frequency. If question form A, for instance, as in the table,

Question Form	% Affirmative Replies	% Negative Replies
A	80	20
B	70	30
C	60	40
D	50	50
E	40	60

secured the highest proportion of affirmative answers, it may be discarded as a leading question. Question E may be discarded for similar reasons, since it obtained the highest proportion of negative responses. In these terms Question C appears to be the most neutral form. This summary does not take into account the "don't know" replies. The fewer indecision answers that are obtained, other things being equal, the better the wording. If 40 per cent reply "Don't know" to a question, the placing of those 40 per cent into one or other category of response could change the entire pattern of reaction. In these terms the question producing least indecision is superior.

This means that in the above example, if question forms B, C, and D all produced the same proportion of indecision responses, then C, because of its middle position in affirmative replies, is the best form.

d. *Testing sequence influences.* The test-tube study may also be designed to show which sequence is best, in terms of both lack of bias and the proportion of respondents able to answer a particular query. If a sequence influence is suspected, then the test-tube study may be designed to indicate the superior sequence.

In this case the four or five possible sequences are arranged on different questionnaire forms, and comparable samples of respondents are obtained for each form. Responses to the various questions are compared for the forms in terms of extent and direction of bias, and indecision. Bias in the order of queries will be revealed by the proportion of affirmative and negative answers to each; if there is any lack of logic to respondents in the order, then proportion of indecision answers will tend to be high. Both bias and improper psychological order will be revealed by such a test.

e. *Suggestions for additional subject matter.* Although by this time the scope of the survey should already have been decided, occasionally a spontaneous comment by a respondent will provide suggestions. In one study of public opinion toward the food industry, a question had been asked as to whether the respondent was favorable or unfavorable about a number of specific food industries. The test-tube study provided a comparison of the specific food industries in terms of public approval and disapproval. The resulting table showed the sponsor that he needed a similar measure of approval and disapproval toward the food industry in general, as well as opinion about a few other industries against which to interpret the results.

f. *Suggestions for elimination of questions.* Some of the questions may have been employed in the test-tube study only because they appeared to have value in the analysis of results to other queries. On one study it was believed that answers to a series of questions would differ between those who thought that we should or should not give Britain active military aid (before our entry into the war). Since the test-tube study showed that such a relationship did not exist, the question on aid to Britain did not tie in with purposes of the investigation and was eliminated from the survey which followed.

g. *Checking adequacy of field workers' instructions.* In some cases the instructions for investigators may not be clear despite the testing procedure. The pre-test workers are all exceptionally competent individuals and may not have had the trouble understanding directions that the more usual sort of worker will. For this reason it is common practice to have conferences of test-tube workers after their field experiences, so that their reactions to their experiences and to the instructions can be discussed. Such conferences commonly reveal situations which have not been handled adequately in the instructions, since the survey supervisors could not foresee all such situations.

h. *Checking plans for tabulation and summary.* Since the test-tube survey usually includes questionnaires in the thousands, it will be essential to tabulate the results, and probably to write the summary. This in itself is a definite "plus" for the test-tube study, since there is always the tendency for the researcher to neglect this summary aspect until he is forced to consider it.

Preliminary tabulations and summary may show other flaws in the study which are revealed by no other method. In one study it was only the summary of the test-tube survey which revealed that the client was interested in one small concern not included separately in tabulations (it was placed in *miscellaneous*) of replies. Such an omission would have been expensive to rectify in the final study once tabulations were complete.

This preliminary summary may indicate important cross-relationships of replies which might be neglected without the test-tube study. Chapter 12 shows the situations in which machine and hand tabulations are advantageous. If the cross-relationships are many, then machine tabulation is usually preferable. But without preliminary tabulation the number of cross-relationships may not be obvious. Once hand tabulation has been completed, it is difficult to convert the entire tabulation procedure to machine work. Summary on the test-tube study will facilitate the decision of hand *vs.* machine tabulation.

i. *Checking internal consistency of results.* When the questions are tabulated, it will be possible to make a reasonably thorough analysis of results. The reactions of those in low-income groups can be compared with those secured from high-income groups. Persons in the former group could be expected to be more conscious of brand differences in price than those in the higher brackets; if this were not evident on the survey, the researcher would have to review each step to find the explanation. If greater-than-chance variation is present in some of the questions, there may be a flaw in phrasing, interviewing, or sampling. Methods for making reliability analyses are discussed in Chapter 14.

Summary. Where feasible, the test-tube study is a desirable step in the development of a study. Once the test-tube study has been completed, the investigator is prepared to undertake remaining steps in the survey procedure. These are described in successive chapters.

References

*(1) AMERICAN MARKETING ASSOCIATION. *The Technique of Marketing Research.* New York: McGraw-Hill, 1937. Chapter 4.

(2) BLANKENSHIP, A. B. "Pre-Testing a Questionnaire for a Public Opinion Poll," *Sociometry*, 1940, 3, 263-269.

(3) BLANKENSHIP, A. B. "The 'Sample' Study in Opinion Research," *Sociometry*, 1940, 3, 271-276.

(4) BROWN, L. O. *Market Research and Analysis.* New York: Ronald, 1937. Chapter 7.

(5) LINK, H. C. *The New Psychology of Advertising and Selling.* New York: MacMillan, 1934. Chapter 3.

(6) ROSLOW, SYDNEY, AND BLANKENSHIP, A. B. "Phrasing the Question in Consumer Research," *Journal of Applied Psychology*, 1939, 23, 612-622.

CHAPTER 8

Securing a Cross-Section

∿∿

THE basis for any measurement by the survey technique is the assumption that a distribution of answers from a small segment of the population will resemble the distribution of replies that would be obtained if the entire population were questioned. This assumption is valid only when the small segment resembles in various ways the entire population from which it is drawn.

A simple illustration will clarify this statement. A container holds 10,000 marbles, 5000 white and 5000 black. If the marbles are thoroughly mixed, and then 100 are drawn from the container (mixing preceding each draw), these will tend to contain (with minor variations) half of each color. This would be the *random* method of drawing the sample.

Suppose that it is known that, regardless of color, 8000 marbles are large and 2000 small. A different method of selecting the sample of 100 can then be used. A total of 80 large and 20 small marbles may be drawn, and this procedure is one of controlled or stratified sampling. The distribution of one of the characteristics of the total universe is known, and the sample is selected so that this characteristic will be distributed in accordance with the known information.

In the *random* method the persons interviewed are so selected that each individual in the total population will have an equal chance of being questioned. The assumption here is that such a sample will tend to resemble, in distribution of characteristics, the universe from which it was selected. In the *controlled* or *stratified* procedure, certain facts are known about the population beforehand, and the sample of respondents interviewed is selected deliberately so that the characteristics of this group will arbitrarily be similar to the characteristics of the total population.

In actual surveys either procedure can deteriorate to an accidental method. Where there is no rigidly controlled procedure for obtaining the sample, the group interviewed will be representative of nothing except the interviewer's own personal inclinations and biases. The field worker is likely to make his calls within a restricted area, and predominantly within his own age and standard-of-living group.

The population from which the sample is to be chosen must be defined before the survey is started. In the opinion poll the universe may be voters, or it may be adult members of the population. In commercial surveys it is more common for the public to be some small segment of the general population. A manufacturer wishing to estimate the potential market for a food mixer could eliminate single women at the outset.

THE RANDOM SAMPLE

1. *The method.* The random method is one giving each item in the universe an equal chance of being selected. When there are lists of the universe available, it is relatively simple to select each 10th or 20th name, so that any name on the list has an equally good chance of being selected. This selection of each 10th or 20th individual can also be managed by interviewing only in every 10th or 20th home.

2. *Advantages and disadvantages.* The random sample procedure is the only practical method in a telephone or mail survey. It is usually true that if there is a list of prospective respondents available, only their names and addresses are available, so that a stratified sampling is impossible.

The random method is useful with populations neither too great nor too limited in scope. A publishing company which sends advertisements through the mails finds it simple to send a mail questionnaire to every eighth person on the list when required. It is impractical to attempt a sampling of the entire country with the random method. There are many difficulties of transportation and of selection of respondents in interviewing every 100th or 1000th family.

With extremely limited populations there is little point in selecting a random sample. One drug manufacturer wanted to learn the retailing methods of his outlets. Only 30 per cent of the drugstores in New York City handled his goods, so it would have been pointless to secure a random sample of New York drugstores for his purpose. Some 70 per cent of the interviews would have been worthless. However, the manufacturer had available a list of the stores handling his goods, and that was a different matter. A random selection of interviews could be obtained with this reduced list, true, but there was already some control, so this was not a purely random method.

In practice the random method of call, when a field worker is used, may deteriorate to the accidental method. The field worker, for instance, has been told to question every tenth household within a given area. The Jones family, of exceptionally high income level, refuses to answer. The interviewer goes around the corner, where homes are less pretentious, and co-operation is easier to get. Distortion of the random sample has started.

Distortion of the random sample in personal interviewing can occur in another way. The random sample a field worker obtains at noon will not be the same sample he gets at 10 P.M. It is women who are at home and answer the door during the day, while men will tend to answer the door in the evening.

Refusals to co-operate can also distort the random sample. Two investigators (5) have found that housewives and persons of low educational status tend to refuse to answer questions. Persons "not at home" can distort the random sample. The same investigators (5) found that the "unavailable" group was composed predominantly of males, included more industrial workers than those of any other group, and tended to concentrate in lower income levels.

3. *Application of the random method.* One practical application of the random method is that followed in radio-audience measurement, as obtained by C. E. Hooper. Hooper's sample is selected by using the telephone directory of each city included in the study, and telephoning to every xth residential telephone on

the list. This procedure probably obtains a sample of telephone owners who are reasonably representative of the entire list of such owners.[1]

The usual application of the random method is in the mail survey. It is a fairly simple matter to send questionnaires to every 10th, 50th, or 100th name on the list. But there is a difference between a *random mailing* and a *representative return*. It has been shown in Chapter 4 that those who reply may not be entirely typical of those to whom the mailing was made.

THE CONTROLLED OR STRATIFIED SAMPLE

1. *The method.* When the controlled or stratified sampling method is used, certain characteristics of the population are known in advance, and the sample is so selected that the distribution of these characteristics is similar to proportions of the total population possessing such features. The method will be described in some detail in a later portion of this section.

2. *Advantages and disadvantages.* Use of a controlled sample requires previous knowledge of the distribution of characteristics of the population. Sometimes the distribution of such characteristics simply is unknown. There are no representative figures available on distribution of family incomes within the United States, yet many surveys undertake to allocate interviews in terms of such a factor. A partial solution to this particular problem will be discussed under the application section.

The stratified sample method also requires the investigator to know beforehand what relationship exists between answers to queries and the particular variables of control which are under consideration. *It is only those variables exerting some influence upon replies which must be controlled.* Preliminary study, perhaps of the test-tube type, will reveal this sort of relationship. Although the controlled sample has a few minor shortcomings, its advantages are great. Only by use of the stratified sample can the research organization make certain before returns are in that the sample will resemble the population from which it is drawn.

[1] Minor distortions may occur because of such factors as non-listing of certain numbers, disconnected telephones, and apartments which make use of switchboards, so that no individual residence number would be listed.

The method insures more careful consideration of the sample to be obtained. In one survey in a small community, the purpose of the study was to measure attitudes of home owners toward air conditioning. In obtaining a random sample, new homes of those who lived several miles outside the city were overlooked. Result was that only owners of the relatively older homes in the community were approached. Since age of the home was found to be a factor related to attitudes toward air conditioning, this omission was a serious one. Use of a stratified sample would automatically have raised the question of the possible relationship of age of home to attitude before interviewing had started, and would immediately have made apparent that these near-by homes should be included. The controlled sample technique provides some assurance that important sampling characteristics will not be overlooked.

3. *The basis for controlled sampling.* The basis for any controlled sample is advance knowledge of how certain characteristics are distributed in the population to be studied. It might be worth while to consider some of these characteristics and to see how an effort is made to control them in some of the studies which have been undertaken.

The American Institute of Public Opinion (Gallup poll) controls its sample of respondents in six ways—(4) proportions of voters: from each state, of each sex, from communities of various size, from each age group, from various income groups, and from each political party. There may be other controls, such as nationality and color. A few of these controls, as applied to specific surveys, will be cited.

a. *Geographic distribution.* On the basis of latest Census figures, it is possible to distribute the proportion of respondents properly on a state or sectional basis. In one survey it was necessary to distribute a total of 2000 questionnaires geographically across the country so that replies would represent each section to the extent of population in that area. The 1940 Census was consulted, and distribution of the 2000 interviews made accordingly.

b. *Sex and age.* The Census is also the source of most recent sex and age data. In one survey the reactions of adults in certain

selected cities to questions about airplanes and aircraft manufacturers were being obtained. Preliminary investigation showed a
marked difference in the replies of older and younger people, and
of men and women. It was obvious that both sex and age had to
be controlled. Census data for each of the cities were consulted.
With this as a start, it was easy to obtain the proper proportion of
interviews within each age bracket.

c. *Standard of living*. In many cases replies to a question are
related to economic level of the respondent. But there are few
reliable figures available on family income in the United States.
Economic conditions have changed during wartime, throwing the
1940 Census figures out of line.

The field worker can judge standard of living of the respondent
during the course of the field work by: (1) obtaining various clues
of status during conversation (the descriptive method), or (2) inquiring as to income of his interviewee (dollar classification).

In the *descriptive procedure*, the field worker collects various
data to place the respondent somewhere on a scale in terms of
standard of living. One method of defining these descriptive terms
to the field worker is to inform him that each of the groups comprises so many per cent of the family population. Look at the
description used by one firm:

The A group is the highest 10% of the population in terms of income.
These homes will be those in the very best sections, usually having two
or more cars, nine room house or larger, and servants' quarters. The persons in this group will be largely successful business men and professional people, executives, etc.

The B group comprises the next 30% of the population. It will generally
include one-family and some two-family houses, containing eight rooms
or less, and a few of the better-class apartments will also fall within this
class. Wage earners of this group will be employed in business or the pro-
fessions, or else will be well-paid clerical workers or skilled factory workers.
This is the upper middle-class group.

The lower middle-class group is the C group, composed of the next
40% of the families. This group will be mechanics, factory workers, and the
lower-paid business, clerical and professional persons.

There still remains the lowest 20% of the population, and this is the
D group. These people have very few autos, and practically none have
electric or automatic refrigerators. The slum element of your town will
be included here, as well as the tenement sections. Most negro and foreign-
language sections fall into this group.

The descriptive procedure may use other approaches (13), such as rent or rental value of the questionee's residence. This procedure might appear more objective, hence more reliable, than the "intuitive" method described above, but actually both methods give comparable results.

One researcher (7) has found that different indices of economic status are frequently interchangeable. Respondents were asked for whom they had voted in 1936. The entire sample of respondents was then broken down into economic groups by two separate methods: by "intuitive" ratings of investigators and by ownership of luxury items (telephones and cars). Results are shown in the accompanying table.

| | Percentage Voting for Landon | |
	Intuitive	Ownership[a]
High income level	42.5	40.2
Middle income level	21.7	28.0
Low income level	15.9	15.3

[a] Under the ownership method, the highest group was composed of those who owned both telephone and car, the middle group of those who owned one or the other but not both, and the low group of those who owned neither one.

For practical purposes the economic influence on the 1936 Landon vote can be measured by either method. It seems relatively safe to assume that in general either method will provide similar results.

The method of *dollar classification* is also used for describing economic status in some studies. Gallup interviewers show the respondent a card on which income brackets are shown, and the interviewee is then asked to designate into which group his or her family falls.

d. *Other controls.* Other controls such as urban and rural distribution of calls, occupation, nationality, religious affiliation, education, and party membership are sometimes used, where such factors may be related to replies.

In these days, of course, it is difficult for the usual investigation to include the proper proportion of rural calls, since gasoline and tire rationing have entered the national scene. But in peacetime this is an important and common control.

The Census has made available the proportion of persons in various occupations, and normally this is another check upon returns. In days of war, however, the occupational scale has been knocked askew; there are relatively few peacetime occupations remaining. It seems probable that the industrial reorganization due after the war will so change existing occupational patterns that the 1940 Census never will be applicable for such a purpose. Normally, however, this is also an item upon which representativeness of the sample may be checked.

Nationality is often an important factor. Those born in foreign countries sometimes have different ideas about American institutions and behave differently from those born in this country. Those who are naturalized citizens sometimes react differently from those who are aliens.

Religious affiliation may cause differences in behavior and attitudes. Many of those in the Pennsylvania Dutch religions, for instance, are conscientious objectors, and their attitudes about the war could be expected to be different from members of other religions. Anyone sampling opinion about the war in the farm areas of Pennsylvania would have to be certain that he obtained calls in proper proportion from these groups and others. A survey on birth control would require careful religious allocation so that the proper proportion of Catholics, whose church opposes birth control, would be included.

One's ideas, attitudes, and behavior will be conditioned by the nature and extent of his education, among other factors. Reading interests, for instance, have been shown to be related to educational background. Union membership is related to an individual's views about capital and labor, as well as government. The particular union to which the respondent may belong can influence his attitudes on such subjects as the company or the craft union.

This discussion of the various controls of the sample presupposes that the various characteristics of the population to be surveyed are known. The Census is one source of material, but this material quickly gets out of date. The survey organization which has been in operation for a number of years is likely to have as reliable and up-to-date information as any other source. If it makes frequent studies of a well-controlled type it will know what proportion of the residents of Omaha have children within each age group. Public opinion polls, in particular, have much evidence of this nature. Most of their work is done with either the general or the voting population, so that they are in a better position than anyone else to estimate what proportion of the voters will go to the polls, what proportion of each socio-economic group will cast ballots, what proportion of men and women will vote, etc. However, the problem of setting up a representative cross-section of voters cannot, as Katz (6) makes clear, be solved by past performance. Rain will affect adversely the Republican vote, since a high proportion of rural voters are Republican. Although women normally go to the polls less frequently than men, they can be expected to turn out in greater numbers if there is a ballot composed largely of women candidates.

In addition to previously collected information as a source for setting up control data, the United States Department of Commerce biannually publishes a volume entitled *Market Research Sources*. This lists a number of places from which survey and market information may be obtained. Various periodicals have gathered information about population characteristics in general, and in regard to their own subscribers in particular. Newspapers frequently have conducted comprehensive studies on the total population of their communities. Chambers of Commerce and trade organizations sometimes have sampling data available. Universities commonly make studies among selected portions of the population, and are glad to provide such information to those who can make use of it. Broadcasting companies ordinarily know the nature of the market which they can reach. Possibly of greatest importance in the commercial survey is the aid that the sponsor of the study may be able to give in defining his market.

The group to be surveyed in a commercial survey is frequently a specific segment of the population rather than the general population. The company for whom the survey is to be conducted may know the characteristics of this special segment. Sales records of the concern, its mailing lists, or previous surveys may all aid in defining the group. The client may even have more than names and addresses. He may be able to define, in at least a general way, the economic characteristics of his customers. If only the customers of the concern are to be approached, the company can usually state immediately the areas in which its products are distributed. If the product is sold only to one sex, as in the case of corsets, the population is further defined. The surveyor must always make sure in considering such evidence that the limits are factual, and not merely opinions of the client. Otherwise the sample of respondents is likely to be distorted.

The controlled sample is possible only when the characteristics of the population are known before the survey is undertaken.

4. *The application of controlled sampling.* Use of the controlled sampling procedure in survey work is not always simple. There are a number of steps in the method: definition of the population to be sampled, obtaining of required data about the population, decision as to what factors should be controlled, consideration of compound sampling factors, assignment of interviews to supervisors and field workers, and checking the returns.

a. *Definition of the population to be sampled.* The sample must be described both in general terms (whether the general population, voters, customers of a particular concern, or members of a labor union) and in specific terms (towns and localities to be covered, sex distribution of calls, urban and rural interviews, age distribution, etc.). The nature of the population to be studied will tie in with the purposes of the investigation; it is an aspect of the objectives of the study.

b. *Obtaining required data about the population.* Methods and difficulties of obtaining the required data about the particular population have already been discussed and need not be repeated here.

c. *Decision as to what factors should be controlled.* There will be little reason to control those factors whose distribution in the population is not known. The survey interviewer would waste time by inquiring at what age people were married. Not only would it be difficult to obtain reliable data for the whole population on this point, but many respondents would refuse to answer the question. Only those items about which the investigator may inquire, or items which he can observe, may be included as factors to be controlled. Sometimes only trial interviewing will reveal whether it is practicable to inquire about certain items.

Critical judgment must be used in selecting the factors to be controlled. There should be good reason for suspecting that a factor is related to responses before it is included in the survey. No possible controls which might be correlated with answers should be overlooked.

d. *Consideration of compound sampling factors.* In the use of the stratified sampling method there is a difficult problem facing the surveyor—that of compound sampling. The more factors there are to be controlled, the greater the number of cross-relationships of such factors there are to be considered. For instance, the relationship of age and standard of living is an interesting one. In a particular survey, the distribution of interviews by age might be required as follows:

	% of Interviews
20-29	24
30-39	20
40-49	19
50-59	16
60 and over	21

In the same survey, the 100 interviews might be distributed as follows on an economic scale:

	% of Interviews
High	30
Medium	40
Low	30

When plans are made for the interview assignments in this study, it will *not* be sufficient to assign merely the total number of calls to be made in each age group and in each economic group. There is a relationship between these two factors. The upper economic group will tend to be older, since it takes some time under our system to accumulate wealth.

Assignment of ages within each economic group must be different; otherwise the assigned sample will be biased by making the high group too young. *In any case where there is an interrelation-ship between sampling factors, distribution of interviews must be planned with such relationship in mind.*

How can such relationships be foreseen? Experience in the field will make the researcher aware of the more obvious relation-ships, such as income and age. For less obvious patterns the prob-lem may become difficult. Continuous surveys such as the Gallup poll will, through accumulated sampling information, know what interrelationships of sampling data to expect. In extended surveys it is sometimes possible to make use of the test-tube study to learn about such patterns. For instance, one organization always makes a random survey in a community before any "final" survey is undertaken there. From this random study it is possible to obtain all sorts of sampling data and to determine the relationships of the sampling factors. It is a relatively simple matter for the organ-ization then to control the relationship of the sampling factors in the sample of respondents ultimately selected for further question-ing.

e. *Assignments of interviews to supervisors and field workers.* Since this step is a portion of the procedure of sending out materi-als, it is discussed in Chapter 10.

f. *Checking the returns.* Although this final step must always be employed when the stratified sampling method is used, it is also applicable to the random sampling procedure. For that reason it will be discussed as a separate section.

CHECKING THE RETURNS

The two chief steps in the checking of returns are (1) inspec-tion of returns against quotas, and (2) checking the representatives of the sample.

1. *Inspection of returns against quotas.* Where the personal interview method has been used, whether the random or controlled method of sampling has been applied, each field worker will have received particular quotas. Quota allotment is detailed in the case of the stratified sample. The quota and return must be compared in detail, to make certain that the field worker has met his precise assignment. Any deviation from the assignment, whether in ran-

dom or controlled sampling, will contribute to distortion of the obtained sample.

2. *Checking representativeness of the sample.* Whether the random or stratified method has been used, there must always be an effort to find out the extent to which the specific sample resembles the population it is intended to represent.

In the case of a mail survey it will be possible to check sectional returns against mailings, so as to make sure that the proportions in each are similar; it may also be possible to check sex and age distribution of replies.

With the stratified sample, all of the controlled factors must be compared in distribution within the sample with similar known figures for the population from which the sample was drawn.

Comparison of uncontrolled factors with known distribution of the characteristics in the population may not reveal perfect agreement. There is some little leeway permitted, since any sample will include some chance error. The following chapter will show what sort of variation is permissible in this respect.

Some future survey is likely to go wrong because sufficient factors have not been foreseen as possible response determinants. The age and economic condition of one's parents at time of death has not, to the writer's knowledge, ever been controlled on any survey. Yet it is entirely possible that such a factor is related to one's attitudes toward an old-age pension scheme. If a split on voting behavior occurs on some other basis than the noncontrolled items, a pre-election poll of the future might be just as wrong as the *Literary Digest* was in 1936.

The nature of the sample is tremendously more important than its mere size. Many surveys have been inaccurate because of the inadequacy of their cross-sections. No known survey has ever gone wrong because of the number of questionnaires collected.

The number of calls is an important factor; these statements are an effort to place it in its proper perspective. Reasons for the importance of sample size and determinants of sample size are outlined in the next chapter.

REFERENCES

(1) ALDERSON, WROE. "Marketing Classification of Families," *Journal of Marketing*, 1941, 6, 143-146.

(2) BROWN, L. O. *Market Research and Analysis*. New York: Ronald, 1935. Chapter 10.

(3) CROXTON, F. E., AND COWDEN, D. J. *Applied General Statistics*. New York: Prentice-Hall, 1940. Chapter 2.

(4) GALLUP, GEORGE. *The New Science of Public Opinion Measurement*. Princeton: American Institute of Public Opinion, no date.

(5) GAUDET, HAZEL, AND WILSON, E. C. "Who Escapes the Personal Investigator?" *Journal of Applied Psychology*, 1940, 24, 773-777.

(6) KATZ, DANIEL. "The Public Opinion Poll and the 1940 Election," *Public Opinion Quarterly*, 1941, 5, 52-78.

(7) LAZARSFELD, P. F. "Interchangeability of Indices in the Measurement of Economic Influences," *Journal of Applied Psychology*, 1939, 23, 33-45.

(8) McNEMAR, QUINN. "Sampling in Psychological Research," *Psychological Bulletin*, 1940, 37, 331-365.

(9) ROPER, ELMO. "Classifying Respondents by Economic Status," *Public Opinion Quarterly*, 1940, 4, 270-272.

(10) STANTON, FRANK. "Problems of Sampling in Market Research," *Journal of Consulting Psychology*, 1941, 5, 154-163.

(11) UNSIGNED. *Average Income—and the New Tax*. New York: Macfadden Publications, 1942.

(12) WARNER, LUCIEN. "The Reliability of Public Opinion Surveys," *Public Opinion Quarterly*, 1939, 3, 376-390.

(13) WELD, L. H. D., ET AL. "Report of the Committee on Income Classifications," *Journal of Marketing*, 1942, 6, 375-386.

(14) WILKS, S. S. "Representative Sampling and Poll Reliability," *Public Opinion Quarterly*, 1940, 4, 261-269.

CHAPTER 9

The Size of the Sample

THE airplane is one of the most mechanically perfect machines of our years. Hour after hour the large commercial transports continue their tasks with few mechanical failures; when the machines do falter, the deficiencies can frequently be traced to the human rather than the mechanical element.

For perfection on this level there is little room for deviation in the measurement of each part. Yet even when a part of this sort must be so accurate in size and shape, some little tolerance is permitted. In some parts one ten-thousandth of an inch is the greatest variation allowed from specification.

The many sources of error already outlined in survey procedure make it fairly clear that accuracy of questionnaire studies can never reach any such levels. Even where all details of procedure in surveys are scrupulously planned and controlled, there will be some "chance" error entering into results. No survey results are absolute. The survey includes only a sample of the population total, and merely by operation of chance laws alone some error may be expected to enter into results.

Data obtained from one sample will seldom agree perfectly with those from another sample obtained simultaneously in the same manner. If it is assumed that responses for the total population from which the sample has been drawn provide a degree of "true" measurement, then errors arising from chance alone will tend to cause some deviation between sample results and the "true" figures.

Provided all other things are equal (even though they never are!), the larger the sample of respondents obtained, the greater are the chances that the survey results will be close to the reactions that would be obtained from the universe (the total population from which the sample has been selected). It is knowledge of this principle and of its functioning that provides the basis for pre-determining the number of respondents required in a question-naire survey.

The laws of chance, to be described in this chapter, have been developed and subjected to thorough tests in fields other than the survey procedure. In the questionnaire field these "laws" are still largely theory; additional evidence is required to demonstrate that they operate as hypothesized. Most of the demonstrations of per-formance of the laws have been in fields where the samples obtained were random; in the survey field it has already been demonstrated that there is no truly random procedure.

The application of these "laws" is, nevertheless, a prerequisite to the survey. Only by use of the hypothesis can the number of the required respondents be predetermined. The degree to which the so called "laws of chance" do hold true with the collected data can always be checked when returns are analyzed.

RELATION OF SAMPLE SIZE TO ACCURACY

One of the purposes in using the laws of chance error is to pre-dict how many questionnaires should be collected. The first prob-lem is to have the sponsor (or someone else in a position to know) make an estimate of how much accuracy is required in the results. If the purpose is to get only a rough idea of relative market posi-tion, then an error of 5 to 10 per cent in the results for the parti-cular brand may be acceptable. If the survey organization has the task of predicting what percentage of the population will vote for a particular candidate, results must be more accurate than this.

The size of the sample has no effect in reducing any bias present in the sample. Only when the sample is representative of its uni-verse does the addition of respondents reduce chance error. In other words, increased size of sample reduces errors of chance; increased representativeness of the sample reduces errors of bias.

Sampling error varies with two factors: the size of the sample, and the proportion of replies in a given category.

1. *Accuracy of returns is directly proportionate to the square root of the size of the sample.* With a given proportion of replies within a category, the accuracy of that result will vary directly with the square root of the number of cases upon which the percentage was computed. With 400 cases as a base, the accuracy of the result may be within 4 per cent.[1] To double the accuracy—to bring it within 2 per cent, the number of cases would have to be quadrupled to 1600. This fact may be expressed in another way. If the error is .85 with 5000 interviews, it will be reduced to .60 with 10,000 questionnaires, and to .42 with 20,000 returns.

When the number of questionnaires reaches 5000 or above, it requires the addition of many replies to make any appreciable difference in accuracy. Only below this point does the application of this principle have much practical value.

2. *Accuracy of returns increases as the proportion of replies within a category moves away from 50 per cent.* With the same size of sample, a category of response into which 50 per cent of the answers fall will have less accuracy than one which receives either 10 per cent or 90 per cent of the replies. For example, if 50 per cent of respondents reply that they have been up in an airplane, that 50 per cent figure will have one-fourth again as much chance error as a 20 per cent or 80 per cent affirmative reply.

The degree of variation in accuracy with different percentages will be dependent, however, upon the number of cases. As the number of interviews increases, the variation due to percentage of replies within a category diminishes.

Use of Appendix Tables for Sample Size Determination

In the back of this book there are two tables. Table 1, after Link (8), shows two standard errors, given in percentages, related to the proportion of replies within a category, and the number of cases in the sample. Table 2, after Brown (2), shows the number of cases required to provide results within certain accuracy limits, related to the percentage of replies within a given category.

[1] This error will always be expressed as a probability, that is, as being accurate within 4 per cent in so many out of 100 surveys. Probabilities are discussed at a later point in this chapter.

Both of these tables were developed from the same basic formula, which will be discussed shortly. Although this chapter will not define a standard error in statistical detail, a layman's definition of the term is necessary so that practical use of the appendix tables can be made.

The laws of chance are expressions of probability. When, in survey work, it is reported that the results are accurate within 5 per cent, that statement is meaningless. If it is stated that the results are accurate within 5 per cent in 95 times of 100, the statement assumes statistical meaning. When there is no criterion against which to check the accuracy of survey results, the only alternative is to express probable accuracy, and to give an indication of what is meant by "probable." Use of the standard error is a description of the probability of the error.

Use of *one* standard error as a measure of accuracy means that the resultant accuracy figure will be a proper expression of reliability in 68 per cent of the cases. If 100 surveys be made, 68 surveys would give results so close to one another that they would fall within the range described as one standard error. The use of three standard errors increases the probability to .99 plus. Two standard errors is an expression of probability to the extent of .95.[2]

Many of those in the research field today are using two standard errors—95 per cent probability—as the most desirable indication of probability. One standard error at 68 per cent is too low for practical use. Three standard errors, when used as a criterion, greatly increases the number of cases and the cost, without proportionate increase in accuracy, so that use of two standard errors appears a practical mid-point. A measure that will be right in 95 out of 100 cases is reasonably accurate for the usual survey. It is for these reasons that both of the tables in the back of the book are expressed in terms of two standard errors.

Let's look first at the Link table to see how it may be used. We assume that the required accuracy of the study has been placed at 5 per cent. It is expected that from 25 to 35 per cent of the replies will fall within a given category of response, so we may

[2] The Link table may be decreased to one standard error by dividing each cell entry by 2. The Brown table may be decreased to one standard error by dividing each cell entry by 4.

look under the heading, "30% or 70%." In terms of two standard errors, 5 per cent accuracy will require between 300 and 400 interviews. With 400 returns and 30 per cent category response, the chances will be roughly 95 in 100 that the results are accurate within the 5 per cent figure.

The same problem can be used to illustrate the way in which Brown's table can be applied. The heading "30% or 70%" should first be located. Since the range of error is 5 per cent, this figure is located on the left-hand column. At the intersection of the proper row and column it is learned that exactly 336 interviews would obtain the range of accuracy desired. The example makes it clear that for usual prediction of the number of cases required for particular accuracy, the Brown table is simpler to use than that of Link. The Link table is especially useful when returns are complete and it is desirable to estimate the range of error for a specific percentage.

As an example of this latter case, a study may consist of a total of 1000 calls. The particular percentage may be 40. The error (expressed in terms of two standard errors) will then be 3.10 per cent.

OTHER FACTORS INFLUENCING SAMPLE SIZE

The degree of accuracy required when the entire sample is utilized is not the only factor that will influence the choice of the number of cases. Additional influences will be (1) the base upon which the percentages are calculated, (2) statistical probabilities and practical considerations, and (3) the other percentages within the study with which the particular figure is to be compared. The role of each of these considerations will be discussed.

1. *Accuracy depends upon the base on which the percentage is computed.* In some instances it is necessary to take only certain cases from the total sample and to work with these. When this happens, the percentage figures will be based upon this sub-sample. One survey, for example, asked a question about the last brand of a particular commodity purchased. All questionnaires naming a particular brand were analyzed, and the replies to other questions were compared to replies of persons who had bought other brands.

When percentage figures were obtained from this limited sample, the range of error had to be computed from the number of cases in the sub-sample, rather than from the number of cases in the entire survey. This factor had to be taken into account at the time of the planning of the study, so that the total number of cases would provide sufficient respondents in the sub-category to give the required accuracy.

As the number of comparisons between various sub-samples increases, the number of cases within each sub-sample will naturally decrease, thus raising the probable error. In the survey mentioned above, if the brand of commodity of particular interest were to have been compared with each of a number of its major competitors, then the sub-samples would have been greater in number, while the respondents in many of the sub-samples would have decreased, requiring additional interviews for the same degree of accuracy. This example shows how thorough the planning of the study must be, and how it must take into consideration even such far-distant factors as the way in which the results are to be analyzed.

2. *Statistical probabilities and practical considerations must be weighed.* Strict adherence to use of such tables as those in the back of this volume without regard for the specific situation may lead the inexperienced technician into difficulties. It might be found that among 1000 persons 95 per cent had listened to a recent speech by President Roosevelt, while a qualitatively poor dance band was heard by only 5 per cent. Obviously these two listening figures will have the same standard error—.62 per cent.

From a practical point of view, however, the smaller figure is subject to more fluctuation than is the larger. Subtraction of 49 listeners from the Roosevelt audience would still give Roosevelt a rating of 90.1 per cent, but if the other program lost 49 listeners, it would have a rating of .1 per cent! The same standard error for complementary percentages may have a different significance. Data in the tables must always be considered from such a point of view.

3. *The percentages within the study to be compared must be considered.* One study was designed to compare the market standing of a particular product with that of its competitors. The par-

ticular brand was used by 25 per cent, and that of the chief competitor by 20 per cent. Since there was a total of 1000 questionnaires, it was known that on the basis of two standard errors the 25 per cent was accurate within 2.74 per cent, the 20 per cent within 2.52 per cent. Obviously there was enough overlapping of the two ranges of error that it was dubious that the two original percentages were statistically different. There is a method possible by which the chances of a real difference can be calculated.

The formula used is:

$$\sigma_{\text{diff}} = \sqrt{\sigma^2{}_a + \sigma^2{}_b}$$

The symbol σ stands for standard error. "Diff." means difference, a is the first percentage, and b the second percentage. In words, the formula would read that the standard error of the difference is equal to the square root of the sum of the squared standard errors of the two percentages. Here is how the formula would be applied in the illustration listed. The sum of the two squared errors $(1.37)^2$ and $(1.26)^2$ is 3.4645. The square root of this sum is 1.86, so 1.86 is the standard error of the difference.

The difference itself (25 per cent—20 per cent) is 5. For final measure of the reliability of the difference, the difference (5 per cent) must be divided by its own standard error (1.86 per cent). In this case the resultant "critical ratio" is 2.68. Reference to a table such as Table XIV in Garrett (5) shows that there are 99 chances in 100 that this is a reliable difference. Although it should by no means be taken as dogma, a critical ratio that approximates 3 is commonly used as a measure of significance. Such a figure provides evidence that the difference will stand up in over 99 per cent of the cases.

THE BASIC FORMULA

The formula from which the two tables in the Appendix have been derived is:

$$\sigma = \sqrt{pq/N}$$

In this formula, σ is the standard error of the percentage, p is the percentage itself, q is 1.00 minus p, and N is the number of interviews. The formula therefore reads that the standard error of a percentage is equal to the square root of the percentage times the percentage subtracted from 100, all divided by the number of cases. Where the number of cases is 1000 and the percentage is 20, the standard error would be:

$$\sigma = \sqrt{\frac{20 \times 80}{1000}}$$

The actual computation results in a figure of 1.26; for verification the appropriate figure in Link's table can be divided by 2.

Brown's table has been derived from the same formula in different form. Since Brown's problem was to derive the number of cases in each instance, he wanted to start with N on the left-hand side of the equation. By doing this, he was able to arrive at the revised formula:

$$N = \frac{4pq}{(2\sigma)^2}$$

This is a statement of N in terms of two standard errors, the form of the table provided in the Appendix. For one and three standard errors the formula could be appropriately modified.

Use of an illustration will show how this formula is applied. With two standard errors as a criterion, results within 5 per cent are required on a given survey, and it is estimated that some 40 per cent of respondents will answer in a given way. Substitutions in the above formula would then be:

$$N = \frac{4(40 \times 60)}{25}$$

The total number of questionnaires required would thus be 384, which is the entry appearing in Brown's table under the appropriate column and row.

These formulas are useful with infinite populations, and have been developed from that point of view. In statistical practice there is a somewhat different formula to be used when the population studied is limited (9). This will not be presented here for several reasons. In the first place it is sometimes difficult to decide when a particular population is finite or infinite. There is no hard and fast line that can be drawn. In addition, even when working with a finite population, it is not always possible to determine the total number within that group. Suppose that only mothers of children from 18 months down were being interviewed on their habits of child-feeding. It would be impossible to make an estimate, even from survey results, of the total number of mothers in the population who would fall within such a category.

Moreover, since the corrective value of the finite population formula decreases as the population increases, it is rarely that the survey technician has a great deal of use for the formula. Most surveys these days are not based on only a few cases; it is seldom that a survey is conducted with less than 500 questionnaires. In addition, the use of the general formula with limited populations makes the surveyor overestimate the standard error, and there can be little objection to such a procedure.

There is also a specific formula to be used with stratified samples, but in practice it is seldom used by those in the field. The interested reader can refer to McNemar (9) for this formula. It might be pointed out that the formula reduces the standard error in a stratified sample when the stratified control is related to the particular response, and not otherwise. Although the stratification formula leads to greater precision in the calculation of the standard error, few would object to the use of the more general formula with its more liberal quantification of error.

In cases in which the number of interviews to be collected must be estimated with relation to stratification, and it is desired to make use of this special formula, it is possible to do what Brown (2) did in the case of his computation—to set up N on the left-hand side of the equation and proceed from there. It isn't as simple as it sounds. For most cases the tables in the Appendix are accurate enough.

REFERENCES

(1) AMERICAN MARKETING ASSOCIATION. *The Technique of Marketing Research*. New York: McGraw-Hill, 1937. Chapter 20.

(2) BROWN, T. H. *Use of Statistical Technique in Certain Problems of Market Research*. Cambridge: Harvard Press, 1935.

(3) CROXTON, F. E., AND COWDEN, D. J. *Applied General Statistics*. New York: Prentice-Hall, 1940. Chapters 12 and 13.

(4) DANIEL, CUTHBERT. "Statistically Significant Differences in Observed Per Cents," *Journal of Applied Psychology*, 1940, 24, 826-830.

(5) GARRETT, H. E. *Statistics in Psychology and Education*. New York: Longmans, Green & Co., 1926. Chapter 3.

(6) HOLZINGER, K. J. *Statistical Methods for Students in Education*. Boston: Ginn & Co., 1928. Chapter 13.

(7) HOOPER, C. E. "The Size of a Radio-Listener Sample," *Printers' Ink*, January 2, 1942.

(8) LINK, H. C. "How Many Interviews Are Necessary for Results of a Certain Accuracy?" *Journal of Applied Psychology*, 1937, 21, 1-17.

(9) McNEMAR, QUINN. "Sampling in Psychological Research," *Psychological Bulletin*, 1940, 37, 331-365.

(10) STANTON, FRANK. "Problems of Sampling in Market Research," *Journal of Consulting Psychology*, 1941, 5, 154-163.

CHAPTER 10

Preparing and Distributing Materials

‹‹‹

THE preparation and distribution of materials varies somewhat with the particular method of data collection. Use of the personal call or the telephone interview requires somewhat different handling in this stage from the mail questionnaire.

THE PERSONAL AND TELEPHONE INTERVIEW

In both approaches there are a number of elements to consider in preparing and distributing materials: (1) the questionnaire, (2) field workers' instructions, (3) the assignment of calls, and (4) timing of the study.

1. *The questionnaire*. Informal interviewing and pre-testing define the form and order of the questions but do not ordinarily have much to do with format. Both format and the particular mechanical means used for duplication warrant some thought.

a. *The duplication process*. There are four principal methods which can be used for reproducing the questionnaire: typing, with carbons; reproduction through use of a stencil-type machine; type setting; and photo-offset.[1] Selection of the particular method will depend on the nature of the individual survey. In terms of clarity of reproduction, typing is poorest (considering the carbons), while type set and photo-offset jobs (the latter having identical clarity with the original copy) are best. The practical number of copies available by use of each method ranges from least with typing to greatest with type set or photo-offset material. Cost of each method varies so greatly, depending upon the total number of copies and

---

[1] Photo-offset is a process by which a negative of the original page is made, and copies are then printed from that negative.

the physical layout of material, that no comparisons can be given here.

Typing is useful in surveys where few questionnaires are required. Typeset or offset processes are practical where the number of questionnaires is in the thousands. In such a case the unit cost will be low, and the result will be a clear questionnaire. In surveys which require questionnaires numbering perhaps 10,000 or less, the stencil-type process is useful. Unit cost is usually lower than for printing, and the stencil should not require more than one replacement. Of course there is some sacrifice in clarity of the finished product.

Clarity is important; whatever the method used, it must meet a minimal requirement of producing copies that are easy to read. If the questioner has to scrutinize the blank each time he asks a question, the interview is not likely to run smoothly.

b. *The format.* The questionnaire must be so laid out that it is simple for the questioner to follow. It is common practice to leave spaces between questions. Each question is numbered so that the investigator's task is simplified. Since the questionnaire usually includes a certain number of "contingent" questions (questions which are to be asked only if the person answers another question in a particular way), it must be clear just when these are to be included in the interview. Such questions may be indented under the basic question, as illustrated on this page, or they may be placed below the appropriate answer and "boxed" for additional aid, as the illustration on the next page indicates.

---

1. Have you ever been up in an airplane? Yes_____ No_____

   (If 'yes' ask Q's 1a, 1b, and 1c; if 'no' ask 1d.)

   1a. How long ago was the last time?_____

   1b. How many trips have you made on regular airline ships?_____

   1c. How many hours have you flown altogether? _____

   1d. Would you like to fly? Yes_____ No_____
      (If 'no' to 1d.)
      1e. Why not?_____

---

1. Have you ever been up in an airplane?

Yes_____   No_____

1a. How long ago was the last time?_____

1b. How many trips have you made on regular airline ships? _____

1c. How many hours have you flown altogether?_____

1d. Would you like to fly?

Yes_____   No_____

1e. (If 'no' to 1d.) Why not?

Condensation of the physical length of the questionnaire can be important. Especially in a personal interview, *absolute* length (time required for the questioning process) may not be as important as *apparent* length. Many respondents become annoyed when the page of the questionnaire is turned, and ask, "How much more is there to this, anyway?" When the same series of questions is asked without the turn of the page there is less likelihood of such comments.

Several techniques may be used to condense the physical length of the questionnaire. The veri-type and printing procedures use space efficiently and often make it possible to condense physical size. Use of legal-size paper can sometimes prevent the necessity for page-turning. Sufficient space for recording answers must be allowed, even for short-answer queries. Comment questions require more room. Amount of space provided for replies has an influence on remarks made. One company which had respondents themselves fill in the blanks (1) requested additional comments at the end of the question-list. Some forms had only three spaces for comments, others had five. The smaller space elicited comments from 8 per cent, the larger from 13 per cent.

c. *The content.* The questionnaire consists of the questions, arranged in proper order. There are still a few problems of exactly *what* to include on the sheet.

Some means of informing the field workers exactly what are the questions and exactly what is for their own information must be provided. One common practice is to instruct field workers to read each question as far as the question mark—that anything past the question mark or in parenthesis is there merely for the field worker's instruction or for his aid in recording replies.

These two practices make it possible to include some of the more important instructions directly on the face of the questionnaire. Points of questioning which are worth reiterating and stressing can be placed on the face of the questionnaire.

Sometimes the introduction to be used by the field worker is placed at the top of the questionnaire form, so that the interviewer can read off even this material to the respondent.

2. *The instruction sheet.* Preparation of the instruction sheet for the investigators is a complicated process. There are a number of points which must be covered amply in the instruction sheet.

a. *The* general *purpose of the survey.* The field worker can do a more competent job if he knows the general purpose of the investigation. Under such conditions he can work more intelligently and adequately. Too specific a description of the purpose is not desirable, since this could bias the results. It might be disastrous to tell investigators that the purpose of a study is to compare consumer attitudes toward dentifrice brand A with those toward brand N. Possibility of unintentional bias in such a situation is too great.

b. *Whom to interview.* Interviewers must be told specifically whom they are to question. In a study to be made among pipe smokers the investigators must be told to talk only with men. Where the study is one with a general cross-section of the population, such a fact should be stated in the instructions. The instruction sheet also states definitely whether the controlled or random method of sampling is to be followed, and just what procedure is to be used in obtaining the particular type of sample.

c. *Where to make the calls.* The instruction sheet must define the *general* locale of field work (the town and/or neighborhood) as well as the *specific* place (home, business offices, or street questioning).

d. *When to make the calls.* The specific dates for interviewing are the first problem. The instruction sheet should also cover a second aspect—a suggestion as to the best time of day for reaching the group it is necessary to approach.

e. *An opening.* The instruction sheet should suggest an introduction for the investigator to use when approaching his prospective
respondents. The approach used by the Gallup workers runs:

"I am interviewing people to get their views for the American Institute
of Public Opinion—the Gallup poll. Every week, in every state, we ask
representative people their opinions on questions of national importance.
I'd be glad to have your ideas on a few questions. I don't want your
name—just your opinions." (3, p. 133)

With the Gallup poll this is sufficient. The problem of securing
respondent co-operation is more difficult in the ordinary commercial
study. Some organizations follow the policy of using a college or
university connection as reference.

f. *Observations.* Any observations to be made by the field force
should be stated on the instruction sheet. In one case (1, p. 159)
a publication wanted to secure information to confirm or refute the
claim of a rival that it alone served the "educated," "clean," "thrifty,"
"intelligent," and "responsible" persons of the community. In order
to obtain information on this point the field workers were instructed
to estimate the respondent's degree of possession of each of these
characteristics. The observations had to be made carefully and in
standard fashion in order to have any significance, so standards of
classification were outlined carefully on the instruction sheet.

g. *Obtaining and recording sampling information.* Since the crux
of the entire problem of securing a representative group of respondents is the degree to which they possess the characteristics of the
population from which they were drawn, obtaining and recording
sampling information by each field worker is vital. The particular
characteristics to be measured will vary with the purposes and
nature of the investigation.

It is common for the interviewer to record the sex and age
(approximate or actual) of the respondent, his economic level
(approximate or actual), and the locality in which the interviewing
was conducted. Other sampling data will vary with the particular
study, and may include some or all of the various sampling controls
outlined in Chapter 8. Such sampling information, however, is
vital whether controlled or random sampling is used. Without it
there can be no check upon the degree to which the obtained

sample is representative of the total population from which it was presumably drawn.

h. *Emphasis on careful supervision and inspection.* The instruction sheet should state that the work of the interviewer is being carefully supervised and inspected (and this should be factual). Each field worker should be warned both personally and on the instruction sheet that follow-up interviews are always made on a portion of the calls he reports. That is why it is necessary to record the street address (and perhaps the name of the respondent) along with other sampling data at the time of the original interview. Honesty is a serious problem among investigators, and every effort should be made to see that the work is honestly performed. This point will be further discussed in the chapter concerned with field work.

i. *Method of payment.* The instruction sheet should also describe the method of paying the worker. He should be informed whether he will be paid by the piece-rate (so much for each completed interview), by the number of hours required for the work, or whether a combination of the methods will be used. Relative merits of each of these systems are discussed in the next chapter.

j. *Instructions for specific questions.* The instruction sheet must always contain detailed instructions for the handling of any particular question. The few general instructions for the technique of asking questions will be outlined at the start of the next chapter, and these also should be included in the questionnaire.

3. *Example of an instruction sheet.* On pages 128 and 129 there is illustrated an actual instruction sheet, used by the writer in a personal investigation. It will be noted that this sheet covers all of the points mentioned in the outline:

The general purpose of the survey
Whom to interview
Where to make the calls
When to make the calls
The opening
Observations
Obtaining and recording sampling information
Emphasis on careful supervision and inspection

INSTRUCTION SHEET—IRVINGTON STUDY

Remuneration. These interviews will be paid for at 10c per completed call, *providing* the interviewer completes his ten full assignments, 30 calls per day from June 10 to June 19, inclusive. It is so important that each worker remain on the job for 10 days that failure to do so will mean that the interviews are worthless. This means that interviews must be made, rain or shine.

Read these instructions and the questionnaires before leaving your supervisor. This will save both of us a lot of headaches!

Whom, when and where to interview. Make interviews only in the home. It is absolutely necessary that the exact assignment be carried out in all respects. Only persons 21 years of age or over are to be interviewed. In your assigned territory, call upon every fifth family, that is, skip four homes. In other words, if you are in a territory containing only apartment houses, stop at every fifth one. If you pass a 2 family residence, that counts as two. If you are in an apartment building, stop at every fifth apartment. If you are not able to complete an interview with what would be the fifth family, get the next door neighbor; then start counting again. If you need a man, and a woman answers the door, ask for the man of the house. If no man is available, do not make the interview. The procedure may be necessary in order to obtain the proper number of interviews with persons of each sex. Do not make interviews with more than one person at a time. If two persons answer together, use the answers of the one who best helps you to complete your assignment. No more than one interview is to be made in one home.

Economic status. The sections and streets in which your interviews are to be made will be given you by the supervisor. All of the interviews assigned you are to be in one economic group (note assignment). This means that if a residence in your territory does not belong to the economic group assigned you, DO NOT make any interviews there. Briefly, Class A homes are those in the very best sections, having usually 2 or more cars, 9 room house (or larger), and servants' quarters; B Class consists of 1 and some 2 family houses, some apartments, 75% owning cars; C Class includes homes of mechanics, factory workers, etc., mostly 2 family houses; D Class includes the poorer sections of the city—foreign language and colored population, tenements, persons engaged as day laborers, service workers, car-washers, people on relief, etc. This is almost the slum element of the city.

Legibility. Please use soft black pencil and write legibly.

Questions must be read word for word to the person interviewed, exactly as they appear on the interview blank. Read the entire question to the interviewee as far as the question mark. You will note that certain questions vary somewhat from form to form, so it is absolutely necessary to read all questions word for word.

Recording the response. Check the proper response in the space provided in the right-hand margin.

Name. Wherever possible get the name of the person interviewed, either from the name on the door, or by asking. This facilitates follow-up calls.

Explanations to interviewees. Do not explain the meaning of any of the questions to the person being interviewed. If the person asks for an explanation of the question, simply reread the question.

Only the questions above the dotted lines are to be asked of the person interviewed. The remaining information is to be filled in by the interviewer without asking, simply by observation.

Don't know. If the person interviewed doesn't know the answer to a question, or refuses to answer, check "D.K." on the question.

Follow-up calls. Be sure to record the sex and age of the person interviewed, type of home, street address, and all other information required at the bottom of the blank, since a number of these calls will be made again by another interviewer as a check on accuracy.

Rotation of questionnaire forms. The purpose of this study is to measure the effect of asking people about the same issue in different ways. For that reason, it is absolutely essential that you rotate the questionnaire form used. Begin with a particular questionnaire form ("A" for example), and when you have completed an interview using that form, then make the next interview on the next lettered form ("B" for example), until you are ready to start a new series of five. Even if you go from one district to another, rotate the interview forms in unbroken order.

Introduction suggested. "How do you do. We are making a little study of how people feel about certain social questions. For example . . ." (read question 1)

Thank you!

Method of payment
Instructions for specific questions

4. *The distribution of interviews.* The general problem of the distribution of interviews will have been settled at the time the nature of the sample was considered. Discussion here refers to the purely mechanical details of assigning each investigator a proper segment of calls so that the sum of all investigators' work will equal the size and nature of the desired sample.

Distribution of interviews involves more than mere allotment of calls by geographic area and locality, although these are parts of the problem. The general nature of the population sample will first have been defined, and details of sampling will have followed. Assignments to supervisors and/or interviewers must be made so that the collective sample will contain the proper distribution of desired characteristics. Where supervisors are used to control the field force, the assignments are made to them, and they then assign each of their workers a proper sample so that the total will agree with the supervisor's assignment. Where the interviewing organization sends assignments directly to field workers, the home office makes the individual assignment. On an adjoining page a sample of an assignment sheet is presented. Naturally this sheet will take on different form with other studies. The present sheet is obviously for use with a stratified sample, since it so definitely states the number of respondents to be obtained within each sub-category.

5. *Timing the study.* Interviewing dates must be specified on the instruction sheet. The only way to eliminate interviewer tardiness is to have the interviewing dates clearly understood. A concomitant point is that the date on which the completed blanks are to be turned in to the supervisor or to the home office must be stated.

Dates of interviewing must be specified for an additional reason. It has been found that a Roosevelt speech can change sentiment almost overnight. Rugg (4) cites many illustrations of how the news causes rapid shifts in opinions. Unspecified dates for interviewing may result in spread of field work over such a period of time that shift in public reaction has occurred during the course of the investigation. Results from such a study are difficult to evaluate.

Another aspect of timing is selection of a period during which

INTERVIEWER ASSIGNMENT—DENTIFRICE STUDY

City _____*Atlanta*_____

You are to secure a total of __40__ interviews, which are to be distributed as follows.

A INCOME GROUP __4__ calls. The A respondents must be divided as follows.

Between 20 and 30 _____ men, __1__ women

Between 31 and 40 __1__ men, _____ women

Between 41 and 50 __1__ men, _____ women

Over 50 _____ men, __1__ women

B INCOME GROUP __12__ calls. The B respondents must be divided as follows.

Between 20 and 30 __1__ men, __2__ women

Between 31 and 40 __2__ men, __1__ women

Between 41 and 50 __2__ men, __2__ women

Over 50 __1__ men, __1__ women

C INCOME GROUP __16__ calls. The C respondents must be divided as follows.

Between 20 and 30 __2__ men, __1__ women

Between 31 and 40 __3__ men, __4__ women

Between 41 and 50 __3__ men, __2__ women

Over 50 _____ men, __1__ women

D INCOME GROUP __8__ calls. The D respondents must be divided as follows.

Between 20 and 30 __2__ men, __1__ women

Between 31 and 40 __1__ men, __2__ women

Between 41 and 50 __1__ men, __1__ women

Over 50 _____ men, _____ women

respondents will feel co-operative, and yet an interval which will produce meaningful replies. As a general rule surveys should not be conducted over holiday periods. Even during wartime it may be assumed that many individuals will "go away" over Christmas, and such a fact could produce a biased sample of respondents. Chances are that too high a proportion of guests will be interviewed, while the interviewer will miss those residences locked up over the period. There is another complicating factor here. People are probably a little more favorable toward everything in general over the Christmas period, so that they may tend to be generally more favorable toward any issues inquired about by the field worker than they would be over a normal period.

Interviewing dates are influenced by the nature of the particular study. An investigation intended to measure reaction to ice-cream use by those who used it during any season of the year could not be conducted over the winter. Ice-cream use is seasonal in nature. Summer is the time when people buy ice-cream, and summer is the period during which people will be best prepared to answer queries about their ice-cream habits.

The study must be so planned that the interviewers will have the easiest time possible to obtain their sample of respondents. Sufficient time must be allowed them to complete their calls. Part of the predictive error of the 1940 Gallup poll was apparently due to overlooking of this fact. In order to get a last-minute prediction, the Gallup field force was assigned the usual three-days' work, but this time it was to be completed in one day of work—a Sunday. The workers found it difficult, in some cases impossible, to complete the assignment in the required time. As a result, the blanks turned in underweighted the lower economic groups, thus causing an over-prediction of the Willkie vote.[2]

The period selected for the study should be advantageous from the field worker's point of view. In the case of a study in which men are to be interviewed in their homes, allowance must be made for the fact that men are at home only during the evenings and over weekends. In an investigation in which women are to be

[2] Upper groups tended to vote for Willkie, lower groups for Roosevelt.

interviewed, a shorter period of time will be required since the interviewer can work all day on weekdays.

If it is a question of securing some particular age group, there is again the problem of the best time for field work. Children of school age will not be at home during school hours, and they retire early in the evening. Some of them do come home after school in the afternoon, and many are around home on Saturdays, so either of these times may be fruitful. If it is the young lady of the family, between 21 and 30, who is to be approached, evening is likely to be a poor time. If she has a job, daylight interviewing will not be applicable. She may be at home on Saturdays or Sundays. Once the marriage has occurred, the situation may have changed. More frequently both will now be at home evenings, and the young woman is likely to be at home all day in the bargain.

The oldest group can be reached at almost any time of day. When a man or woman reaches the age of 60, he or she seldom works, and can be found at home (retired or living with relatives). This fact explains why it is poor technique for the field worker to attempt to secure a cross-section of men by interviewing in homes during daylight hours. His sample will tend to be biased toward the upper age groups. Younger men will be at work.

Although most investigators are aware of such facts as these, it is the responsibility of the survey organization to make clear in the instructions the probable best time of day or week during which the particular group of respondents may be reached.

THE MAIL QUESTIONNAIRE

Several of the detailed steps of preparing and distributing materials will be different from the outline presented when the mail questionnaire is used. There is no field worker; the questionnaires are sent directly to the potential respondents, so that any explanations must be made either directly on the questionnaire or in an accompanying letter. There is no opportunity for a field worker to attempt to obtain co-operation or to explain question meanings (where permissible). These points now have to be covered by the printed word to the prospect.

1. *The questionnaire.* The questionnaire will have been tested

for wording and sequence, but there remains more than the mere problem of duplicating the blank. It must also be of such appearance and make-up, and consist of such questions, that the recipient will be motivated to reply. The physical appearance must be neat.

a. *The duplication process*. The four chief types of duplication process mentioned as available for telephone or personal interviews were: typing (with carbons); reproduction through use of a stencil machine; typesetting; and photo-offset. Individual typing of questionnaires for mail surveys is out of the question, but it is possible to substitute here an electrically typed questionnaire. This is not expensive, and has exactly the appearance of an individually typed questionnaire.

Duplication by use of a stencil-machine is ordinarily not desirable on the mail survey; it makes the recipient feel that he has received a form inquiry. A typeset or photo-offset questionnaire is useful. Either has a pleasing appearance. Choice of the particular method will depend on the requirements of the survey.

b. *The format*. The layout of the questionnaire for the mail survey is considerably more important than in the case of the telephone or personal interview. The recipient must be stimulated to return the completed blank, and its general appearance will be one of the determining factors. The questionnaire must appear interesting and be laid out so that it looks simple to answer. Space for entering the replies should be clearly indicated, and in general short-answer questions should be the rule. Blocks for marking the proper reply, as in voting ballots, will aid in making the questionnaire appear simple to answer.

Space must be provided for the recording of corollary information, such as sex, age, and income, where these are desirable. Without some of this information, representativeness of the sample of those who do reply cannot be checked.

c. *Content*. In discussing the content of the telephone or mail questionnaire, we made the point that some of the instructions could be placed directly on the face of the questionnaire sheet. This is more important with the mail questionnaire. In this case each direction should be given at the point of the questionnaire where it is important. While it is true that some of the directions may also be mentioned in the covering letter, the recipient cannot be expected to refer to the letter at the time he is answering the questionnaire. The question blank itself must be an entity which anyone, picking it up without any further instruction, can fill out.

Some of the questionnaires which have been successful in stimulating a high proportion of replies have been those employing humor. This is really a means of giving the respondent some reason for answering the series of questions. This motivation may take other forms—it may stimulate pride or interest. Along with this, the questionnaire must not be too long. In general, respondents simply will not answer a long questionnaire.

2. *The letter*. The survey organization itself must make a direct appeal to the prospective respondent for his co-operation in the form of a letter—one which must present good and sufficient reason for the individual to reply. Executives will require a short letter, to the point. A person who has just bought a new product will probably be so interested in it that he will respond to a brief request for co-operation by the manufacturer. The language must correspond to the type of person for whom the letter is intended. It is difficult to list general rules about the letter, since the writing will vary so much with the nature of the respondents.

In some cases the sponsoring organization cannot well use its own letterhead. A few of the larger companies in this country are disliked by a sufficiently high proportion of the people to prevent them from obtaining a representative reply to any mailing they might make. In such cases it is common for the interested organization either to hire a survey organization, which then uses its own letterhead, or to use the letterhead of a "front" organization. Use of the name of a college or university also aids in the stimulation of replies.

Frequently it is possible to write a "homey" letter signed by an individual; in such a case the returns are mailed to that person. This was the approach used in several surveys which were highly successful in the proportion of responses obtained.

3. *Increasing the returns*. The usual person is more likely to open a first-class piece of mail than mail which arrives second class. The latter may be an advertisement. A stamp provided on the return

envelope seems to stimulate more replies than an envelope providing for addressee-paid postage. The personal approach seems to stimulate replies throughout all aspects of mail questionnaire work. The typing of the letter will produce a greater proportion of replies than stencil production of a letter. A typed envelope addressed to the respondent will make a better impression than one which is duplicated in the usual way.

New developments in reproducing make it possible to meet such requirements at relatively low cost. Letters can now be duplicated in typewriter style, with names of respondents typed on the top. The slight increase in cost is more than repaid by the increased returns.

Sometimes it may be desirable to offer premiums for replies; where this is done it is possible to include a much longer and much more "personal" questionnaire.

4. *The distribution of the mailing.* The distribution of the mailing will vary with the nature of the survey. A random method of selecting names can be used where the mailing list of customers of Company XYZ is complete for a particular city. Where a national list of names is available, some selection of names is not only possible but usually necessary (owing to size of the list). With this kind of mailing list it may be desirable to sort the names on a sectional basis, and then to make a random selection within each area.

Some provision must be made for checking the distribution of returns against mailings, to insure that the two are similar. The postmark will provide the clue for purposes of comparison.

Sometimes it is necessary to have the respondent identify himself. This may cut down the proportion of replies, but occasionally there is no help for it. One direct-mailer sent an acquaintance of ours a letter with a business-reply card. This card, in common with others of its kind, had the usual series of bars across the right- and left-hand sides of its face. There were no spaces provided for identification of the person replying.

This particular recipient returned the card without indication of his identity. Within two days there was a salesman in his office. The respondent had been traced through the placement of a minute check in the series of bars. There were so many variations of markings possible that the salesman reported he could identify any one of 10,000 persons to whom the card had been sent.

This method requires a lot of detail work, and probably a great deal of expense. Where identification of the respondent is required without his knowledge, the method may be applicable to survey work. Since it provides an additional means of identifying characteristics of persons replying, it is worth noting.

REFERENCES

*(1) AMERICAN MARKETING ASSOCIATION. *The Technique of Marketing Research*. New York: McGraw-Hill, 1937. Chapters 8 and 9.

*(2) BROWN, L. O. *Market Research and Analysis*. New York: Ronald, 1937. Chapter 9.

(3) GALLUP, GEORGE, AND RAE, S. F. *The Pulse of Democracy*. New York: Simon and Schuster, 1940. Chapter 7.

(4) RUGG, DONALD. "American Morale When the War Began," Chapter 11 in Goodwin Watson (ed.), *Civilian Morale*. Boston: Houghton Mifflin, 1942.

(5) SAUNDERS, A. G., AND ANDERSON, C. R. *Business Reports*. New York: McGraw-Hill, 1940. Chapter 5.

(6) WEAVER, H. G. "Consumer Questionnaire Technique," *American Marketing Journal*, 1934, 1, 116-118.

CHAPTER 11

The Process of Interviewing[1]

~~~~~~

A DISCUSSION of public opinion polls was on the air (7), and this was given as an example of the questioning procedure in an opinion poll:

Interviewer: Have you heard of the Dies Committee?
Respondent: Yes, I have followed it very closely.
Interviewer: Do you think Congress should provide money to continue the Dies Committee another year?
Respondent: I think a lot can be gained by Congressional investigations, but I don't like exactly the way the Dies Committee is going about it to do their job.
Interviewer: Then you would vote "no." Is that right?

The last query was a leading question. In similar situations the respondent might be influenced to commit himself in a direction opposite to his sentiments. This example provides one small indication of ways in which the field work can go wrong.

Bias is one of the greatest potential dangers of any survey in which field workers participate. There are other possible dangers— qualitatively poor field work, and dishonesty.

1. *Interviewing bias.* In one study (3) three field workers using the identical questionnaire in the same community obtained a comparable sample of respondents. On four of ten questions asked there were real differences apparent in the three sets of results, differences explicable only in terms of interviewer bias.[2]

[1] This chapter is written from the point of view of the personal interview approach. The material applies to telephone field work with but little modification. The chapter has no place in the discussion of mail questionnaires, since no interviewers participate.

[2] For a critical study showing *lack* of interviewer bias, see A. B. Udow, "The 'Interviewer Effect' in Public Opinion and Market Research Surveys," *Archives of Psychology*, No. 277, November 1942.

In another study Katz (11) analyzed results of a poll made among the laboring class in Pittsburgh. Nine field workers were from the white-collar class and eleven were working-class investigators. When samples of respondents were equated for the two groups of interviewers, there were significant differences in the two sets of results.

Both of these studies were conducted in the field of opinion measurement. Baker and Stanton (2) performed an experiment on the same subject in the field of memory questions. Material to be learned was presented to several university psychology classes. Each student reported separately at intervals of 4 and 18 days following the learning. At these times of "check-up" 5 trained field workers were put in charge, and none of the 5 knew what material was originally presented. Each interviewer was provided with a key of "correct" answers (some right and some wrong) and was told to check the recognition of each subject in standard fashion. At both intervals more of the responses that were correct were in the direction expected by the interviewer's knowledge than were contrary to this direction. Interviewers' "knowledge" of the "correct" reply influenced the results, producing bias in results.

Preconceptions of the interviewer can affect survey accuracy. These preconceptions may produce biased results by incorrect handling of the questioning process, errors in recording replies, physical indications during the course of questioning, and "pushing" respondents for a reply.

a. *Incorrect handling of the questioning.* Slight unintentional changes in the phrasing or sequence of questions can influence the replies obtained. If the field worker explains the meaning of the inquiry where the question is not understood by the respondent, there is danger of obtaining a biased or misleading reply.

b. *Errors in recording replies.* With short-answer questions there will normally be only a small proportion of recording errors. Chances of bias in writing replies received to free-answer questions are greater. Field workers report that after a few calls they know fairly well what answers will be given by those yet to be interrogated. Psychological experiments in other fields indicate that a person perceives (in this case hears) pretty much what he expects to perceive. Where the response differs a great deal from previous replies it is still possible for distortion to occur.

c. *Physical indications during questioning*. Vocal inflections and muscular movements of the interviewer during the questioning may also cause bias in the respondent's remarks.

d. *"Pushing" respondents for replies*. Pressing a respondent for an answer can also bias results. One survey organization had been asking a particular question periodically for a number of years. In one study it was observed that the proportion of "don't know" answers decreased some 10 per cent, owing entirely to the inadvertent omission of the "don't know" category for the interviewer to check. The question asked of respondents was identical with its predecessors. Apparently this one omission convinced the field force that they were not to accept "don't know" answers, so they probably pushed respondents into definite replies.

e. *Sampling errors*. Bias sometimes results from the sample of respondents obtained by the field worker. It can occur even in the controlled sample. In the Katz experiment (11), discussed previously, inexperienced field workers told to interview laboring persons obtained a slightly better-educated group, higher occupational levels, higher economic status (and hence lower union membership) than other interviewers who had had previous field-work experience. Apparently the new workers wanted to do the best possible job, hence interviewed those whose opinions they thought would be more valuable. Some of the new workers were Jewish, and tended to obtain a higher proportion of Jewish questionees.

There is greater danger of a sample bias with random sampling—the interviewer may work within his own age and economic groups.

Many surveys require the interviewer to estimate such factors as age or standard of living. Some workers may consistently over- or under-estimate one or both of these, thus introducing a constant error into the judgment and causing sampling bias.

2. *Qualitatively poor field work*. Generally poor field work can make survey results of little value. Such flaws as these occur: no replies to some questions, or inconsistent replies, even to the extent that "yes" and "no" are entered for the same question. Poor inter-

viewing is indicated in many other ways, some of which will be discussed in later portions of this chapter.

3. *Dishonesty*. Dishonest field work is dangerous, since the results may be used as a basis for a program by business or government. Every organization in survey work has had the problem of dishonesty once or more. The topic will be discussed in some detail later in this chapter.

Problems of bias, poor work, and dishonesty are all important in consideration and control of field work. The interviewer *can* influence the results he obtains. Such an influence should be minimized. Field workers should be trained extensively and intensively—should be warned about the possibility of their influencing the results. They should be taught and made to practice certain principles of interviewing.

PRINCIPLES OF INTERVIEWING

Interviewing is more of an art than a science. The procedure requires constant adjustment of the field worker to the particular respondent and to the general situation. To get past the butler to interview a wealthy dowager will require a different technique from the approach used with the mother of a relief family who has five young children all at home and squealing.

Though there can be great variations in approaches and handling of the interview, there are a number of general principles which the investigator should follow.

1. *He should make a few trial calls before beginning his assignment*. Trial interviewing by each worker provides insurance that the survey organization will have its calls completed in the way it expects. The good worker checks back with his supervisor to make sure that he has properly followed instructions on these trial calls. Sometimes he will discover types of responses not adequately covered in his detailed instructions. Such issues must be settled by those in authority before the field work proceeds.

2. *The interviewer must follow his instructions carefully*. Every survey agency has had the experience of discovering an entire set of questionnaire returns to be worthless because some field worker has not followed his instructions carefully. Some questionnaires are

necessarily complicated. Only the workers who carefully digest their instructions will do acceptable work on such a job.

3. *The calls on respondents must be properly timed.* The survey organization always specifies the dates on which field work is to be conducted, but that is only part of the problem. The field worker must so time his calls that he may best approach the type of respondent required.[3] The least-experienced investigator knows that Monday morning is a poor time to approach housewives, since the family wash is the most important thing in the world at that time.

4. *The obtained sample must be precisely in line with the assignment.* Chapter 8 has explained the importance of controlling such factors as the proportions of respondents from various geographic areas, economic groups, and other strata. The research group can instruct field workers about the proportions of each group required, but it is the investigator who "makes or breaks" these quotas. Bias can result if his sample is not secured in precisely the way indicated.

At the start of the interviewing, the field worker using the controlled sample approach usually waits to see what sort of respondents he obtains by chance. After making a few calls, he can see what types of respondents he is missing, and can concentrate his efforts on locating people who comprise his missing categories.

Sometimes the research staff instructs the interviewers to use the random method of obtaining respondents. The interviewer may be instructed to call at every tenth residence in an area.

In practice this method is somewhat difficult to control. The investigator may discover that the tenth family lives in an apartment house guarded by a ferocious-appearing doorman. There is a temptation to skip the apartment house.

Obtaining co-operation of prospective respondents is one of the most difficult yet important aspects of the interviewing process. Questioning will not be completed if the field worker gets off to a bad start. Most survey organizations use a particular approach (see Chapter 10), depending upon the nature of the interview. The clever field worker varies this approach so as to get most efficient

[3] See Chapter 10 for a detailed discussion of timing.

results with the particular "prospect" with whom he is dealing at the moment.

In time of war the problem of obtaining respondent co-operation is magnified. Our government has warned against giving information to strangers, and respondents are taking that warning to heart. One survey of workingmen's attitudes toward a number of industrial concerns was undertaken eight months after the entry of our country into the war. Field work was being handled by young men. One evening a respondent became suspicious that a field worker was collecting information about war-producing plants. Police were called, and the investigator was hauled off to the police station, despite his explanations. His draft registration card was asked for; unfortunately it had been lost one hour before! An F.B.I. man was called in, and the young man was quizzed for several hours, with no effort being made on the part of the authorities to check with the interviewing organization. In the morning the police checked with the field worker's draft board, and he was then released. Interviewing offers strange occupational hazards these days.

The rationing situation also makes people hesitate to tell either what they have or what they intend to buy.

There are two reasons why respondent co-operation is a necessity: so that no bias in the sample will result from the failure to secure "non-co-operative" people, and so that those who do reply will give answers which are carefully thought through (rather than quick responses designed merely to get rid of the questioner).

Even with field workers doing their best to interview everyone approached, there is some danger that the obtained sample may not be the best possible cross-section. Gaudet and Wilson (10) found that refusals tended to come from housewives and persons of low educational status.[4] Of a total of 2800 original calls, second interviews were attempted with each respondent. On the call-back the unavailable group tended to be principally males, and included more industrial workers than other groups.

6. *The question must be asked word-for-word as written on the question blank.* Previous chapters have shown what can happen

[4] In terms of expected refusals as estimated from proportion of each group in the sample.

when an apparently minor change in phrasing or sequence is made. Occasionally field workers who are too clever modify both phrasing and sequence in order to secure co-operation. Sometimes respondents give answers which do not refer to the specific question asked, so the investigator is tempted to ask a leading question to point up the issue, to explain the query to the respondent. Because of this fact, many "don't know" replies in the work of one interviewer may actually indicate more careful interviewing than a number of detailed answers in the work of another.

7. *The investigator must make a favorable impression on the respondent.* The interviewer must be courteous, pleasant, and tactful throughout his work. He must be assured and conversational, though entirely businesslike. His personal appearance must be attractive, his dress adapted to the class of respondents whom he is questioning.

Nervous mannerisms or indistinct speech can cause a great deal of annoyance to respondents. The worker's English must be good; otherwise he will annoy persons who speak good English. He must not have the habit of interrupting conversation.

In other words, the field worker must act constantly as a public relations man. He can never, regardless of how he is treated, lose his temper or show any annoyance.

8. *The field worker must be neutral during the questioning.* Possibilities of interviewer bias were outlined at the start of this chapter. The point requires no additional discussion.

9. *The surveyor should repeat the question if he does not understand the response given.* Repetition may secure a more meaningful reply. The field worker should not attempt to edit or interpret ambiguous replies, but should write down on his questionnaire blank everything the respondent says that appears pertinent. This means not only careful checking of a *yes* or *no* in the correct spot on the blank, but faithful reproduction of pertinent details of answers to free-response queries.

10. *The investigator should write neatly and legibly.* Poor writing may make completed questionnaires undecipherable, hence worthless.

11. *The interviewer should accept and record only replies which*

are adequate. A reply must be true to be valuable. An immediate reply may not always be accurate. In one case this direct question was asked: *Is the manner in which coffee is packed of importance to you?* (1) A number of respondents gave an unequivocal "No" to this query, yet subsequent questioning showed that in almost every instance some feature of packaging was important to the person replying. The persons conducting the field work must be instructed to alter an obviously untruthful or mistaken answer to the response for which there is clear and definite evidence. An adequate reply is a full one as well as true. The investigator must give his respondent an opportunity for complete expression and should record as much of the reply as possible.

12. *The field investigator must make sure that he has recorded all of the desired information*. The competent interviewer doesn't skip questions, doesn't miss recording any of the sampling information. Omission of such items confronts the surveying organization with the problem of what to do with a "no answer" group of responses.

Who Is a Good Interviewer?

Each interviewing job is somewhat different from every other survey. Some organizations, it is true, conduct only one type of survey. Gallup concentrates on political and social-issue polls, but even these change from study to study. It is difficult to summarize qualifications for interviewing when the work varies so much. Different kinds of surveys seem to require various sorts of field workers. A study among mothers to measure reactions to baby foods obviously requires the use of women investigators of approximately the same age as the mothers to be approached. A study designed to uncover real reasons for a strike will require some rough-and-ready male workers to mingle among picketers. Yet these investigators will need sufficient intelligence to uncover the basic motivations underlying the superficial and standardized responses that may be given by the strikers.

Despite the apparent differences in interviewing procedure, there is a common core. All of the work involves the approach of prospects, the securing of co-operation, the asking of questions, and the recording of replies. Because of this similarity in the survey situation, there is agreement on a few traits required by investigators. They must have the appearance and manners to react favorably upon those approached. The investigator should be an extrovert—one who enjoys talking to people, who can gain their confidence, and who is both pleasant and courteous.

An investigator must be healthy. The field worker for the usual survey must be of fairly high intelligence level. If he is not reasonably intelligent, even with detailed and specific instructions he will have no idea how to handle a complicated procedure. He will not know how to manage a situation not covered by his instructions.

A number of writers list the lack of bias as a desirable trait. Unquestionably it is, but to the psychologist it appears a trait highly modifiable by training. It seems pointless to select interviewers before training on such a basis.

One exploratory study (5) attempted to obtain objective information on the characteristics of poll investigators. An interesting descriptive sketch of the typical interviewer is quoted:

"Miss Jane Doe, aged 30, is a Protestant. She is in good health, and has lost no time from work during the past two years. She has completed 14 years of schooling, and has had a little 'professional' training in the bargain. She completed grammar school at 13, high school at 17. While in school her favorite subjects were English and social science. She particularly disliked mathematics and foreign languages.

"Miss Doe is a fairly active member of her community, where she has lived for 14 years, with her parents. She belongs to one club, but is not an officer. She formerly belonged to other clubs, and had been an officer. She has made speeches in public, and before clubs.

"There is a telephone in her home, but she does not own a car. She owes no outstanding personal debts; in fact she carries some personal insurance. Miss Doe is somewhat better than average in many traits. In intelligence, for example, she is superior to 60% of persons with equal education; in vocabulary she is superior to 66% of her friends with equal education. Indications are that she is slightly on the aggressive or dominant side. She is average in terms of home adjustment, emotional adjustment, and occupational adjustment, and is a little better than average in terms of health."

The good and poor workers—on the basis of judgments by their supervisors—were compared in these characteristics, with some interesting outcomes. The good pollers were higher in intelligence and vocabulary than the poor workers, and the good workers were better adjusted all around.

How Can Interviewing Be Improved?

Some indications of the answer to this question have already been given. There are four methods: (1) careful selection of field force, (2) proper training of investigators, (3) supervision, and (4) method of payment.

1. *Selection of field force.* Where possible, interviewers should be personally selected by one or more members of the central office staff. Dependence on an outsider who has scarcely seen the office will mean that selection is being made by one who has little idea of the specific problems in which the office is interested. Selecting workers by correspondence alone is worse, since it is impossible to judge accurately the characteristics of a person merely by letters and recommendations.

Field workers must be selected by personal interview. The discussion with the applicant should be revealing enough to determine whether he is intelligent, extroverted, honest, healthy, and capable of following directions. Personal references of the applicant should be checked for verification of his statements and worth. The interviewer should be chosen with regard for the particular type of survey being undertaken.

2. *Training investigators.* Training of the field force is as important as their selection. The interviewer who shows greatest potentiality cannot do good work without proper training. Investigators not only must receive general training in interviewing technique, but must be trained specifically for the particular job at hand. Suggestions of what to include in the general training will be found at the start of this chapter; all of the listed principles of interviewing are techniques which the well-selected field worker can learn.

One organization is doing an especially thorough job of training its field force. A new worker is brought into the central office and works around there for several weeks until he gets the general "feel" of survey work. At the same time he is supervised carefully in his learning and is given some material on survey techniques to be digested. At the end of this preliminary period he is sent into the field under close supervision, with detailed instructions as to how to operate. At intervals he returns to the office for additional training and experience.

For any specific survey the best instruction is that given on the scene of operations. This task falls to the supervisor and is, in fact, part of the process of supervision.

3. *Supervision of field force.* Direct supervision of field workers is desirable; no investigator can be depended upon to do his work precisely in the manner the home office desires if the matter is handled by the postman. Personal supervision must be of high quality; supervisors must be selected even more carefully than the field force. Supervisors must have all of the characteristics required for good interviewers, and must possess other characteristics as well. The supervisor must not only be a person who can select his own field workers when the occasion arises, but he must be an individual who arouses the confidence of his workers; he must be a leader. He must be a person who can properly train his workers, a person who will see that the questionnaires sent to the home office are in the desired form. He must have had extensive experience in all aspects of survey work. He must understand the drafting and testing of questionnaires; he must grasp all the principles and problems of the sampling procedure. He must comprehend thoroughly the purpose of the particular study, and should understand how the material is to be used after it reaches the home office. Without such knowledge he will not be able to select, train, and check his field staff. He will not even recognize the difference between a good and a poor interview.

The good supervisor will make sure that his investigators understand the questionnaire and directions for the study before it is undertaken. The competent field manager will also make the interviewer question him (the supervisor) with the interview blank so that he can determine how well the field worker is following directions. It is good training here for the answers to be made as difficult as possible, so that the interviewer is forced to use a great deal of discretion. When the supervisor detects a flaw in the asking of questions, in the recording, or in any other aspect of procedure, it is simple to show the interviewer just what mistake was made.

Following this "test," the field worker should conduct a few test calls in the presence of the field supervisor before he does any interviewing on his own. The supervisor should accompany the worker, whether new or experienced, on his first few calls. This is a further check to insure that the field worker is following instructions.

Psychologists have found that honesty is not a constant trait. Practically all of us will be dishonest if the circumstances and motives are right for that dishonesty. The most moral person will tell a "white lie" to save the feelings of a friend. Dishonesty in the interviewing situation is of a different sort, but here too it is a variable quality. Field workers who have been honest for many studies have been known to "go wrong" suddenly.

The best way to control this is to create a situation in which it will be difficult, if not impossible, for the dishonesty to occur. At the beginning of the day the supervisor can drive the field worker to the territory in which he is to work, and then pick him up at a given point and time in the evening. This will make it virtually impossible for the field worker to fill out his own schedules. Most survey organizations make it a point periodically to check the calls made by interviewers. The agency may have a check interviewer repeat every tenth call listed by the original worker, to make sure that the investigator was actually there. Other agencies send postcards to the people the field workers claim to have interviewed.

Psychologically, it is sound to make motivation so strong that interviewers will not be tempted to be dishonest. The best possible motivation would seem to be a fair and considerate treatment of the worker.

The supervisor must make sure that the quota assigned by the home office has been met in every detail. All sampling characteristics should be checked against the assignment. Each questionnaire must be completely filled out. Are any blanks definitely unacceptable, and if so, must additional interviews be made? Does the work of any of the investigators appear biased? The supervisor must answer all of these questions to his own satisfaction before he can confidently forward the work of his questioners to the home office.

4. *Payment of the interviewers.* Quality of the field work will vary with the method of paying the worker. Probably the best method of payment is on a salary basis, but few organizations have the volume and scope of work to keep a full force of investigators busy. Interviewers are frequently paid on piece-rate, but when an interviewer runs into a bad day—people just aren't at home, or they just won't seem to co-operate—he will become discouraged. This can result in failure to complete the assignment, poor work, or dishonesty. It is probably better to pay by the day. This way the workers know just how much they may expect, and there will be no dissatisfaction on pay.

Paying a daily rate has its own disadvantages. A good worker, able to complete a large number of calls within a short period of time, is penalized for his proficiency. The poor worker is actually paid a higher rate per completed call. Under a daily rate there is some danger of "soldiering," or performing the work more slowly than if the pay were piece-rate.

A possible solution seems to be a combination of the piece-rate and wage system. The investigator can be told that he is expected to complete a minimum of so many calls per day, and that he will be paid so much for that day's work. When he is able to complete more than the quota for that day, he will be given a bonus in accordance with what he was actually receiving per interview. Where he falls under his quota for a particular day he will still receive his full day's wage, since this may be caused by unforeseen circumstances. An interviewer who consistently falls below the standard, of course, cannot be retained on the field force. This may involve more "cash on the line," but the saving will more than repay the investment in terms of loyalty and quality of work.

Offer of a bonus can also be made on the basis of the quality of the work. The usual daily rate can be paid, with the offer of a stated bonus for each day that the worker meets such requirements as the quota, high quality of interviewing, and the like. This system stresses the quality of the work and is an effective inducement.

REFERENCES

*(1) AMERICAN MARKETING ASSOCIATION. *The Technique of Marketing Research*. New York: McGraw-Hill, 1937. Chapters 8, 9, and 10.

(2) BAKER, K. H., AND STANTON, FRANK. "Interviewer-Bias and the Recall of Incompletely Learned Material," *Sociometry*, 1942, 5, 123-134.

*(3) BINGHAM, W. V., AND MOORE, B. V. *How to Interview*. New York: Harper, 1941. Chapter 10.

(4) BLANKENSHIP, A. B. "The Effect of the Interviewer upon the Response in a Public Opinion Poll," *Journal of Consulting Psychology*, 1940, 4, 134-136.

(5) BLANKENSHIP, A. B., MANHEIMER, D. I., AND OTIS, J. L. "Characteristics of Opinion Poll Interviewers." Paper given before American Psychological Association, 1941.

(6) BROWN, L. O. *Market Research and Analysis*. New York: Ronald, 1937. Chapter 11.

(7) CHICAGO ROUND TABLE DISCUSSION. Testing public opinion. November 5, 1939.

(8) COUTANT, F. R. "Supervising the Field Investigation," *Market Research*, 1938, 8, No. 6, 19-21.

(9) COUTANT, F. R., AND DOUBMAN, J. R. *Simplified Market Research*. Philadelphia: Walther, 1935. Chapter 4.

(10) GAUDET, HAZEL, AND WILSON, E. C. "Who Escapes the Personal Investigator? *Journal of Applied Psychology*, 1940, 24, 773-777.

(11) KATZ, DANIEL. "Do Interviewers Bias Poll Results?" *Public Opinion Quarterly*, 1942, 6, 248-268.

(12) PFIFFNER, J. M. *Research Methods in Public Administration*. New York: Ronald, 1940. Chapter 9.

(13) ROPER, ELMO. "Sampling Public Opinion," *Journal of the American Statistical Association*, 1940, 35, 325-334.

(14) SCRIVEN, J. E. "Why Successful Salesmen Fail as Investigators," *Management*, November, 1929, 33, 58.

(15) SNEAD, R. P. "Problems of Field Interviewers," *Journal of Marketing*, 1942, 7, 139-145.

(16) UNSIGNED. "Listening Post," *Advertising Age*, February 23, 1942.

(17) UNSIGNED. "Sizzle Needed in Census Spiel, Is Wheeler's Opinion," *Advertising Age*, April 10, 1940.

(18) WECHSLER, JAMES. "Interviews and Interviewers," *Public Opinion Quarterly*, 1940, 4, 258-260.

*(19) WHITE, PERCIVAL. *Marketing Research Technique*. New York: Harper, 1931. Chapters 7, 8, 9, 10, and 11.

CHAPTER 12

Summarizing the Results

THE purpose of summarizing results is to bring out succinctly the significance of the mass of data collected on the study. Summary is designed to give meaning to a volume and range of individual replies received on a survey. This meaning, expressed in terms of conclusions from the study, takes place from a process of examination and classification of replies.

EXAMINATION OF QUESTIONNAIRES

Editing of questionnaires has two main purposes: elimination of errors in the data, and preparation of the data for tabulation. The editing is handled in the office in which summary work is to be done. Any changes of replies made during the editing process should be indicated on the particular questionnaire sheet in colored pencil or ink, so that it is possible to differentiate the response originally written on the blank from the notes made in the office.

Since the editing may vary with the point of view of the person doing the work, it is well to limit the number of workers who perform this important task. As problems arise during editing, the solution should be recorded, so that the principles followed in the particular process of editing will be recorded for future reference and guidance.

1. *Returns should be compared by area and investigator.* Substandard work of one or more investigators or areas frequently comes to light by such a technique. This is one of the surest methods of discovering dishonest work. The reports of a dishonest field worker usually vary so greatly from those of any other worker that they immediately stand out.

If reports of one worker tend to follow a pattern, rather than indicating variation in reply, there is additional reason to suspect dishonesty. Individual replies tend to be specific, and are not likely to fall into a standard pattern except where the short-answer question has been used.

The editor should discard the work of any investigator whose reports are definitely below average,[1] or useless for some other reason.

2. *Incorrect answers should be discarded.* Careless or unintelligible answers are apparent to the editor who knows the background of the specific questionnaire issues. On a questionnaire concerned with silverware, a question about respondent ownership of sterling, plate, or both was included. This was followed with queries about the maker and pattern of each set. Some respondents gave the names of plate makers and sterling patterns as referring to the same set; these had to be changed so that the particular pattern was placed under the correct heading.

In another survey respondents were asked what brand of a particular product they had last bought, and at what kind of store they had purchased it. A few stated that they had bought brand X through mail order houses. Since this brand was not sold through mail order concerns, such answers had to be discarded.

In some surveys it is desirable to measure consumer reaction as such, regardless of correctness. In such cases the obviously incorrect answers would not be discarded, but would be carried in the summary with appropriate indication of their incorrectness. In one study the products used to clean toilet bowls were being investigated. Each housewife was asked the brand of product she used for this purpose, and this query was followed with the question: *Is this a product made especially for toilet-bowl cleaning?* Since one of the purposes of the investigation was to determine the proportion of housewives who thought a general cleanser was made specifically for toilet cleansing, the answers to this question were not "corrected."

3. *Inconsistent answers must be corrected or discarded.* The answers to two or more queries within a single questionnaire are

[1] In terms of omission of replies, fullness of response, inconsistency, etc.

sometimes found to be inconsistent. In one mail study the question was asked: *How many times in the past year have you bought_____?* This was followed with the inquiry: *About how long ago was the last purchase made?* Some of the respondents stated in reply to the second question that they had not bought any of this commodity for a year, yet mentioned in the first question that they had bought it twice during the past year. It was assumed in this study that the answer to the latter question, since it referred to more recent behavior, probably was more correct, so the answer to the first question was discarded.

4. *Where possible, incomplete answers or no replies should be filled in.* In many questionnaires there is an interlocking series of questions, so that even if the respondent doesn't answer one query or doesn't answer it fully, the editor finds it possible, through other answers on the subject, to write in what the answer should have been. The method may be used only in cases where there is no room for doubt.

In the silverware questionnaire, some respondents did not state whether they owned sterling, plate, or both. The question on makes and patterns owned was usually answered fully, so that it was possible to fill in the proper answer to the ownership question.

5. *Where the reply to a question indicates a modified or qualified response to another question, the change should be indicated.* This is similar to the preceding point. The difference is that the two questions may not produce contradictory answers, but the reply to one, rather, qualifies the answer to the other. It is not unusual for a respondent to give a definite and unqualified answer to a short-response question, and then to modify that answer in replying to another inquiry. In one study this question was asked: *Do you think that American industry is doing all it can for the war effort?* Then followed the question: *Why (or why not), in what way?* A few respondents said they did not believe that industry was doing all possible. When asked why, they mentioned such points as "union coercion," "lack of government planning," etc. These questionees were not objecting to the effort of the industries, but rather to something outside their control which prevented their greatest production for war. These modifying replies really changed the

earlier response, in so far as the intent of the question was concerned. A category of response to the first question had to be established to include those who felt that some force outside of industry's control was keeping them back.

6. *Numerical answers must be converted to similar units.* Surveys frequently include questions which obtain replies in terms of numbers. The last-purchase question, inquiring the period of time since the last purchase of an item was made, is common. Some people reply in terms of days, some in weeks, some in months, and some in years. For ease in the tabulation of replies, the editor should convert all such answers into the same terms.

7. *Where numerical answers are to be tabulated in classes, the editor should indicate the proper classification on the blank.* This point of editing saves the tabulator time and annoyance, and probably makes for greater accuracy in summary. The editor is usually a more responsible and more highly trained person in the usual research organization than is the tabulator, so that responsibility should be his.

8. *Answers should be allocated to the proper category of response.* This point refers to the free-response type of inquiry, where the respondent's reply is limited only by his own imagination and vocabulary. This sort of question is likely to elicit such a variety of answers that the usual tabulator will be helpless. The editor must develop the proper classification of replies as he goes through a portion of the returns. This problem of categories will be discussed in the next section of this chapter. Once the classifications of replies have been developed, the point of editing is the proper time at which to indicate the category into which the answer falls.

The editor should indicate these categories, using colored pencil or ink for the purpose. These should be noted on the questionnaire for several reasons. Without it any retabulation of the responses will be difficult, and may not agree entirely with the first tabulation. The entry of the category on the face of the questionnaire will make for a consistent point of view; it will not matter how many tabulators work on summary of the question—allocations and results will be identical.

9. *The editor should indicate which of the replies are worth verbatim reproduction.* Even in short-answer queries the respondent frequently makes comments so pertinent that the research director may want to include them somewhere in his report. Comments may be important for reproduction either because they are typical of the answers obtained or because they are so significant they should not be lost in the shortened form of answer common in summary tables. Sometimes a single remark may be worth the price of the entire investigation. One remark can suggest a new product or a new use for an existing product, or a new copy idea for use in advertising. The editor must have imagination and judgment so that he will not overlook such significant replies.

CLASSIFICATION OF REPLIES

Classification of responses is the basis for all summary work; without classification no summary is possible. In brief, classification is "... a matter of grouping data on the basis of such likenesses or differences as time units, space units, or other inherent qualities" (*13*). The classification of answers in terms of time or space units is usually not a difficult process; it is the "other inherent qualities" that are tantalizingly difficult to categorize. It is in the free-response question that problems of classification arise.

1. *Requirements for a classification.* One authority has stated that in order to be satisfactory, a classification must be (a) articulate, (b) psychologically adequate, (c) logically correct, and (d) psychologically pertinent.[2]

The objective of classification is to give meaning to the mass of answers too numerous to report individually. Statements are grouped into classes (i.e., a number of other statements) which are similar in meaning. There is an apparent contradiction here: If only a few groups of responses are used, it means that a number of relatively different items must necessarily be included within each group. If each category is strictly limited to some specific type of reply, then a large number of classes will result. The use of "articulate" cate-

[2] This discussion of requirements for a classification is based largely upon material in Chapter 11 of *The Technique of Marketing Research* (*1*).

gorizing is applied to solve this stalemate. The process employs the gradual development of classes. At first only a few groups of responses are defined. Each group is then subdivided and the process may be carried as far as necessary. This process of articulation is of great practical value. It makes for easier comprehension on the part of the person who is reading the summary. It can be adapted to the number of cases used. The process of articulation can be extended to the point where the number of cases in the sub-category of lowest frequency is still indicative of reliable results.[3]

The classifications must be psychologically adequate. The categories selected must represent the best possible scheme for comparison of the responses. Any psychologically adequate classification scheme will leave no item outside of the categories, and at the same time every class used will be significant. A psychologically adequate classification scheme also provides categories which are not overlapping.

To be logically correct the classification must not include groups which have been added together under different aspects of classification. A classification of cameras used by respondents could not include movie cameras, Eastman Kodaks, box cameras, and those with f3.8 lenses. The categories are not only overlapping; they are not made on the same basis.

The classification must be psychologically pertinent. The respondent must be considered. Lazarsfeld (1) cites a case in point. At the time of his study in Vienna, little wash was sent to the laundry; even women of good circumstance took pride in doing their own washing. A laundry concern wanted to know how to obtain converts, so they asked women who sent out washing why they did so. Among the answers was a variety of statements, referring to such reasons as illness and desire to save time. The first step in classifying these responses was the observation that women sent out their laundry either for some particular occasion (such as having guests), or for a general purpose (such as the saving of time and work). The table of responses was divided as follows:

[3] See Chapter 9 for a statement of the relationship of number of cases and reliability of results.

	%
Occasions	81
Gave up maid	30
More family members, guests	19
Housewife took job	18
Housewife became ill, older	14
Advantages	19
Saving of time and work	13
Cheaper	6

Obviously this difficult portion of the summary work is not a procedure which can be left to a clerical worker; it is a part of the work which only those thoroughly qualified in survey research can handle. It is essential for the qualified person at least to make and set down the standards of the classification to be used; this can be done only after a list of responses to a given question for 100 or more questionnaire blanks has been made. One of the reasons why it is essential for the qualified person to make this preliminary classification is that frequently on the same study there are other comparable free-response queries which must follow a similar classification scheme in order to be of value.

2. *Considering the meaning of a reply*. At the time the classification is started it will be necessary to decide just what each response means. Adequate classification is impossible without knowledge of what is being classified.

One of the problems here is a "don't know" answer. Just what does "don't know" mean?[4] In knowledge questions the reply has significance. In reply to the question *What company makes the Airacobra?* a "don't know" reply means only one thing—that the respondent is ignorant of the particular information. In behavior and opinion questions the "don't know" response is more difficult to interpret.

Consider the behavior question *What brand of coffee did you buy last?* Persons who answer "Don't know" have bought *some* brand; it is known that all of the "don't know" answers to this query are distributed in some fashion or other among all coffee brands

---

[4] See Chapter 1 in Zeisel (16) for a discussion of the meaning of a "don't know" answer.

mentioned specifically by those giving a definite answer to the question. The meaning of such an answer is then in doubt; the "don't know" response to such a question can actually mean any one of a number of brands.

A similar fact is true for almost all behavior questions to which "don't know" is obtained as a reply. Zeisel (16) mentions another illustration. The question *How many hours have you listened to the radio during the last week?* was asked. Some 30 per cent of all radio listeners replied, "don't know." Those who gave such an answer were then asked, *Was it approximately one hour or less, more than one hour but less than five, or more than five hours?* A total of 80 per cent of the "don't know" group replied that it was more than five hours—in other words the number of hours was too high to be remembered.

In the case of opinion questions, the "don't know" (or "no opinion") answer is fully as difficult to define. One paper (7) assumes that a "don't know" answer reflects neutrality on a subject. On the other hand, Benson (2) has shown clearly that in the case of pre-election polls, a secret ballot technique obtains from 9 to 14 per cent fewer "don't know" answers than the usual interviewing procedure. Roslow and Blankenship (12) have demonstrated a similar reticence on the part of respondents to commit themselves. When the question appeared to be innocuous, 24 per cent more people were willing to give a reply than when the same question was phrased differently.

There is evidence indicating that many "don't know" replies reflect lack of knowledge of respondents about the particular opinion issue. It is common to find that lower economic groups give many more "no opinion" replies than do higher groups. Since psychological studies have shown that the lower the economic group, the lower the intelligence (in general), this would appear to indicate that many "don't know" replies reflect ignorance. A preliminary study by Manheimer and Blankenship [5] supports this point of view.

These investigators asked 80 persons a series of 12 questions before our entry into the war. All questions related to information

[5] Unpublished paper.

about the Japanese-Chinese situation. Preceding the information questions was one on attitude—whether the United States should continue to send war materials to China. The half of this group less informed on the situation gave 75 per cent of all the indecision answers. Among the informed group there were 14 per cent "no opinion" replies, while the proportion was 50 per cent in the uninformed group. Degree of information was related to standard of living.

If a "don't know" answer is susceptible to so many interpretations, it is simple to see that definite answers themselves may often be difficult to define. One indication of the difficulty of interpreting definite answers is provided by the experiment of Ghiselli (5). When this investigator asked one group of respondents to reply to an attitude question in terms of "yes" and "no," the proportion of answers was different from those of a group who answered in terms of four steps—degrees under the "yes" and "no" categories. Fewer were willing to reply under the straight "yes-no" setup, and those who did reply to this form were less favorable toward the proposal.

Even before classification is started, some effort to interpret replies must be made in order for a meaningful and significant group of categories to be obtained.

FACTORS TO CONSIDER IN PLANNING TABULATIONS

A point of view is necessary before summary of results can be planned. Many factors are important in determining the point of view which will dominate the tabulations: the purpose of the investigation, possible cross-tabulations, the speed with which the results are required, the order of question summary, and the problem of hand versus machine tabulation.

1. *The purpose of the study.* The first and most important consideration in the planning of the tabulations is the purpose of the investigation. What is its principal objective? How was each question designed to help answer the problems raised?

In one study the purpose was to determine the degree of consumer use of a mail-order catalogue, with particular reference to its editorial section. It was desired to learn whether people read and made use of this section, and if so, in what way. The questions were all designed to produce answers which would bear upon these basic issues. In planning the tabulations it was necessary only to remember that every tabulation had a part to play in throwing light upon one or more of the primary purposes of the research. A mere summary of the answers to the question *Did you cut out and use the figures on page 12?* would have meant little in itself. These replies assumed meaning only when they were considered in relation to the number of persons reporting that they had read that section of the material. It was consequently necessary to plan the tabulations so that the answers would be shown in relation to the number of people who had read that section.

2. *Possible cross-tabulations must be considered.* The example just mentioned bears directly on this point. The issue concerns which questions are to be tabulated alone, and which will be valuable only when shown in relation to other inquiries. The straight tabulation shows a one-dimensional breakdown of replies and is illustrated by the accompanying table, shown in Zeisel (*16*).

MORTALITY FROM CANCER

	%
Die from cancer	11.3
Die from other causes	88.7
Total	100.0
(Cases)	(1,330,496)

This table describes deaths only in one dimension—cause (in this case cancer). Such a tabulation answers one question: the chances of eventual death by cancer.

Why do 11.3 per cent of the population die of cancer? This question can be answered only by further fractionation of the data. Age might be one of these, and when age is taken into consideration the following table results:

MORTALITY FROM CANCER
SHOWN BY AGE GROUPS

	Ages Below 55 Years	55 Years and Over
	%	%
Die from cancer	9.1	12.6
Die from other causes	90.9	87.4
Total	100.0	100.0
(Cases)	(498,724)	(830,616)

The table indicates that age is a factor in cancer deaths—that chances of dying from cancer increase with age. Addition of a third factor—sex—produces the following breakdown of the data:

MORTALITY FROM CANCER
SHOWN BY AGE GROUPS AND SEX

	Ages Below 55 Years		55 Years and Over	
	Men	Women	Men	Women
	%	%	%	%
Die from cancer	5.9	13.5	11.5	14.2
Die from other causes	94.1	86.5	88.5	85.8
Total	100.0	100.0	100.0	100.0
(Cases)	(283,166)	(215,558)	(456,738)	(373,878)

It is clear from this breakdown that the proportion of women dying from cancer shows little change as age increases. But with men, the proportion of cancer deaths almost doubles from one age group to the other.

Although this example clarifies the need for fractionation of the data, it provides no clues as to rules for breakdowns. The clues for the direction and extent of cross-tabulation will be provided by the individual in charge of the research, and will depend in large part upon his imagination and insight in relating analysis of results to the purposes of the investigation.

3. *The speed with which results are required will affect the planning of the tabulations.* The deadline for the summary of results may be one week from the time in which completed questionnaires are in the hands of the home office. This sort of case will make imperative the assigning of many more than the normal number of office workers to summary of results. Work on other investigations may have to be postponed temporarily. This kind of pressure accounts for the frequent evening and week-end working of those in the survey field.

4. *The order of question summary.* Sometimes the deadline can be met by supplying the sponsor of the study with the results of what he considers "key" questions. Some questions will be more important than others, and these should be summarized first in any

case. The survey technician should plan to summarize the questions in order of their importance for purposes of the study.

5. *Hand versus machine tabulation.* This question should also be answered at the time that plans for tabulation are made. Since there are so many factors in the selection of one method over the other, these will be discussed in a separate section.

HAND VERSUS MACHINE TABULATION

1. *The technique of hand tabulation.* Hand tabulation is the simple summary of replies by a hand-recording process which requires the entry of a tally mark for each interview for each question. Suppose, for instance, that this question had been asked: *Do you believe the present government is helping or hurting business?* There could be five categories of response here: helping, hurting, both, neither, or don't know. The tabulator looks at the response to this question on each of the interview blanks, and records the reply in the appropriate space on his tabulation sheet. The usual system is to enter each case as a stroke (/), and to use a cross-bar to mark the fifth case (⫽⫽), so that the group of five entries will make for greater ease in adding all the cases entered within each category.

2. *The technique of machine tabulation.* Machine tabulation is the conversion of every response to a number, punching the number on a card, and running all cards through a machine in order to obtain the figure representing the total number of times each figure was punched. The final summary of figures is then changed back into the categories of answers originally obtained.

Consider the government-and-business question just mentioned. The five possible answers are: helping, hurting, both, neither, or don't know. Let's see how this is handled on a typical "punched card."

On the following page is shown a typical card. This particular one contains 80 columns of digits across the card. Each column has 12 possible positions. Although the numbers 0 to 9 are the only ones printed on the card, there are two more positions at the top of the card for special use, referred to as positions X and Y, or 11 and 12.

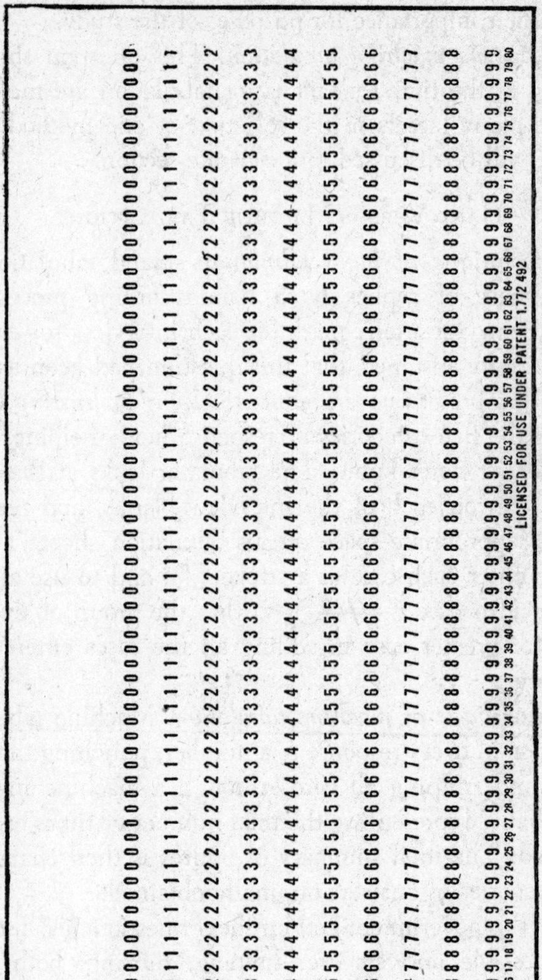

Reproduced by permission of International Business Machine Corporation

For our particular question we must decide upon a location on the card in which to punch the various answers received. One card is reserved for a single questionnaire throughout the process. The unused space on the card may be utilized for other questions. Since in the case of this particular question there are five possible replies, five digits on the card must be used to handle the answers. A sixth space might also be provided for the "no answer" group. Column 5 can be the one selected for our purpose.

It has been decided that a "1" on column 5 means that the individual has replied "helping" to the question. The number 2 would mean "hurting," 3 would indicate "both," 4 "neither," 5 "don't know," and 6 "no answer." For every interview collected the appropriate hole will be punched in the card.

When the 1000 cards for the question have been punched, they are ready for machine-running. This procedure might reveal the following distribution of punched numbers on column 5:

1. 300
2. 300
3. 150
4. 150
5. 100
6.   0

Conversion of these numbers to the original categories produces the following table of results:

Helping	300
Hurting	300
Both	150
Neither	150
Don't know	100

In this particular case not all of the 12 spaces on the column have been used; possibly some other question with only a few categories of reply can be placed in remaining positions on the column. Ordinarily, however, this is not desirable unless the questionnaire is so detailed that all space on the card is required. When the results of one question must be shown in relation to the answers received on another query, confusion in machine-running can easily result if more than one question is punched on a single column.

Occasionally 12 spaces are not enough to handle all the categories of response to one question. Questions on brand use frequently result in mention of more than 12 items. Make of automobile owned is a good illustration. One possibility is to use additional columns as required, but with only 12 spaces per column this uses up a lot of space if there are as many as 25 or 30 classifications.

There is another method for handling the type of question which secures a variety of answers. Two columns may be allocated to such a question. Each combination of numbers on these two columns will then have a different meaning. If columns 45 and 46 are being used to record the make of automobile, the range of replies and the coding numbers used for each may appear as follows:

	Position on Column	
Make of Auto	45	46
Auburn	1	1
Austin	1	2
Buick	1	3
Cadillac	1	4
Chrysler	1	5
Cord	1	6
Chevrolet	1	7
DeSoto	1	8
Dodge	1	9
Ford	1	0
Hupmobile	1	11
LaSalle	1	12
Lincoln	2	1
Marmon	2	2
Oldsmobile	2	3
Packard	2	4
Plymouth	2	5
Pontiac	2	6
Reo	2	7
Rockne	2	8
Whippet	2	9
Willys	2	0
Stutz	2	11
Don't know	2	12
No answer	12	12
None	11	11

An Auburn automobile would then be entered as 1 on column 45 and 1 on column 46. Twelve in each column would indicate no answer to the question.

Now that the general process of machine tabulation has been outlined, the specific procedure may be discussed. The steps in the process are these: (a) deciding the categories of answers to be used in each question, (b) allocation of the necessary space on the card for each question, (c) preparing "codes" from which the clerical help may work, (d) having the clerical workers fill in the codes, (e) punching of the machine cards, (f) the machine work, and (g) conversion of machine results into summary tables.

a. *Deciding the categories of answers to be used in each question.* The process of categorizing the answers has been previously discussed. There is no difference in the procedure merely because the machine method is to be used.

b. *Allocation of the necessary space on the card for each question.* It has already been explained that a single punched card is usually reserved for each collected questionnaire. The first consideration is to provide some means of associating each questionnaire with its particular card, so that if, during the process of running results, the questionnaire for a particular card is needed, it can be found without difficulty. Usual procedure here is to allot the first few columns for identification. Each questionnaire is numbered as it comes in. As the coders work, they number the card in a corresponding manner. But this point is not a portion of the allocation of card space, except in so far as it determines the number of columns which must be reserved for the identification.

One column is usually then assigned for each of the sampling factors: locality of the interview, the age of the respondent, his sex, his standard of living, the investigator, and the like. The remaining columns on the card can be assigned to questions appearing on the interview form. The allocation of space cannot be completed without knowledge of the number of columns required to handle the replies to each question. This problem can be answered only after the "codes" have been prepared.

c. *Preparing codes from which the clerical help may work.* The list of automobiles given previously, and the punches required in the particular columns, is an example of a code. For purposes of identification there is usually a heading on each code to indicate clearly the data and column(s) to which it refers.

This preparation of codes is not always a simple process. Consider the case of "multiple answers," where one individual makes more than one reply to a single question. In the question *Which of these products are made or distributed by General Foods Corporation: coffee, cereal, cocoa, yeast?* a single respondent could name as many as four products. A punch would have to be provided to permit the handling of such multiple answers.

There would be two ways in which this particular situation could be managed. Either a single punch for each product could be made (and thus four punches could occur in the one column), or a code could be set up to provide for the handling of each possible combination of answers.

The first method appears simpler. Providing multiple punches in one column can have objections in such a case. It will be difficult and tedious to run such cards according to the number of products mentioned, and it will be almost impossible to have breakdowns of

CODE SHEET

Q. Which of these products are made or distributed by General Foods Corporation: coffee, cereal, cocoa, yeast?

Col. 50	Col. 51	
1	R	Coffee alone
1	2	Coffee with cereal
1	3	Coffee with cocoa
1	4	Coffee with yeast
1	5	Coffee with cereal and cocoa
1	6	Coffee with cereal and yeast
1	7	Coffee with cocoa and yeast
1	8	Coffee with cereal, cocoa and yeast
2	R	Cereal alone
2	2	Cereal with cocoa
2	3	Cereal with yeast
2	5	Cereal with cocoa and yeast
3	R	Cocoa alone
3	2	Cocoa with yeast
4	R	Yeast alone
12	12	Don't know

any other questions according to the number or type of combinations mentioned by each respondent.

Preparation of a code to handle the various possible combinations of answers to the question would provide greater flexibility in the machine work. If the code were set up as illustrated, then it would be simple, by securing a sort on the first column, and running each of these numbers separately, to count the punches on the second column, and to obtain the entire distribution of combinations of replies. The total number of "coffee" mentions is simply the total number of "1" punches on column 50. To obtain the total number of cereal mentions, the particular combinations including cereal could be added. At the same time it would be simple to sort the cards according to the number of products mentioned by each respondent merely by a sort of the punches made on column 51. All of the "R" punches (which are "rejects" and actually no punches at all in the column) would represent mention of a single product. The "2," "3," and "4" punches represent those persons who named two products. The "8" punch would include cards of those who named all four products.

The coding process is therefore not always simple. It can become complicated where a single individual gives more than one reply to a particular question. It can become complex when there is a wide variety of answers to a single question, since the allocation of columns must always be made economically.

d. *Having the clerical force fill in the codes.* Sometimes the questionnaire itself may be so prepared that the coding is largely automatic. A question on the blank may appear:

Do you believe the present government is helping or hurting business?

> Helping   —(1)
> Hurting   —(2)
> Both   —(3)
> Neither   —(4)
> Don't know—(5)

When the field worker checks the proper answer in this case, the code is already indicated. Where such a procedure is used, there must appear close to the question the number of the column or columns on which the information is to be punched.

More common is the entry on a separate code sheet of the information obtained on the questionnaire. This removes the responsibility of coding from the investigator. In this case the sheet is made up as illustrated. This particular sheet shows column headings for each of the 80 columns that appear on the actual card, though not

CODE SHEET—DENTIFRICE STUDY

Col. 1____	Col. 21____	Col. 41____	Col. 61____
Col. 2____	Col. 22____	Col. 42____	Col. 62____
Col. 3____	Col. 23____	Col. 43____	Col. 63____
Col. 4____	Col. 24____	Col. 44____	Col. 64____
Col. 5____	Col. 25____	Col. 45____	Col. 65____
Col. 6____	Col. 26____	Col. 46____	Col. 66____
Col. 7____	Col. 27____	Col. 47____	Col. 67____
Col. 8____	Col. 28____	Col. 48____	Col. 68____
Col. 9____	Col. 29____	Col. 49____	Col. 69____
Col. 10____	Col. 30____	Col. 50____	Col. 70____
Col. 11____	Col. 31____	Col. 51____	Col. 71____
Col. 12____	Col. 32____	Col. 52____	Col. 72____
Col. 13____	Col. 33____	Col. 53____	Col. 73____
Col. 14____	Col. 34____	Col. 54____	Col. 74____
Col. 15____	Col. 35____	Col. 55____	Col. 75____
Col. 16____	Col. 36____	Col. 56____	Col. 76____
Col. 17____	Col. 37____	Col. 57____	Col. 77____
Col. 18____	Col. 38____	Col. 58____	Col. 78____
Col. 19____	Col. 39____	Col. 59____	Col. 79____
Col. 20____	Col. 40____	Col. 60____	Col. 80____

all of these 80 may be used. The blank after each column number is for the entry of the proper digit(s) corresponding to a particular answer on the questionnaire.

There is a process of coding which is somewhere between the two extremes outlined here: Occasionally it is desirable to have spaces provided for coding right on the questionnaire, even though entry of the answer does not provide automatic coding. The space for a particular code number may be provided in the right- or left-hand margin of the particular question, or at the top or bottom of the questionnaire blank. Each blank has a number shown beside it, for reference to the column.

A few survey organizations give the completed questionnaires directly to the "punchers" of the cards, who mentally convert the answers to code numbers and punch the cards appropriately. This seems a somewhat dangerous procedure because of the many problems of coding that may arise during the course of the process. It seems a great deal safer to have experienced research workers do coding.

e. *Punching of the machine cards.* The next step is to have cards punched from the code sheets. Usually this process is handled by a business-machine concern, such as International Business Machines or Remington-Rand, and will not be discussed here. Though the process is simple, it requires a high degree of selection and training of workers to insure accuracy and speed of operation.

f. *The machine work.* The first decision here is whether only the sorting and counting machine is to be used, or whether a tabulating machine is also necessary. When the sorter and counter is used, all the cards, in miscellaneous order, are placed in a hopper on the right-hand side of the machine. The machine is adjusted to the particular column which is to be sorted or counted. It may then be set either so that the cards will be sorted into piles in accordance with the punch (with which a simultaneous count of each pile may be obtained), or so that merely a count of the number of each punch will result without any sorting process. In either case the machine will handle 400 cards per minute. Whether a sort is desired or not will depend upon the purpose of the summary of that column. Suppose that column 2, in this case punched for socio-economic group, is being considered. No other columns have yet been totaled. It is likely that answers to many of the questions will vary according to income level. Proper procedure in this case would be to sort the cards by income level, simultaneously obtaining a count of the number of cards in each class. Then the cards representing those of each income level can be run separately through the counter in order to determine the distribution of answers to specific questions.

Sorts may not be necessary on answers to some of the questions. Careful consideration of all possible useful relationships between answers to various questions before the machine process is undertaken should give the answer to this problem.

In some cases the tabulating machine will be of use. For this it is necessary to sort the cards to secure the proper classification. Once this basic sort has been made, the cards may be placed in the tabulating machine. This machine will automatically print a sheet containing the total of all categories for any column being run. The machine will handle cards at the rate of 150 per minute. It automatically records total and sub-totals. (On the sorter and counter these figures must be entered by hand after reading the totals from dials on the machines.)

Not all survey organizations send out questionnaires or code sheets to another concern. Some of the large companies have their own machine installations and handle the process from start to finish. In some of the larger cities there are even specialized organizations which will summarize data.

g. *Conversion of machine results into summary tables*. Since this is a largely mechanical task, it will not be discussed here in detail. Preparation of tables is outlined in a later section of this chapter.

3. *Advantages of hand and machine tabulation*. The question arises: Under what circumstances should each be used? Sometimes this decision is based entirely upon the number of questionnaires and the volume of questions, but these points should be relatively minor considerations. The applicability of either method to a study will depend largely upon the nature of that study and its requirements.

Hand tabulation can be used where the number of cross-breakdowns of questions is at a minimum. If the answers to all questions are to be shown merely by locality, hand tabulation will be sufficiently accurate and considerably more speedy (taking into account the number of processes involved in machine tabulation). If the number of questionnaires is particularly small, the hand method will probably suffice. If only 100 questionnaires have been obtained, the use of hand tabulation will be quicker, less expensive, and generally more useful than the machine procedure.

Hand tabulation must be used for comment questions, at least for a number of questionnaires sufficient to insure that the entire range of responses has been provided for. On the free-response query one can never be sure when a new and different type of answer is going to appear during the course of the tabulating. These odd cases are more readily handled if the procedure is by hand. If the questionnaire is full of free-comment questions, it will be virtually impossible to use the machine method. If there are only a few such questions, and the remainder of the questionnaire can advantageously be run on cards, then the few comment questions can be handled by hand in a separate process.

The chief advantage of the machine process is the ease with which replies to questions may be broken down by responses to other queries. Where necessary to evaluate a number of such relationships, the machine process is superior to the hand method. The machine process makes any number of such cross-breakdowns in hours, where it requires weeks of hand work. The extent of such breakdowns is the chief consideration in deciding which of the two methods is to be used.

Checking the Tabulations

Since the checking of the tabulations is similar in the case of both hand and machine summary, it may be logically discussed for both methods under a single heading.

Error in hand tabulation or in coding will damage the value of the study. Some research staffs, for instance, will not allow work to proceed where the material is more than .1 per cent in error. If there are 1000 questionnaires which have been entered on 50 columns—a total of 50,000 code entries—no more than 50 errors will be tolerated. How can such error be detected, and what can be done if the error is greater than this margin?

The natural thing to do in this accuracy check is to use the sampling procedure! If one worker has been working on one question the whole way through the study, take his every 10th, 20th, or 30th blank, depending upon the proportion of his work it is desirable to check. The supervisor, or another careful and accurate worker, should then go over each questionnaire independently and make up his own code sheet. Where there is a discrepancy, it is simple to find out who is in error and what the total proportion of error has been. A record of all errors of the original worker should be kept, and the same process followed for all questions, making certain that a cross-section of the work of each tabulator is obtained. In any case in which the error exceeds the allowable margin, the entire work of the tabulator must be gone over and corrected. This method not only provides for motivation in accuracy but is a good measure of the proficiency of each worker.

Other methods of checking accuracy will be discussed following the section on preparation of tables.

EXAMINING THE DATA

Before tables are prepared, the data should be checked for their accuracy, as well as for their general applicability to the study.

1. *Are the data relevant?* The tabulations may reveal that some of the results are not relevant for the purposes of the study, even though well edited and well handled by field workers. Such data should be discarded.

2. *Is the sample a good one?* During the process of the tabulations, characteristics of the sample of respondents whose reactions were obtained will have been summarized. There is always a possibility that some of the workers have not correctly followed their assignments, or that the sample may be distorted in terms of some characteristics uncontrolled on the study. Material will be useful only if such distortion is corrected. Examination of the sample characteristics is one of the first steps after the completion of tabulations.

3. *Are the data reliable?* Are the responses to the questions consistent, both in terms of comparable sub-samples and in terms of the series of responses given by individuals to related questions? These problems are discussed in some detail in Chapter 14.

4. *Are the data valid?* Does the study measure accurately what it was intended to measure? Answer to this question will depend in part upon the goodness of the sample and the reliability of the data, but there are other problems involved. Chapter 14 also takes up this question.

Preparation of Tables

Once tabulations have been completed and checked, and data examined for accuracy, the next step is to prepare tables for the report. More tables will be prepared than used, for one cannot always determine in advance which summaries will and will not be useful. All possible leads pertinent to purposes of the investigation must be explored.

Purposes of the study must be kept in mind in preparing the tables. The most important information should be the first to be summarized in tabular form. From that point on it is usually clear just how the remainder of the information fits into the mosaic of the study. In preparation of tables, little effort should be made to separate the vital summaries from the less essential ones; this is the problem of the report-writer. However, it is a good idea for the person working on the tables to make a few brief notes on the essentials of the table. The report-writer has to check such notes, but they do make his task easier when it is time for him to review all the tables to learn what they show.

Preparation of tables usually implies the computation of percentages. Only by conversion to percentages do the data assume meaning. Changing the number of cases to percentages permits comparison of data in terms of a common denominator. Usually the material is entered on a sheet which permits the entry of percentages directly opposite each figure. Computation of percentages is facilitated by use of a slide rule, calculating machine, or comptometer. Fortunately for the reader, the operation of these instruments will not be discussed here.

1. *Problems in percentage computation.* There are three chief problems in the use of percentages: (a) deciding the direction in which to compute the figures, (b) selecting the base, and (c) deciding the details of percentages.

a. *Direction in which to compute percentages.* In one survey a question was asked about the present type of heating equipment owned, and another question related to whether the person owned or rented his home. Answers were distributed as follows:

	Home Owners	Home Renters	Total
Hand-fired coal	330	289	619
Coal stoker	93	23	116
Oil	136	42	178
Gas	55	15	70
Coke	6	4	10
Wood	0	7	7
Total	620	380	1000

Most apparent procedure in computing percentages in this table would be to base the figuring upon the total number of home owners (620) and home renters (380). It is unquestionably revealing to learn that while 53 per cent of home owners have hand-fired furnaces, the proportion is 76 per cent in the renting group.

Breaking down percentages in another way will be equally meaningful. It is significant to learn that of all 619 hand-fired coal furnaces (the total of all those in both owned and rented homes), 53 per cent are in homes owned by occupants, while 47 per cent are in rented homes. The interesting example raises other problems. In at least two of the categories ("coke" and "wood") the base of the percentages is so small that the chance error will be large. Percentages computed on these bases lose much of their significance.

It is just for this reason that the base upon which percentages have been figured must always be indicated. Another reason for indicating the base is to make clear to the reader exactly to what the percentages refer. Percentages cannot be verified by an independent worker unless the base is shown. To be significant, any set of results must be subject to verification.

b. *Selection of the base.* Usually it will be reasonably clear upon just what base to compute percentages. There are some situations in which it is difficult to make this decision. One of these concerns the case in which "don't know" responses have been received.

In cases in which the meaning of the "don't know" answer is not clear, it probably should not be included in the computation of the percentages, but should be removed from the base. For instance, with the question *Where did you buy this item?* the numerical distribution of replies might be:

Where did you buy this item?

	No. Replies
Independent super-market	438
Chain super-market	1503
Independent grocery	582
Chain grocery	847
Drug store	200
Don't know	430

The chain super-market received more replies than any other type of store; if the percentage for this category were computed on the base of 4000, which would include "don't know," then the proportion would be 37.6 per cent. Let's consider these "don't know" replies.

Obviously a "Don't know" answer in such a case does not form a category which belongs in the table. These persons bought the item *somewhere*, and if they could remember where, their answers would belong in other categories. The category "don't know" in this particular case includes hidden overlapping with other classifications, and therefore fails to meet one of the requirements of a group of replies. Since this is the situation, "don't know" answers ought not to be included in the computation of percentages. The table should appear:

Where did you buy this item?

	% Replies
Independent super-market	12.3
Chain super-market	42.1
Independent grocery	16.3
Chain grocery	23.8
Drug store	5.5
Total	100.0
(Total answers)	(3570)
(Don't know)	(430)

The "don't know" answer may mean something definite; this depends upon the nature of the question asked and must be decided before percentages are computed.

There is also a problem of determining the base upon which to compute percentages when multiple answers are received. A respondent frequently gives more than one answer to a free-response query or to a check-list question, where alternatives are not mutually exclusive. A person describing the most important qualities of a gasoline tends to mention more than one quality. In such a case there are more answers than there are people answering. Should the total number of comments be used as a base, so that the percentages will total 100; or should the total number of people replying be used as the base, in which case the percentages will add to over 100? The following table of hypothetical answers to a question shows the effect of computing the percentages in these two ways:

Q. Does your fuel dealer ever send you advertising, telephone you, or call on you?

	No. Replies	% Based upon Total Replies	% Based upon Total Persons
Sends advertising	840	56	84
Telephones	50	3	5
Calls personally	310	21	31
No contact	300	20	30
Total replies	1500		
Total respondents	1000		
Total per cent		100	150

Logic forces one to the conclusion that the total number of persons should be used as a base. Mere increase of responses in one category could deflate the secured percentages for a given constant figure in a repeated survey where the same number of respondents was questioned. Similar studies might obtain the number of answers to each category as shown below. Percentages have been computed in both ways in order to effect comparisons.

	Number of Replies		Per Cent of Replies		Per Cent of Respondents	
	Study 1	Study 2	Study 1	Study 2	Study 1	Study 2
Category A	200	200	18	17	20	20
Category B	900	1000	82	83	90	100
Total answers	1100	1200				
Total persons	1000	1000				
Total per cent			100	100	110	120

Examination of the percentages computed on the reply basis indicates that category A has fallen off in importance. This is due only to the fact that more mentions for category B have been obtained; there are just as many category A answers in the second study as in the first. Common sense tells us that category B, according to this method of computation, does not show the real gain in response that has actually occurred. When percentages for the two studies are computed on the basis of total respondents, the results are meaningful. This computation shows just what happened; there was no loss in the frequency with which category A was mentioned, while there was a sharp drop in the frequency of mention of category B.

Another logical reason for basing percentages upon total respondents rather than total answers is that similar tables in the same study cannot otherwise be compared. If the total number of comments is used as a base, difficulties will also arise if the particular question is to be shown in relation to some other question or fact. Suppose it is necessary to show proportions in each income group who gave various types of answers to comment questions. These percentages will have no comparable meaning unless they are computed upon similar bases—the number of respondents in each group. For it is common survey experience that upper-income people give more and fuller answers than those in the lower groups. Therefore, any category mentioned most frequently by the upper groups is bound to suffer when comparison is made in terms of percentages based upon total comments.

c. *Deciding the detail of percentages.* After the base for percentage computation has been selected, it must be determined how detailed the percentages are to be. Should the figures be given in whole per cents, to tenths, or to hundredths? If the total number of cases upon which the percentage is based is so small that the standard error[6] at its smallest will be 5 per cent, then a figure showing tenths of a per cent has little significance. Only when the sample is large enough to give each figure a standard error of less than 1 per cent is it desirable to show tenths of a per cent.

If the study is a one-time affair, not likely to be repeated, it is

[6] Refer to Chapter 9 for a discussion of standard error.

unlikely that computation to tenths of a per cent will be required. In such a case there seems no good reason why the sponsor would be interested in such detail. Where a large number of cases is obtained, and the study is a repeat affair, small changes of less than 1 per cent may be meaningful. This will be particularly true where a slow-but-sure trend is found from study to study.

2. *Types of tables.* The simplest type of table is the one-dimensional affair, which shows results to a single question not related to the answers obtained to any other inquiry. More useful is the two-dimensional table, which shows the relationship of the answers to one question and the answers to another. The example given on page 176, where type of heating equipment was related to renting or owning of homes, was an example of this sort of table.

Tables may be so set up as to show the relationship of more than two variables. However useful these are to the technician in his analysis of results, they seldom are used in the report, since they tend to become confusing to the lay reader.

3. *Checking tables for accuracy.* Each table should be independently recomputed. All numbers and percentages should be added to insure accuracy. All straight totaling must be carefully checked. If the users of dentifrices on one table are shown as 698, another table of dentifrice users broken down in a different way must still total 698. It is impossible to make too many of these empirical checks on accuracy. However, methods of checking internal accuracy vary so much from study to study that no general rules for the process can be stated.

REFERENCES

*(1) AMERICAN MARKETING ASSOCIATION. *The Technique of Marketing Research.* New York: McGraw-Hill, 1937. Chapters 11, 12, 13, 14, 15, and 16.

(2) BENSON, L. E. "Studies in Secret Ballot Technique," *Public Opinion Quarterly,* 1941, 5, 79-82.

*(3) BROWN, L. O. *Market Research and Analysis.* New York: Ronald, 1937. Chapters 12, 13, and 14.

(4) COUTANT, F. R., AND DOUBMAN, J. R. *Simplified Market Research.* Philadelphia: Walther, 1935. Chapter 5.

(5) GHISELLI, E. E. "All or None Versus Graded Response Questionnaire," *Journal of Applied Psychology,* 1939, 23, 405-413.

(6) Jenkins, J. G. "The Questionnaire as a Research Instrument," *Transactions of the New York Academy of Science*. Series II, 2, No. 5, 1940.

(7) Lazarsfeld, P. F., and Robinson, W. S. "Some Properties of the Trichotomy Like, No Opinion, Dislike and Their Psychological Interpretations," *Sociometry*, 1940, 3, 151-178.

(8) Lazarsfeld, P. F., and Stanton, Frank. *Radio Research 1941*. New York: Duell, Sloan and Pearce, 1941. (Good for examples.)

(9) Paton, M. P. "Selection of Tabulation Method, Machine or Manual," *Journal of Marketing*, 1942, 6, 229-235.

(10) Reed, V. D. "Why Market Surveys Fail Sometimes," *Printers' Ink Monthly*, October, 1930, 22, 52.

(11) Reilly, W. J. *Marketing Investigations*. New York: Ronald, 1929. Chapter 16.

(12) Roslow, Sydney, and Blankenship, A. B. "Phrasing the Question in Consumer Research," *Journal of Applied Psychology*, 1939, 23, 612-622.

*(13) Saunders, A. G., and Anderson, C. R. *Business Reports*. New York: McGraw-Hill, 1940. Chapters 6 and 16.

(14) Wagner, I. F. "Articulate and Inarticulate Replies to Questionnaires," *Journal of Applied Psychology*, 1939, 23, 104-115.

(15) White, Percival. *Marketing Research Technique*. New York: Harper, 1931. Chapter 15.

(16) Zeisel, Hans. "Say It With Figures." New York: Harper, 1947. Chapters 1, 2, 3, 4, and 5.

CHAPTER 13

Preparing the Report

~~~~~~

THE purpose of the report is to get readership and understanding, to gain belief, and to secure action. The write-up is the most important part of the entire study to the person who is reading it. The reader measures the worth of any piece of research primarily from the report. It is in the report that the surveyor has an opportunity to describe his methods, his results, and his interpretations of the findings. If the report is a poor one, the organization conducting the study may be judged poor by the reader. If the report is sparkling and apparently reflects the competence of the entire organization, the chances are that the basic research is of high caliber.

This is by no means a contention that the evaluation of a survey should be based upon the report alone. All details of methodology must be known before such a judgment can be made. In practice, however, most people are going to judge the value of a piece of research by the impression made with the report. That is why the research group should spend a considerable amount of time on the preparation of the report. From the standpoint of public relations this is the most essential portion of the study.

The report made by the popular opinion polls will naturally be different from that made for commercial use. The opinion poll commonly has space to present only the highlights of its findings, and the lay reader is not interested in methodological detail. The report of the opinion poll usually does not require any deep thinking about conclusions and interpretations. The commercial report is more difficult and raises more problems; for that reason the present chapter is concerned primarily with the commercial report.

There are two distinct types of report: that written for general circulation (among prospective advertisers for a particular medium, for instance), and that written only for the use of a client. Some of the reports written for general circulation may be published in trade journals or popular magazines. But most reports are prepared for the private consumption of the client for whom the study was undertaken. This type of report will naturally be different in many ways from the report written for general circulation. If the report is to be circulated among the research staff of the client, many more details of procedure and results will be required than if it is to be read only by top management of the company. This chapter can deal only with the broad outlines of the report, however; no attempt will be made to suggest procedure for specific cases. The nature of the case will always be unique so that such effort would be pointless.

Steps in the report are: drawing of conclusions, making of recommendations, preparing the report, and the use of visual aids in the report.

The Drawing of Conclusions

Conclusions are factual statements and generalizations about the survey results. One reference (1) cites an excellent illustration of the sort of generalization sometimes possible. In the laundry study mentioned in the preceding chapter, it was observed that Viennese housewives did not regularly send out laundry, but did send it out on special occasions such as loss of the maid and appearance of guests. All situations had a common denominator—some emergency. From all the details of the findings it was possible to state, as a generalization, that the housewives sent out their laundry in times of emergency.

There are several steps to be followed in the drawing of conclusions: (1) consideration of the facts, (2) setting up of test conclusions (3) testing of these tentative conclusions, and (4) formulation of final conclusions.

1. *Consideration of the facts*. The first problem in considering the facts is to make a selection of the data.

Each portion of the material must be carefully weighed to determine its significance, the part it has in this drawing of conclusions.

Some points in this process of weighing the evidence have already been mentioned—reliability of the material, representativeness of the sample, and the validity of the data.

Lack of evidence regarding some of the data should not be overlooked. Mail surveys are still conducted, and usually there is an effort to measure the characteristics of those who respond. There is seldom any real test as to the representativeness of those who reply to mail questionnaires, even though their ages, sex, and locality be known. Evidence points to the fact that those most interested in the subject will be those who tend to reply to such a questionnaire, and this fact must be realized when there is an attempt to draw conclusions from mail surveys. The particular mailing list used must also be considered. The entire detailed procedure must be carefully considered not only during the whole process of the study but especially at the time test conclusions are to be made.

Relationships discoverable among data are the basis for the drawing of conclusions. It usually is less significant to find that 19 per cent of the sample use a particular brand than it is to find that among men, for instance, the proportion is 25 per cent, while it is only 13 per cent with women. All important relationships within the data must be established before conclusions are drawn. The data must be fractionated and refractionated.

In the above illustration, a tentative conclusion would be that the factor of sex is relatively important in the use of this product—that men use it twice as much as women. Analysis of these data by sex of the user could conceivably show the following relationship:

PROPORTION OF USERS

	Among Men	Among Women	Among Total Group
From 20-29 years	15	27	21
From 30-39 years	20	20	20
From 40-49 years	25	13	19
From 50-59 years	30	6	18
60 years and over	35	—	17

This tentative conclusion is now shown to be misleading, since the influence of the sex variable is related to that of age. Among men, the proportion of users of the product tends to increase with age. Among women, the proportion of users tends to decrease with age. The differences between the age groups within each sex would suggest also that age is not quite so important in the use of the product among men as it is with women, since the differences run 5 per cent with the men against 7 per cent for the women.

Crespi and Rugg (8) have an interesting illustration of the fractionation process for the drawing of conclusions. It would appear at the start that to understand from survey data the role of income level in responses is a simple problem. It might seem that the only requirement to determine this influence would be a summary of results within each income group. But practically all surveys show that few variables are independent—they are associated to some extent with other factors. For purposes of illustration, the assumption may be made that the particular survey data are related only to age and income level. The following table shows the distribution of replies in the various age and income groups:

% OF "YES" REPLIES IN EACH GROUP

Wealthy	60%	Over 50	63%
Above average	50	40-50	55
Average	47	30-40	50
Below average	45	Under 30	45
Poor	45		
On relief	43		

The obvious conclusion might be that answers to this question were related to both age and income level. This conclusion would be incorrect. Since 90 per cent of the wealthy group is composed of individuals of 50 and over, while the other income groups contain people distributed more evenly among various age groups, much of the dispersion of answers apparently acounted for by income level might be due to age, or to a relationship between income level and age.

The solution of this problem of evaluating determinants is not to hold age constant for all income groups, or any other similar step. This would be adulterating the sample, since in the public certain characteristics are definitely interrelated. The experienced investigator will have some idea of which of these characteristics are related, and to what extent. If he sees that differences occur when results are broken down by some sampling characteristic, his problem then is to know whether the determinants is related to some other characteristics, or whether it is independent. If the attribute is not related to others, the conclusion will be simple enough to make. If it is related to others, further analysis will be required.

Fractionation of data is not necessarily the answer to all the surveyor's problems. Jenkins (*12*) cites a case in which he had prepared all sorts of analytical tables and charts from results. Another worker, in reviewing his data, showed how a "beautifully unifying theory" was possible to consolidate all of the data. This example indicates that, although fractionation is basic, thought and insight into the situation are also required for the process of drawing conclusions.

2. *Setting up of tentative conclusions*. Once all data have been properly summarized and thoroughly considered, the researcher is prepared to set up tentative conclusions. The purposes of the investigation must be kept in mind so that any generalization will be pertinent to the problems raised.

Fractionation of results, the basic process of analysis, is a factual process. The making of generalizations, on the other hand, requires a mental assimilation of the results, with, perhaps, the generalization of "a beautifully unifying theory." Usually this process of drawing conclusions is a matter of proper classification of the various results obtained on the survey. Once this classification has been well achieved, the conclusion tying up all the facts should be reasonably obvious.

On a study concerned with various aspects of aviation, it was suspected that men would have more knowledge, more experience, and more favorable attitudes in general than women. Analysis of the results showed this to be fact. Analysis also revealed that in general, within both sex groups, the younger persons were those with more experience, more knowledge, and more favorable attitudes. It was only a process of thinking which suggested the third aspect of this analysis, with the resultant unification. Since all the analyses revealed a similar basic relationship, it was suspected that the various questions were closely related to one another, and that there were persons with different degrees of air-mindedness, as defined in terms of responses to these questions. Analysis showed this to be fact, and this air-mindedness analysis was the one which unified all the results on the investigation.

3. *Testing of the tentative conclusions.* The tentative conclusions must be checked so that they can be justified in light of the data. Does all of the available evidence tie in with the conclusion? Is the evidence sufficient to justify the conclusion? Are there any inconsistencies in the material which might make the conclusion questionable? Are the conclusions reached in harmony with the major evidences of the report, rather than an emphasis upon minor points in the results? Are the conclusions free of bias and the pre-conceived notions of the surveyor?

Conclusions must be tested by careful consideration of the opposite or negative conclusions. A cigarette study conducted a few years ago showed that cigarette X was overwhelmingly preferred to any other brand. The obvious conclusion was that cigarette X was the one most highly regarded by consumers. This was not the entire story. Cigarette X was also named as the brand toward which people were most unfavorable—it led all other brands in this connection. Both of these facts had to be considered before conclusions were drawn, since on the surface they appeared to be conflicting. Actually they were not at all conflicting—there was evidence that brand X was best known of all the brands of cigarettes, and naturally it tended to be named by a great number of respondents in any connection.

4. *Formulation of final conclusions.* Once these tentative conclusions have been subjected to all possible tests, and still stand up, the researcher is prepared to state them as "final" conclusions resulting from the data of the study. Once more the surveyor must make sure that the stated conclusions tie in with the purposes of the study. Do the final conclusions meet the everyday test of "common sense"? Do they tie in with facts from other sources, independently obtained? One practical test of the conclusions is to see if an independent worker, using the same evidence, comes to the same results. Reference and conversation with others will always aid the researcher in checking these conclusions.

MAKING RECOMMENDATIONS

Recommendations refer to the action suggested by the results. The process of recommending is an interpretive affair. Recommendations must tie in with other "accepted" data and policy. They must be "practical" in the sense that there is at least a reasonable chance that they may be followed.

1. *The pros and cons of recommendations.* Some of those in the survey field feel that the survey staff has no right to make recommendations, while others argue just as strongly that a survey should not be called complete until interpretations of the results have been made. One writer (2) has stated that the survey should be similar to a barometer (prediction) rather than like a thermometer (mere measurement). Jenkins (12) makes a stronger statement in his contention that the survey which does not interpret its findings is of little value. T. H. Brown (5) argues that conclusions are useless unless they are placed in an interpretive context, and of course at that point they become recommendations.

One of the largest research firms in the country (in terms of volume of work) argues that it never makes recommendations based upon survey findings because the people within its organization could not possibly interpret the findings as competently as men in the industry for whom the study was undertaken. The argument seems to boil down to the idea that research agents cannot grasp the problem well enough to make recommendations following the study. If the surveyor has no more conception of the problems of the industry than this, he has little reason to be in the survey field. How can he develop his cross-section, plan and test the questionnaire, and do the hundred and one other odd tasks connected with the study if he lacks the unifying concept of the purpose of the investigation? How can he have even a verbal discussion with the client about the problem?

Arguments about the pros and cons of recommendations favor the former. Interpretation is the most critical aspect of the entire survey process. Few interpretations can be made without arrangement and rearrangement of the data. Executives who read the report have little experience, training, or inclination to study and rearrange the detailed data, and to arrive finally at the proper course of action. The problem is one for the research agent. Survey work which stops short of recommendations is of little value. One research firm, whenever it obtains a new client in a field different from those in which it has worked previously, adds a man to the staff who is experienced both in that industry and in the research process. This seems as close to the ideal solution as the usual survey organization can come. The advertising agency is in a favorable position here. In the advertising business there are men from all fields who are available for consultation with the research staff. Between the experts and the research men there is little difficulty in reaching recommendations which are related to the facts and situation of the industry for which the survey has been conducted.

2. *Standards for recommendations.* First question here is whether the conclusions are supported at more than one point by the evidence. It is dangerous to use one isolated fact from a survey as sole support for a recommendation. The recommendation should have support at a number of separate places within the survey. Support from outside sources should also be sought.

The data must be examined by the interpreter in such a way that he will be certain there are no great exceptions to his recommendations within the data. One study showed that more people preferred popular music than any other sort of music on the air. It might be expected that the recommendation for the client to use this type of program could follow. However, the same survey indicated that the client's product was one that was purchased predominantly by higher-income groups, and these groups liked somewhat "heavier" music. In this case a real search through all of the evidence had to be made before any recommendation was possible. The particular problem required a great deal of evidence outside the survey. The client had to make sure that he could obtain a good network hour on the best network (in terms of audience), and that he would be able to secure attractive talent for the proposed show.

Recommendations must be practicable. They must be concrete suggestions and predictions which make sense to the client. Sometimes there are individuals within the client organization who may be expected to give opposition to almost any recommendations coming from an outside source. Such persons can be handled by permitting them to give help in arriving at the recommendations. Particularly where the evidence is irrefutable, and apparently suggestive in only one direction of action, this is a useful procedure. In any case, the suggestion should be concrete. The concrete gains which can be expected from the proposed course of action can be stated to help get across the idea of tangibility.

Through any study the ultimate aim of the surveyor is to obtain action as a result of his findings. Any aid possible in securing such action helps to "sell" the survey field to business, and appears entirely justified, in so far as the procedures and conclusions meet standards of scientific scrutiny.

3. *Form of the recommendation.* The recommendations should be positive and definite. The proposals should not be too sweeping if the data from which they have been developed are meager and limited. The particular form of the recommendations will always be dictated by the data of the study. In a large number of recommendations, the most important should be those presented first, so that the reader will not have to proceed through a mass of minor detail in order to discover the major interpretations. Conclusions and recommendations should be shown in order of importance.

The nature of the recommendations will vary in accordance with the point of view from which the data are being considered. The same survey results shown to two competitors might lead to different recommendations for each, depending upon the nature of the business and the distributive organization. From the results of a single survey one silverware concern might be told that its present policy of advertising was sound, and that the scope of its efforts might be expanded. A competitor might be informed that his advertising was not correctly directed toward his market, and that he was not making use of effective appeals.[1]

PREPARING THE REPORT

There are a number of problems to be settled in the final preparation of the report. The material to be included is the primary prob-

---

[1] In practice the same survey is not usually shown to competitive organizations, of course.

lem, and style of writing is important. Use of visual aids will be discussed here, but reference to other sources, particularly Saunders and Anderson (*14*) will aid those who demand a discussion of style.

1. *Outline of the report.* The first step for the survey technician is to outline the material that is to go into his report. This simplifies preparation of the report and aids in thinking about the method of developing the material for presentation.

a. *Statement of the problem* of the investigation will be the first consideration. What was the study intended to accomplish? Did any change in ideas of the objective occur during the course of the study? Early statement of the objectives of the research will help to develop the remainder of the report with these purposes in mind. It is important to write up the entire study with proper emphasis upon the purposes of the study and the way in which the procedure and results help answer these objectives.

b. *Description of the method* is the next logical material to be outlined. The details given here will depend upon the individuals for whom the report is designed. A research staff will require full details. Top executives will demand a minimum of such material.

The most complete description of the method should include a discussion of the questionnaire and how it was developed, the instructions to field workers, the number and type of field workers, the distribution of calls, the dates of the field work, the supervision of the field work, and other pertinent details. If any new methods have been used, or if any specific adaptations of existing procedures have been made, these should be described.

One desirable procedure seems to be to present all procedural details, so that they are available if anyone is interested. They are presented either in the body of the report (when designed for a research staff), or in an appendix (when designed for top executives or laymen).

c. *Presentation of results.* The question of the amount of detail to present in the results can be answered only when the type of reader of the report is known. Some research staffs always present complete results, placing the detail in an appendix when it is suspected that the primary readers of the report will not be interested.

The type of table to be presented has already been discussed in the preceding chapter, so does not warrant repetition here.

d. *Conclusions and recommendations*. Although these are logically last in the outline, they may be first in the actual presentation, depending upon the nature of the audience for whom the report is intended. Logically, however, they follow from consideration of the results and other known facts about the client and the market, so they should be the very last point for consideration in the outline.

e. *Arrangement of items*. The particular order in which these major points are included in the report, and the emphasis they are given in the write-up, will depend upon the readers for whom the report has been written. For top executives, who have neither the time nor the inclination to spend effort in going over detail, it is sometimes good policy to condense the results, conclusions, and recommendations into a few short paragraphs, leaving all other details for appendices. Sometimes important information, not directly related to the major purposes of the study, comes out of the study. This would interrupt the flow of principal arguments if placed in the body of the report. An appendix is the proper place for it.

When the report is designed for a research staff, the emphasis will be different. The material will probably require no appendices, and will, in most cases, follow the order given in the outline.

Visual Aids in the Report

In addition to style of writing, there are several ways in which the report may be made more interesting, dynamic, and clear. Well-considered typographical variations, illustrations, and graphs and charts are a few of the visual aids which may help to complete the report.

1. *Typographical variations*. Judicious use of typographical variation helps in making the material interesting and readable. Use of indented paragraphs and statements is justified to help emphasize an important point. Underlined and capitalized statements and phrases not only help to make the material more interesting, but aid in "getting across" the important aspects of the investigation. Un-

derlining and capitalizing must be used cautiously rather than indiscriminately. Some businessmen may find time to read only the underlined and capitalized material. The use of such material must permit a grasping of the essential facts if such a method of reading is followed. This problem calls for considerable ingenuity on the part of the writer.

2. *Illustrations*. Educational psychologists have performed many experiments which show that illustrated material is better and more readily learned and understood than material without illustration. This may be partly because illustrated material is of more interest than mere reading matter with tables.

Use of illustrations in the report requires ingenuity. Too many illustrations may tend to minimize the attention which each one receives. Some readers may concentrate upon the illustrations and neglect the report.

Form of illustrations varies with the nature and purpose of the particular material to be demonstrated. It may be a photograph intended to typify some point made in the report. It may take the form of a chart or graph, and there are many variations of kind. It may be a curve or line graph, in which a continuous line shows the frequency distribution in terms of some characteristic. It may be a bar chart, where each point in the distribution is indicated by means of a solid bar. In special cases it may be a ratio or logarithmic graph. The material may be plotted in circular form—the pie chart. A map may be used for illustration of geographic points. More recently the pictorial graph, which illustrates quantities with drawings of the concrete variable in different sizes, has become popular.

Principles to be followed in the construction of any of these illustrations can be found in such sources as Brown (4) and Coutant and Doubman (7).

CHECKING THE REPORT

Since the material and the report have been prepared rather carefully, with check-ups during the course of the work, this final scrutiny may be devoted to the material within the report itself.

1. *Editorial material*. The relevancy of all presented data must be

checked, in an effort to detect errors of omission and commission. Purpose of the investigation should once more be compared with each portion of material presented, to see that the most important information has been included and that of little value omitted.

The checker must also make sure that the treatment of the material is entirely sound—that reasoning used is logical. Is there a proper analysis of cause and effect? Are any analogies used applicable in the particular situation? Are the conclusions sound and relevant, and do they follow from the results? Are the recommendations consistent not only with the results obtained but also with facts known about the industry and the particular client?

Arrangement of the material must be checked. It is possible that some modification of the order would make the report clearer or more effective.

2. *Technical material.* Style of the report should have one final check. The style must be persuasive, interesting, and clear, and the written material must be free from grammatical or spelling errors.

Is the material in consistent and standard form? All tables, for instance, must be laid out comparably, with similar headings and consecutive numbering. A rapid scanning of the figures in the tables will permit one last cursory check on their accuracy.

Finally the report should be scanned to insure that all the usual contents of a summary have been included: title page, table of contents, description of procedure, results, and conclusions and recommendations.

When all this has been done, the report may be placed in the hands of the printer or typist who is responsible for its duplication. For practical purposes it is now out of the hands of the researcher.

REFERENCES

*(1) AMERICAN MARKETING ASSOCIATION. *The Technique of Marketing Research.* New York: McGraw-Hill, 1937. Chapters 15, 16, and 17.

(2) BALCHIN, N. M. "A Psychological Approach to Market Research," *Human Factor,* 1933, 7, 375-385.

*(3) BLEYER, W. G. *Newspaper Writing and Editing.* Boston: Houghton, Mifflin, 1932. Chapter 5.

*(4) BROWN, L. O. *Market Research and Analysis*. New York: Ronald, 1937. Chapters 14 and 15.

(5) BROWN, T. H. "Interpretation of Market Data," *American Marketing Journal*, 1935, 2, 217-223.

(6) BUSH, CHILTON. *Reporting of Public Affairs*. New York: Appleton-Century, 1940. Chapter 1.

(7) COUTANT, F. R., AND DOUBMAN, J. R. *Simplified Market Research*. Philadelphia: Walther, 1935. Chapter 6.

(8) CRESPI, LEO, AND RUGG, DONALD. "Poll Data and the Study of Opinion Determinants," *Public Opinion Quarterly*, 1940, 4, 273-276.

(9) EDMUNDS, HARRIET. "To Get Your Story Over Quickly, Say It with Charts," *Industrial Marketing*, May, 1939.

(10) JACKSON, REGINA. "A Case for Charts," *Market Research*, 1938, 8, No. 2, 15-18.

*(11) JENKINS, J. G. *Psychology in Business and Industry*. New York: Wiley, 1935. Chapter 15.

(12) JENKINS, J. G. "The Questionnaire as a Research Instrument," *Transactions of the New York Academy of Science*. Series II, 2, No. 5, 1940.

*(13) REILLY, W. J. *Marketing Investigations*. New York: Ronald, 1929. Chapter 21.

(14) SAUNDERS, A. G., AND ANDERSON, C. R. *Business Reports*. New York: McGraw-Hill, 1940. Chapters 9, 10, 11, 12, 13, 14, and 15.

(15) SMART, W. K. *Handbook of Effective Writing*. New York: Harper, 1931.

CHAPTER 14

Measuring the Adequacy of Surveys

WHEN a new serum or treatment of disease has been developed, the measure of its efficiency is somewhat drastic. Patients suffering from the particular malady are divided into two similar groups (in terms of such factors as age and sex, seriousness of the malady, and stage of the disease). One group is treated by the new method, and the other group does not obtain the new treatment, even though there is reason to believe that the treatment might save lives. Differences in recovery are observed as a measure of efficiency of the new procedure.

In the survey field no such drastic measures of efficiency are required. But there are two principal questions which need to be answered:

1. Is the information obtained actually representative of the reactions of the total population which the survey is intended to represent?

2. Is the information obtained consistent?

The first question refers to the problem of validity, and the second to that of reliability. Validity is the extent to which the survey measures what it intends to measure. If the survey is designed to measure brand-buying behavior, the questions can be checked against actual purchases. A pre-election poll can have its results checked for validity against the election returns.

Reliability refers to a comparison of the consistency of survey results. There are several methods of securing such a measure. Results to the same questions submitted to the same respondents over a short period of time may be compared. Responses of similar samples of respondents on the same study can be compared. Breakdowns of question results within a particular study will indicate the degree to which there is "internal consistency" of the data.

The distinction between the validity and the reliability of surveys may be demonstrated by the straw vote of the now defunct *Literary Digest*. The 1936 survey on presidential choice did not measure what it intended to measure—voting sentiment of the American public. It mispredicted the presidential winner, and consequently lacked validity. On the other hand, very little difference occurred in the week-by-week expressions of preference, so that the reliability of the results was reasonably high. Of course in a survey in which high validity has been demonstrated, high reliability will almost of necessity be a concomitant. Without giving reliable results, it is doubtful that a survey could provide valid returns.

The layman assumes that all surveys are accurate because of the success of pre-election polls in their predictions. This conclusion is not necessarily justified. Since almost every survey is unique, some validity measure should be obtained for each type undertaken. Only constant empirical checks can show that surveys in general possess high validity. On the other hand, practically every survey undertaken gives evidence of high reliability, so it is reasonable to assume that surveys in general are reasonably reliable. But there are still unanswered problems in survey reliability.

The topics of validity and reliability will be discussed in that order.

The Validity of Surveys

One of the most crucial tests of the significance of any survey results is whether they are representative of the reactions or behavior of the group the sample of respondents is intended to represent. In some cases it is not possible to measure reactions or behavior of the entire population from which the sample has been drawn, but in such situations the people in the sample itself can be studied to determine the accuracy of their responses as against their behavior.

Some standard of objective behavior or opinion is necessary in order to compute validity. Checking survey responses against this behavior provides an indication of accuracy. Among the specific procedures which have been used in measurement of accuracy of survey results are the comparison of (1) candidate election returns and poll results, (2) referenda returns against poll results, (3) brands of goods possessed by respondents with those they report during questioning, (4) observed reading behavior with that reported during questioning, (5) known market data against questionnaire replies, (6) sales due to advertisements against ranks of those advertisements by respondents, and (7) other behavioral indices against question replies.

1. *The use of candidate election returns as a criterion.* Some polling organizations have presented lists of their election predictions on candidates as compared with actual election returns. Gallup and Rae (7) include the following list to show the accuracy of the Gallup pre-election polls:

	Error in % Points for the Winner
1937 Detroit mayoralty	2
1937 New York mayoralty	4
1938 Kentucky primary	2
1938 South Carolina primary	2
1938 Georgia primary	2
1938 Maryland primary	2
1938 Maine gubernatorial	2
1938 New York gubernatorial	.5

In a presidential election the prediction for total popular vote could be perfect, yet there could be major state-by-state errors which might make the prediction of electoral votes inaccurate. The state-by-state vote must be considered in determining any measure of validity in a presidential poll. In 1940 Gallup indicated this state-by-state error in the following manner:[1]

	GALLUP SURVEY Roosevelt %	ACTUAL ELECTION Roosevelt %	Deviation
Kansas	43	43	0
Louisiana	86	86	0
Maryland	59	59	0
New Jersey	52	52	0
Wyoming	53	53	0
Alabama	86	87	1

[1] As presented in releases following the election.

As a final indication of accuracy, Gallup summarized and averaged all of the state deviations. In 1940 this "average error" was 2.5 per cent.

Chief fault of this measure is that it fails to consider the direction of the error. In 1940 the Willkie vote was over-predicted in 35 of 43 states (5 were "on the nose"). In addition, among the 8 states erring in Roosevelt's favor, the average error was 1.9 per cent, while the average over-prediction in the states where Willkie was credited with too high a proportion was 3 per cent. The total percentage deviation for all states in which the Willkie vote was over-predicted was 106, while the similar figure for the Roosevelt over-production was only 15. The total error favoring Willkie was thus seven times as great as the total error favoring Roosevelt.

Gosnell (8) has used a correlation technique[2] for measuring the accuracy of candidate polls. In 1936 the three major presidential polls rated as follows: Gallup, .972; Crossley, .970; and the *Digest*, .908. Since perfect agreement between returns and prediction would have been 1.000, it can be seen how closely each of the polls approached perfection. There are a few obvious deficiencies in this method. One or two extreme disagreements between state predictions and returns can lower the correlation coefficient greatly, making the poll appear a great deal worse than it was. Or, as in the case of the *Digest* poll, the correlation validity can make the poll appear better than it was. Because the correlation validity can be misleading, it does not seem of great use.

Is the general use of election figures compared with candidate polls a useful method of determining survey validity? It is unquestionably an accurate measure of finding out how precise the specific poll was. But several factors may affect the casting of ballots, thus distorting the number of votes received by each candidate. A rainy day may keep away the rural vote. Transportation difficulties may keep away those who live some distance from the voting booth. Party activity may get out a disproportionate number of voters for one candidate. During times of war the young men in the armed

---

[2] The theory and practice of correlation will be found in any standard statistical reference.

forces are not likely to cast votes. Even dishonesty at the polls must be considered as a possible source of distortion.

The common accuracy with which candidate polls predict returns is a tribute to those conducting the surveys. This high validity of predicting candidates, however, is not an indication of high validity of other sorts of surveys. The type of question asked on the candidate poll and on other surveys is different. Candidate polls are not identical with social- and political-issue polls, for the latter kind of questionnaire study concerns more abstract issues. Almost everyone will be willing to express a choice for a candidate; this is not nearly so true in the case of the issue polls, in which the "no opinion" vote is commonly higher than in the candidate poll. Candidate polls are different from market investigations in the type of material included in questioning.

This is not the only difference. Pre-election polls concerning candidates include only voters in their sampling. Other surveys may include a cross-section of the entire public, or a cross-section of some particular portion of the public, as described in the chapter on sampling procedure.

The number of respondents whose opinions are obtained on the pre-election poll will generally be greater than on any other sort of survey. It is in these polls that the public will judge the organization conducting the survey. This means that the organization has to use every available means to make its accuracy as great as possible. Increasing the number of interviews is one of the methods followed.

Even though comparison of the pre-election candidate poll with election returns is a reasonably accurate indicator of the validity of a particular survey, it may not be assumed that this high validity indicates high validity for other surveys.

2. *Use of referenda returns as a criterion.* Some questionnaire studies are designed to predict referenda outcome, and when the validity of such polls is computed, it is partial answer to the criticism that validity of candidate polls does not indicate validity of issue surveys. It is true that the Gallup referenda polls show roughly the same margin of error as his candidate polls. His result on the 1937 Maine sales tax was 5 per cent in error, as an indication.

Factors which distort the candidate election can also operate in a referendum. In addition, there is usually less interest on the part of the public in voting on a referendum than in voting for candidates, so that the voting population probably will not turn out to the same extent. Moreover, the number of interviews collected on this sort of poll will be higher, as in the candidate poll, than on the normal type of survey where no accuracy measure is obtainable. The issue poll is still different in the nature of the queries (and usually in the sample of respondents) from the market survey type of study.

3. *The possession of branded goods as a criterion.* Following an interview in which ownership of various branded items has been inquired about, some researchers have been able to determine the actual brands owned. The researcher may check with the retailer with whom the respondent deals in order to determine the brand of the last purchase. He may be able to get into the home of the respondent in order to compare ownership with brands reported during questioning. Both methods have problems.

It is difficult to get into the home in order to list brands, and sometimes after the home has been entered, it is impossible to determine brands. Many housewives remove flour, coffee, and other goods into canisters, destroying the original package in which the goods came. In the grocery method the clerks may not keep careful enough records for the researcher to determine brands. Despite these difficulties both methods have been used with some success.

Jenkins and Corbin (*12*) have made the most comprehensive study of the store type. In their study they included questions and store checks on some 13 products, and it was found that from 62 per cent to 100 per cent of the individual replies agreed with the brands purchased.[3] Group measures of validity were not reported.

In another survey (*3*) the questionnaire method was checked

[3] This method is not a check on accuracy of the *method*, or total results, but only a measure of the accuracy of individual replies. The point here is that some of the errors in individual report of brands may be expected to cancel out by compensating inaccuracies in other persons' replies. Since it is the method which is important, this total accuracy is more important for our purposes. Naturally the group validity can be expected to be somewhat higher than the corresponding individual validity.

against both the pantry inventory and the laboratory store method. Four products were included in this study conducted in Mt. Pleasant, Iowa. In this case the total validity of each question was not computed; it was simply noted that the drop in accuracy from method one to method two was 17 per cent for soap, 18 per cent for cleansers, 42 per cent for coffee, and 40 per cent for cereals. Variations were explained by the investigator as due to the fact that people do change around in their buying habits more than they report on a questionnaire. So pronounced was this shifting tendency that the store results were not close to the survey results.

Another paper (19) reports the investigation of a validity study of several other brand questions, one of which concerned the brand of flashlight cells last bought. Following the completion of the questioning, 852 respondents were induced to produce their flashlights. Although 62 per cent reported buying brand X, only 55 per cent actually possessed this brand. This particular report gives no over-all validity figures.

In the same report a question about the make of razor used by respondents was included, and 125 answers were distributed among three brands. When razors were inspected, 92 per cent of these responses were correct.[4] Prestige value of one brand of a commodity may operate to produce too many responses for that brand. The result is well illustrated by *Kodak*, a brand name for Eastman cameras, which has become a generic term popularly used to designate all cameras. *Frigidaire* is another brand name which has been so well sold to the public that it now means any kind of electric refrigerator.

Brown (5) asked a number of respondents what brand of a certain commodity they used. Following the reply to the question, he offered each respondent a new package of the product in exchange for the old one in his home. In the case of 8 brands among those who stated that they had a particular brand, the proportion who actually had that brand varied from 43.2 per cent to 100 per cent, depending upon brand. This provides a rough indication of the question's validity, but doesn't permit computation of an over-

[4] This is not a validity index for all results to this question, but only for these three brands.

all validity figure.[5] Here, as in other cases, it is well to consider the prestige value of the various brands mentioned.

Most studies of brand questions indicate fairly high validity. These high figures do not indicate high validity of other sorts of questions. One difference has already been shown—the prestige value of certain brand names. There are other differences. A brand question refers to past behavior, while other sorts of surveys, such as the candidate or referendum poll, concern future behavior. Brand-buying is an activity carried on by almost every housewife; her opinion on social and political issues may be an entirely new experience!

3. *Use of observed reading behavior as a criterion.* Some questionnaire studies are designed to measure what people have read. The Curtis Publishing Company, publishers of the *Saturday Evening Post,* for instance, conduct continuous surveys inquiring which portions of their publications the respondents have read.

It was natural for two of the individuals of this company to become interested in the problem of the accuracy of the individual's report. Can the respondent identify accurately the portions of the magazine which he has not read? Ludeke and Inglis (*16*) devised a clever experiment to measure accuracy of such reports. Without her knowing it, the person reading the magazine was observed, and notes were made as to which editorial matter she did and did not read during a period of one hour and a half. Since the participants did not even know that this experiment was designed to check accuracy of their reading reports, there was little opportunity for such a factor to influence results.

Each participant was interviewed in her home from twenty-four hours to fourteen days after this observation, with an inquiry about the portions of the magazine she had read. Field workers did not

[5] The method used by Brown may have biased the results. It seems likely that only those who had used a goodly proportion of the package would be interested in changing it for the new. Those who had just purchased a new package probably wouldn't be so interested in the exchange. This would mean that those of the group who had bought the package a longer time ago than the average would tend to be those on whom validity figures were computed. Since their memories wouldn't operate as accurately as those who had just bought the product, this study probably secured depressed measures of validity.

know that observation of the respondents' reading had been made.

Each of the 48 women was asked to tell whether she had "seen," "read some," or "read all" of every one of the 59 items in the magazine. Actual percentages of respondents who answered in each category, and who were observed in each category of behavior, are shown in the table. The experimenters' conclusions that the

	Reported	Observed
	%	%
Seen	64.6	67.0
Read some	31.7	33.4
Read all	22.0	18.3

"reported reading behavior did not differ materially from actual reading behavior" is justified from the data.[6]

Reading behavior is a highly specific activity, and all figures for validity of such replies cannot well be compared to those for voting preferences or brand-buying. Going out to the store is not the same sort of activity as sitting down to read a magazine; one is "business" for the housewife, while the other is recreation. Nor can reading behavior be compared with voting behavior. In the case of the poll on voting behavior the respondent is talking about possible future action, while a report on reading concerns past activity.

5. *Use of market data as a criterion.* This procedure is similar to that used to check the representativeness of the cross-section obtained. In checking the accuracy of the cross-section, characteristics of the sample are compared with known data. In the present case known market data are used as the criterion, and survey results are compared with these.

One preliminary form of a question asked among New Yorkers would have indicated that few persons read the tabloid type of paper—most persons reported reading the better class of paper. A subsequent question form, designed to eliminate this prestige factor, secured evidence that the sample of respondents read various newspapers in proportion to actual circulation figures. The first test

[6] These figures represent *group* rather than *individual* data. Agreement of results for a single individual would tend to be lower than this, since some of the individual disagreements would tend to be canceled out in the group results.

showed low validity, while the validity of the second procedure was acceptable.

Such market data are a common means of checking accuracy. A study designed to measure frequency of readership of various publications naturally will require a comparison of the proportion of respondents reporting purchasing (or readership) of each one with the available circulation figures. Although no investigator has yet provided evidence to supply over-all validity indices, there appears to be no reason why such indices cannot be reported in the future.

Even total consumption figures, without brand breakdowns, are rough evidence of the degree of survey accuracy. From one study (18) where a question was asked about the number of quarts of milk purchased from the store each week, it was possible to estimate the total weekly milk consumption in the New York area. Accuracy of the study was indicated by the fact that this projected figure was remarkably close to the known consumption figures. Although this sort of measurement would be difficult to reduce to an "index," it is nonetheless an accurate and useful means of measuring the validity of certain types of questions.

Market data do not necessarily indicate the validity of any other type of question, for reasons already listed.

6. *Use of advertisement-stimulated sales as a criterion.* Many copy tests have the stated purpose of ranking a given number of advertisements in the order in which they will produce sales. Whether or not this ranking determined by a sample of respondents justifies the choice of the most popular advertisement may be determined only by a large number of studies which show the extent of agreement between the ranking of the advertisements and their pulling power in terms of sales. The final degree of effectiveness of the ordinary commercial advertisement is measured by the sales it produces.

First problem here is to control the advertising situation in such a manner that the "pull" of each of the several advertisements may be accurately measured. The particular method of control will vary with the circumstances.

Some idea of the general procedure may be outlined. A number of publications[7] offer "split-run" advertisement facilities. In this method the advertiser can place four (or some other number) advertisements in the same issue. As the publication rolls off the press, the first copy contains form A of the advertisement, the second form B, the third form C, and the fourth form D. By offering the same product for sale in all four advertisements, the advertiser is able to find, through the keyed-coupon method, which advertisement is responsible for the greatest number of sales. It is a short step to compare these results with those obtained on a consumer survey.

This measure of validity has not been reported extensively, probably because the results are usually so confidential in nature. There are a few such measures available. Schwerin (20) found only .5 per cent discrepancy between consumer preference and keyed-coupon returns for two advertisements. Gould (9) found that only two of six advertisements changed rank at all in his study, and in terms of rank-order correlation coefficient, the two results in his study were comparable.

Although Allen (1) gives no percentage results, his study, conducted similarly, showed that the consumer study accurately predicted the relationship between the volume of inquiries on two advertisements.

It is apparent from these results that the validity of the copy-test procedure, as indicated by the keyed-coupon method, is fairly high. The method cannot be applied to all copy, however, since much copy is not designed to sell, at least in terms of coupons. Yet it is difficult to obtain any measure of advertising "effectiveness" outside of coupons or inquiries, so it seems unlikely that the copy-test procedure for "non-selling" copy can ever be validated.

Since measurement of copy-test accuracy by the coupon method is so specific a procedure, there is no justification for assuming that validity of all copy tests have been shown. Consequently

[7] Among others, the *New York Times* Magazine, *This Week* Magazine, the *New York Herald Tribune* Rotogravure Section, the *New York Sunday News* Rotogravure Section, the *New York Sunday Mirror* Magazine Section, the *Family Circle, Pathfinder, Grit,* and *Woman's Day* fall into the group of publications that offer split-run facilities.

these validity studies do not indicate the accuracy of any other questionnaire surveys.

7. *Use of other behavioral checks as criteria.* Preceding discussion has shown that various types of questions are so distinct from one another that validity findings with one cannot be extended, except with a new investigation, to hold true for another type of question. Not only does the nature of the material in questions differ, but the technique may be unique. The method of collecting the information may vary. The type of investigator or the nature of the sample of respondents may not be a constant. Yet there is one thing that all of these validity measures have in common.

They all utilize some sort of behavior as a criterion. Behavior, after all, is the only possible method of determining whether or not the group of respondents is answering the questions accurately. Almost every survey undertaken is concerned with securing from the individual some indication of how he has acted in the past or how he is likely to behave in the future. Pure opinion questions (those entirely unconcerned with behavior) probably can never be validated. For that reason it is encouraging to note a trend toward the type of questions that ask about behavior rather than about opinion alone. As Link (*15*) observes, the survey that cannot be checked by some measure of behavior is probably of little value anyway.

This sort of behavioral check will require a different sort of criterion for almost every issue to be investigated. If enough of these checks are made on sufficiently different kinds of issues, it may be that some indication of the validity of surveys in general will result. At the present time knowledge of survey validity is limited, and the chances are that where low validity has been found it has not been reported. Unfortunately, it cannot be expected that those in a commercial field will ever publish results which are extremely unfavorable to the entire procedure, as some of these might well be.

The Reliability of Surveys

Another aspect of the problem of survey accuracy is the question of whether the technique obtains consistent results. Useful measures of consistency include: computation of agreement between two or more portions of the sample of respondents on the same survey; determining how closely the replies of the same individual agree when he is questioned twice within a short period of time; and examining the internal consistency of the replies—whether the answers to related questions by the same individuals form a pattern of response which is meaningful.[8]

Each of these methods is measuring something somewhat different from each of the others. They are grouped together here because they are all aspects of the general problem of the consistency of survey results. As in the case of the measurement of validity, the object of any consistency measure should be to determine the degree of agreement of group rather than individual results.

Reliability of surveys is important because the validity of surveys is always limited by the degree of reliability. Without high reliability it is impossible to attain high validity.

1. *Group consistency on a single survey.* This is the most common method of measuring survey reliability. With a fairly large sample of respondents, results may be broken down by comparable sub-samples. One method of selecting these sub-groups is to take all questionnaires and divide them, on a systematized sorting basis, into piles of equal numbers. Although this process ordinarily provides similar groups of respondents, similarity on sampling characteristics must be measured if the comparison of question-by-question results is to be meaningful.

Gallup and Rae (7) use this method in showing the extent of differences resulting from the size of sample utilized. In 1936 they asked a total of 30,000 respondents, *Would you like to see the N.R.A. revived?* When the ballots were completely tabulated there was a "no" vote of 55.5 per cent. The first 500 ballots showed the

---

[8] A fourth type of reliability method can be secured by comparing the results of two independently conducted surveys. This does not seem particularly useful. Surveys made by different organizations are usually made with somewhat different techniques, and under different conditions. Upon final analysis, such a method seems to be comparison of two samples, which is one of the methods discussed here. The difference is that in the present discussion of sample comparison it is assumed that all other factors, such as methodology and time, are similar for the samples.

same result within .5 per cent. Here is the difference made by the additional questionnaires:

Number of Ballots		% Voting Against N.R.A. Revival
First	500	54.9
First	1,000	53.9
First	5,000	55.4
First	10,000	55.4
All	30,000	55.5

This particular table obscures the relationship between each set of 500 returns.

Dr. H. C. Link carried this same sort of procedure to its logical conclusion (*14*). In April, 1934, he conducted a nationwide survey on brand-buying habits. The questionnaires were sorted on a random basis into 51 sets of 100 each. Each set contained the same proportion of interviews made in each section of the country. The proportion of respondents replying in any given way to each question was compared for each group. Following this comparison the questionnaires were combined into new sets containing 500 interviews each, and the process was repeated. Finally comparable groups of 1000 interviews each were compared.

This empirical check revealed that the degree of variation followed almost exactly what one would predict from knowledge of the formula, $\sigma = \sqrt{pq/n}$. This experimental investigation showed roughly the values indicated in the two tables reproduced in the Appendix of this book. Similar empirical checks for other types of questions ought to be undertaken, to determine the degree to which the formula holds true in all survey work. At present those in the survey field are forced to assume, for want of a better tool, that sampling accuracy for all types of survey does follow these results.

There may be reason to believe that the formula is not entirely applicable. Standard error calculation assumes that the data being used fall into a curve of normal distribution. Surveys are, however, affected by considerably more than chance factors. There are many unsuspected and unidentifiable influences. The very selection of the sample itself is not on a random basis, as the formula requires. Most studies today are conducted on a controlled sampling basis. Even in Link's basic study there was a selection of cases; interviewers were assigned the localities in which to work (only urban communities were included), and were told how many of each sex to interview.

At present it is safer to depend largely upon empirical checks of group consistency. Starch's stabilization chart (2) is such a method. This is the same procedure illustrated by Gallup and Rae (7). In practice, questionnaires are added to the results until further addition makes no appreciable difference in the findings.

2. *Individual reliability of response*. In some cases the same group of respondents is interviewed twice over a short period of time, and their answers are compared. This procedure apparently began with sociologists and psychologists in university circles who were interested in measuring the "stability" of replies to personal questionnaires (4, 21). In the survey field there are a number of studies using different types of questions which are along similar lines. Curtis (6), for instance, reports that 70 per cent of a group of respondents answered in the same fashion on two mail questionnaires concerned with regularity of their radio listening. More interesting is a measure of how well the two sets of listening figures agree. In other words, what did the two separate summaries of results of listening habits show in the way of similarity? When the percentage of agreement for *group* results is computed in this case, the figure is 92.3 per cent.[9] It is apparent that some of the individual variations in response were compensated by variations in the opposite direction.

Jenkins (11) has made a detailed study of 19 brand-buying questions in order to measure consistency of response. Interviewers went to 150 homes in the upper-middle income group. Some 48 hours following the original call, field workers completed the identical series of questions with 100 of the same respondents (after explaining that the first sheet had been lost). The agreement for various questions ranged from 85 per cent to 97 per cent. Since this was a measure of individual variation in response, group consistency

[9] The "no answer" replies have been omitted in this computation.

was probably higher. Jenkins concluded that ". . . the high reliability of the method was relatively independent of the class of product investigated."[10]

The length of time between the first and second calls will be an important determinant of reliability. If the time is too short, the respondent will probably recall most of his original replies, so that a measure of memory will be obtained. If the time is too long, the respondent may have changed his behavior in the interim. The very process of interviewing on opinion questions may start a person to thinking about an issue to which he has given no previous consideration. In this situation one should expect to find many less undecided respondents in the second survey than in the first, even where the interval is as short as 48 hours. This is exactly what happens.

For the present, at least, it must be admitted that the *general* consistency of response on surveys is unknown. Due to the many varying factors at work in surveys, general figures of this type may never be known. Only by accumulation of many data is there hope of an answer to the problem.

3. *Internal consistency*. This is a rather loose method, not subject to any rigid technique of analysis. There are two methods applicable here: the consistency of interlocking information obtained to one questionnaire, and the consistency of relationship of the individual's background to his answers.

a. *Consistency of interlocking information*. On most surveys there is an opportunity to include related questions, and the results to one of these questions should be expected to tie in with results to the others. A survey was conducted among a group of workingmen who were being asked their attitudes toward a number of industrial concerns in the area in which they lived. Each respondent was first asked a series of five questions relating to various aspects of employment of each of the concerns. The man was then asked whether or not he would seek employment at the particular company if he were looking for a job, and if not, why not. Answers to

[10] Work in different income brackets might provide varying results. Other types of question probably have somewhat different reliability. Consistency may also be dependent upon factors such as type of questioner and length of questionnaire.

this "why not" inquiry agreed almost perfectly, company by company, with the replies given to the first five specific questions. For the company which obtained the greatest proportion of negative replies to question 4, referring to danger of work, replies to the "why not" question were predominantly "danger."

The particular survey will indicate what questions are related, and how the analysis can be made. If desirable, the individual as well as group consistency on labor attitudes could have been determined, but by and large it is the group figures which are more meaningful in survey research.

b. *Consistency of replies to respondents' backgrounds.* The individual's background is always related in some fashion to the replies he gives. Many of these relationships can be foreseen, and analyses made to determine their exact form. One survey indicated that Democrats were more in favor of the changed date of Thanksgiving than Republicans, which reaction was to be expected. In the question: *If you had been a member of Congress during the past two years, would you have supported every bill recommended by President Roosevelt?* Republicans were found to be more opposed than Democrats. On an issue inquiring about approval or disapproval of the proposal to drop striking WPA workers from the rolls, WPA workers were found to be less favorable toward the idea than the general public. On a recent poll concerning attitudes toward "wartime," farmers, as was expected, showed more opposition than the remainder of the public.

It is evident that respondents' answers in general are consistent with their backgrounds. Survey experts ordinarily make such checks as a matter of course, in order to be certain that they are drawing conclusions warranted from their data. Few such breakdowns are seen by others in the survey field; the internal relationship is a matter largely taken for granted in the presentation of results. Common acceptance of internal consistency is well justified; seldom do surveys show results to the contrary.

Certain aspects of survey accuracy are still open to question. The problem of validity is wide open for a real experimental attack, and it appears that the behavior type of criterion is most promising.

Consistency is by no means a closed affair, to be taken as a matter of course. There is some evidence that group consistency in a single survey follows the pattern suggested by the two tables in the Appendix, but additional evidence is required for "final" verification. Individual reliability figures are all high, but more data are needed. Internal consistency, however, is so common that this is no longer a real problem. This is not a suggestion that internal consistency on a particular survey may be neglected; it is still vital to make sure that the data on a study are internally consistent.

REFERENCES

(1) ALLEN, MARSHALL. "A Way to Pretest Magazine Advertisements," *Market Research*, 1935, 3, No. 4, 10-12.

(2) AMERICAN MARKETING ASSOCIATION. *The Technique of Marketing Research*. New York: McGraw-Hill, 1937, Chapter 19.

(3) ARNOLD, PAULINE. "Is There One Best Method for Measuring Customer Use?" *Sales Management*, 1935, 39, 627-629.

(4) BAIN, REED. "Stability in Questionnaire Response," *American Journal of Sociology*, 1931, 37, 445-453.

(5) BROWN, L. O. *Market Research and Analysis*. New York: Ronald, 1937. Chapter 4.

(6) CURTIS, ALBERTA. "The Reliability of a Report on Listening Habits," *Journal of Applied Psychology*, 1939, 23, 127-130.

(7) GALLUP, GEORGE, AND RAE, S. F. *The Pulse of Democracy*. New York: Simon and Schuster, 1940. Chapter 6.

(8) GOSNELL, H. F. "How Accurate Were the Polls?" *Public Opinion Quarterly*, 1937, 1, 97-105.

(9) GOULD, H. H. "A New Idea in Copy Testing," *Market Research*, 1936, 5, No. 5, 15-17.

(10) HOVDE, H. T. "Recent Trends in the Development of Market Research," *American Marketing Journal*, 1936, 3, 3-19.

(11) JENKINS, J. G. "Dependability of Psychological Brand Barometers. I. The Problem of Reliability," *Journal of Applied Psychology*, 1938, 22, 1-7.

(12) JENKINS, J. G. AND CORBIN, H. H. "Dependability of Psychological Brand Barometers. II. The Problem of Validity," *Journal of Applied Psychology*, 1938, 22, 252-260.

(13) KATZ, DANIEL. "The Public Opinion Polls and the 1940 Election," *Public Opinion Quarterly*, 1941, 5, 52-78.

(14) LINK, H. C. "How Many Interviews are Necessary for Results of a Certain Accuracy?" *Journal of Applied Psychology*, 1937, 21, 1-17.

(15) LINK, H. C. "The Problem of Validity vs. Reliability in Public Opinion Polls," *Public Opinion Quarterly,* 1942, 6, 87-98.

(16) LUDEKE, H. C., AND INGLIS, R. A. "A Technique for Validating Interviewing Methods in Reader Research," *Sociometry,* 1942, 5, 109-122.

(17) MENEFEE, S. C. "The Effect of Stereotyped Words on Political Judgments," *American Sociological Review,* 1936, 1, 614-621.

(18) ROSLOW, SYDNEY, AND BLANKENSHIP, A. B. "Phrasing the Question in Consumer Research," *Journal of Applied Psychology,* 1939, 23, 612-622.

(19) ROSLOW, SYDNEY, WULFECK, W. H., AND CORBY, P. G. "Consumer and Opinion Research: Experimental Studies on the Form of the Question," *Journal of Applied Psychology,* 1940, 24, 334-346.

(20) SCHWERIN, HORACE. "Copy Pre-Testing," *Printers' Ink,* November 1, 1940, 67-68.

(21) SMITH, M. "A Note on Stability in Questionnaire Response," *American Journal of Sociology,* 1933, 38, 713-720.

(22) WARNER, LUCIEN. "The Reliability of Public Opinion Surveys," *Public Opinion Quarterly,* 1939, 3, 376-390.

CHAPTER 15

The Case Against the Questionnaire Survey

> It is possible to make a survey prove anything. It is just a matter of picking the right people or establishments to survey, and framing the questions so that the desired answers will be obtained.
>
> —ASPLEY (3, p. 225)

wwwwwwwwwwwwwwwwwwwwwwwwwwwwwwwwwwwwwwwwwwwwwwwwwwwwwwwwwwwwwwwwwwwwwwwwwwww

THIS is the sort of criticism that has been leveled against all kinds of surveys and all sorts of survey organizations.

The very complexity of the survey technique is one reason that criticisms about the procedure have been numerous. Previous chapters have shown how factors such as the wording and sequence of questions, the nature and size of the sample of respondents, the timing of the study, the process of interviewing, and other elements each play a role in determining accuracy. The criticisms which have been made are broader than procedure; there are claims that surveys are detrimental to our way of life. The two types of criticism fall into different categories, and deserve separate discussion.

CRITICISMS OF THE TECHNIQUE

A recent questionnaire (11) was circulated among those in the survey field. One question inquired what the researcher considered the principal defects of present commercial methods.[1] The proportion of respondents mentioning the most frequently-named criticisms is shown below.

Improperly-worded questions	74%
Inadequacy of sample	52%
Improper statistical methods	44%

[1] Although this study is several years old, and concerned commercial research rather than surveys in general, there seems little reason why the results cannot be applied to present-day questionnaire research. The comments should at least be suggestive.

Items such as lack of adequate supervision and checking of field workers, poor exploratory work, classification of respondents on income rather than standard of living, and use of inexperienced investigators also aroused comment.

1. *Are questions likely to be biased?* Several times a bill has been introduced into Congress calling for an investigation of public opinion polls. Columnists have attacked polls. The use of biased questions was usually a major point in these attacks.

It is true that leading questions are sometimes asked. Chapter 5 gave examples of leading questions that were asked on nation-wide surveys. There seems no evidence that any set of poll questions shows definite and constant bias in favor of a particular concept or group. Wording bias is probably present, where it occurs, because of accident rather than intent.

Experimental attacks on the influence of wording are a relatively new procedure in the survey field. Not all sources of wording bias are clearly recognized. As additional experiments of this sort continue, frequency of biased questions can be expected to decrease. At present there is justification for a careful examination of questions used on any particular study, since the chance of biased wording is somewhat greater than negligible.

2. *Do surveys ask questions on which respondents lack a real opinion?* The charge has also been made that some questions are asked about which the public has no opinion, and that results from such questions will be misleading. The issues included should be close to the experiences of those interviewed. As Robinson (*15*) states, a vote on easier divorce or child labor is more significant than one on the tariff or the gold content of the dollar. The public must have knowledge of the subject for the issue to obtain meaningful results. If the public lacks knowledge on the particular subject, "snap" judgments may be secured. These judgments are likely to change after the person has become acquainted with the significance of the issue.

This problem of relating questions with information is one which polls cannot solve, according to Gallup and Rae (8). As far as public opinion surveys are concerned, they think that the ultimate solution of this lack of knowledge rests with the press, the radio, and political parties. Perhaps so, but it is in order for survey technicians to make certain that they don't make an assumption of knowledge on issues where ignorance is the rule.

There are two things that the survey researcher can do here to be on solid ground. Sufficient pre-testing provides clues to the extent of information on the particular issue. Question sequence can be so arranged that the respondent will start thinking about the particular issue before the specific question is asked. If this background of thought on the issue is provided by the question arrangement, there should be little reason for assuming that people will give spot reactions in place of thoughtful answers. The sequence of questions naturally does not offer any advantage with the respondent who just doesn't know anything on the issue.

3. *Is the pre-testing frequently insufficient?* This accusation is largely true. Primary reason for this probably is that so many commercial surveys are rushed for time. The client frequently wants results before the project has had sufficient time to get under way.

Since almost every survey does include issues so divergent from those previously covered, pre-testing is a requisite. No scientific investigation can make use of an adaptation of procedure without exploratory experimental work, and the questionnaire field is no exception.

4. *Does the survey fail to measure intensity of opinion?* Argument of the critics who raise this question runs that a minority of the public might favor the return of prohibition, for example, but that this minority might be so well organized and vociferous that it would do more than its opponents in influencing custom, editorial policy, and even legislation. Present-day surveys are quantitative rather than qualitative. Mere inclusion of the words "mildly" and "strongly" in the question for the respondent to indicate the degree of his feeling is not a solution to the problem.

The only real measure of intensity is a question concerning past, present, or future behavior of the respondent. To find out how strongly a person believes that the Axis powers will bomb the United States, he can be asked, as a corollary question, whether he or any members of his family have joined the civilian defense efforts. Many surveys are today using this sort of approach, and it can be predicted that the proportion of such behavior questions will rise in the future. The problem is another aspect of phrasing the question, an aspect of surveys in which advances are being made every day.

5. *Are the samples of respondents obtained adequate?* This is a question defying general answer, since it always depends upon the particular investigation. Before 1935 there was some justification for this criticism's being made on a wide-scale basis and applying to the work of most organizations. The *Digest* vote went wrong because it sampled too many of the upper-income levels. The Gallup poll hit this same snag in a minor way in both the 1936 and the 1940 presidential predictions. Strangely enough, those who criticize the sample appear to be less interested in its nature than in its size.

Critics who make this charge do not understand that the nature of the sample is considerably more important than its mere size. The millions of ballots collected by the *Literary Digest*, according to the size theory, should have been closer to actual presidential preference than the "scientific" surveys which were operating with the number of ballots at most in the thousands. Assuming that a representative sample of respondents has been obtained, the tables in the Appendix show that it is possible to obtain survey results representative of the view of the entire nation within 5 per cent with less than 1000 calls. Since the chapter on sampling has outlined the steps to be followed in scientific sampling procedure, these need not be discussed here.

6. *Is the average interviewer competent?* A number of faults have been laid at the doorstep of the field force. Some claim that investigators are frequently biased, or that they are insufficiently trained. Both of these criticisms are sometimes true. In the organizations most concerned with careful work, however, the problems of the field force are receiving more attention than formerly, although this is still one of the most neglected aspects of survey work.

Most training of field workers, for instance, is determined at a desk; training of interviewers should be subjected to experimental attack in much the same manner that questions are asked and tested during the course of the pre-test and sample study.

There is room for a great deal of improvement in the competency of the field force. Until the particular organization has shown that its field force is competent, there is good reason to entertain a healthy doubt. Even a highly competent force does make interviewing errors.

7. *Are survey technicians justified in classifying respondents in terms of income rather than standard of living?* The argument here runs that the same income will mean different things in different localities. Where the study is made in only one locality there is no criticism—either income or standard of living may be used. Different localities included in the same study will require application of the standard-of-living classification.

A $5000 income in New York City is different from the same income in a small southern town. The $5000 could buy considerably less in New York. The Alabama $5000 would place the respondent among the group of highest-income people in his area, while the New Yorker with the same amount would be much closer to average income in his community. In terms of probable habits and attitudes, this New Yorker would be identified with an Alabama group of considerably less than $5000. The Alabama $5000 would belong with a higher New York income.

That is why, in survey work, it is more common to talk in terms of standard-of-living groups rather than income groups. If the population is grouped into the upper 5 per cent, the next 35 per cent, the next 40 per cent, and the lowest 20 per cent in each community, then the highest level will be roughly comparable throughout the United States in terms of standard of living and behavior. On the other hand, if all of those with incomes of over $5000 throughout the United States were thrown together, there would be a motley crew representing a variety of living standards. Straight income could be used only if the upper 5 per cent in terms of income in each community were classed together. This procedure could become complicated in a large-scale survey.

The use of standard-of-living classifications in questionnaire surveys is becoming common.

8. *Are inapplicable statistical techniques sometimes used?* The use of inapplicable statistical techniques has sometimes been made as an accusation against those in the survey field. This criticism is

made with some justification. As indicated throughout this volume, statistics is an important tool in survey work, both in the planning of the sample of respondents and in the analysis of results.

Some survey statistics have been totally incorrect in their application. Three sorts of errors of statistical method as applied to survey work are: (a) errors of calculation, (b) errors of logic or reasoning, and (c) failure to describe statistical procedures or raw material. The first type of error, though important, is least significant in a discussion of statistical procedures, and will not be taken up here.

b. *Errors of logic or reasoning.* There can be no reason for using a statistical procedure designed to give results accurate within 1 per cent if the collected data themselves are known to contain more inaccuracy than this. In one case a multiple correlational analysis was applied to survey data, and the statistician claimed that this treatment insured a probable error of 2.49 per cent in the final result. The statement made it appear that the final survey results were accurate within this range. The inference was misleading, since some of the factors known to affect the results were purposely omitted when the survey was undertaken.[2] The application of statistical method cannot and does not increase the accuracy of the raw data.

Some surveys are made to appear highly accurate by the use of figures carried to two decimal places. One study[3] reports that 6.09 per cent of 3016 persons interviewed planned to buy Norge refrigerators. Since the standard error of 6 per cent based on 3000 cases is .43 per cent, it is meaningless to give a percentage figure to the hundredths decimal place.

In some cases statistics used may be sound, but inferences drawn as a result of statistical analysis may be entirely fallacious. One widely circulated report concerning the effectiveness of a particular advertising medium illustrates the point. This survey purports to show that the particular medium sells goods. This is "proved" by showing that a greater percentage of those reached by the medium buy the particular goods advertised in that medium than is the case with those who are not reached by the medium. Statistics presented

[2] This example was cited in (2).
[3] Sources of most of these examples cannot be given for obvious reasons.

show that those reached do buy more of the advertised goods—there is no question of that fact. But the argument falls to pieces when it is realized that the influence of standard of living has not been shown. On analysis of the detailed data we learn, for example, that 23 per cent of those reached by the medium own the advertised brand, while only 21 per cent of those not reached own the product. Final figures result only because there is high ownership of the particular brand in the upper standard-of-living group accompanied by high coverage of the medium. Both low ownership and low coverage are the rule in the lower groups. In other words, there is a serious question as to whether sales of the product were due to income, coverage of the medium, or a combination of both.

c. *Failure to consider or describe statistical procedures or raw material.* Careful collection of statistical data is always required to show that the sample of respondents obtained is a representative one for the particular investigation. One survey organization made two studies on the same subject at an interval of one year. Their reports show that they went to considerable trouble in measuring characteristics of respondents to each questionnaire. Yet the later report makes uncritical comparisons of the two surveys. The surveys were not conducted in precisely the same localities nor were the interviews distributed geographically in the same proportions.

The same sort of failure to disregard statistical evidence was indicated in the failure of the *Literary Digest* straw vote of 1936. It has previously been stated that this failure was due primarily to the biased sample of respondents secured by the magazine—respondents who were predominantly telephone and automobile owners. When respondents were asked for whom they had voted in 1932 there was too high a proportion of Republican responses, but the sponsors of the poll apparently disregarded this fact.

It is questionable whether it is worse to disregard essential sampling characteristics which have been gathered, or to fail to obtain these statistics at all. In one mail questionnaire conducted by an inexperienced organization there was no effort to measure the essential characteristics of respondents. Since survey organizations have consistently reported difficulties in securing a representative sample by the mail procedure, this oversight makes the entire result meaningless.

Surveys have rightfully been criticized for presenting statistics which are inapplicable, or for the failure to present necessary statistics. It is also common to hear the remark that it is impossible to decipher the meaning of the statistics. This is a real point against those in the survey field; if the report is designed for consumption by those who lack detailed statistical knowledge, there is no excuse for presenting a great deal of detail. In such cases it is more than sufficient to footnote the over-all results with the statement of what procedures were used to arrive at the conclusion.

Summary. Despite all of the criticisms that have been made against statistical techniques, there is still general acceptance of survey results. In the field of the opinion poll, for instance, a recent study (12) showed that 85 per cent of Senate and House members believed that polls either wholly or in part accurately measure public opinion. The business survey appears to have fully as wide an acceptance in the business field, although the lay public (owing to their lack of acquaintance with business surveys) probably would not accept such results as quickly as those gathered by opinion polls.

CRITICISM OF THE EFFECT OF SURVEYS
ON OUR SOCIAL SYSTEM

It is more difficult to answer the questions raised about the sociological effects of questionnaire investigations, for many of these criticisms concern points which cannot be answered in terms of fact. Nevertheless, it is valuable to consider some of the points which have been raised here. Since this type of criticism varies for the opinion poll and for the commercial survey, their points should be considered separately. The points outlined here all refer particularly to the opinion poll; arguments concerning the commercial survey have been summarized in the first chapter.

A major point has been that the opinion poll tends to destroy our system of democracy. Although this topic has also been discussed somewhat in the first chapter, some of the specific criticisms are worth consideration here. These are: (1) Polls take power from our legislators, thus changing our system of representative government; (2) the public cannot decide the issues; (3) polls discourage voters from casting votes; (4) election poll results tend to make the losers give up the fight; and (5) there is a rush of voters to get on the apparently winning side.

1. *Do they take power away from our legislators,* and thus change our system of representative government? The *New York Times* has claimed that our form of government calls for the election of representatives to handle controversial and complex issues of government. According to the argument, the polls tend to force our legislators to become mere puppets in the hands of the public. Desire of the legislators to be re-elected causes them to follow the wishes of their constituents rather than their own best judgment.

The argument that polls take power away from our legislators is both true and untrue. It is correct that the legislator will not dare as frequently as he did before to defy public opinion. Significant in this connection is Lewis' finding (12) that 30 per cent of a group of Senators and Congressmen reported that they were aided in deciding desires of their constituents either wholly or in part by the polls. When the question was asked impersonally, 70 per cent believed that other men in public life were aided in deciding their policies through the results of opinion polls.

In another sense the polls have given legislators additional power. They need no longer fear minority groups whose voting power is unknown. It was reported, for instance, that a minority pressure group recently went before a congressional committee to demand that a bill be killed. A member of the committee simply retorted that the people wanted the bill to pass, and that little matter was settled.

The real issue is not whether the power of legislators is being lost. It is more nearly correct to inquire whether the purposes of our government are better served by having our representatives vote without knowledge of public opinion on the issues, or by having them vote with such information at their command. In this connection it is interesting to observe the results of polls and congressional voting behavior during the war crisis. The public preceded congressional action on increased defense expenditures, the draft, increased taxation, and other defense steps. All along during the war crisis the public has been a step or two ahead of Congress.

This approaches the next criticism, which is actually a corollary of the one just discussed.

2. *Is the public capable of deciding issues?* One prominent sociologist (13) has written that ". . . a major problem democracy faces is to persuade the individual citizen that things are not as simple as he has been wont to believe, that he is not as competent as he thinks he is, and that many issues cannot be solved simply by taking positions 'for' or 'against' them and totaling up 'the truth.'" (p.219)

This is a sensible note of caution for opinion surveyors not to oversimplify issues, and not to inquire about issues that are too complex. It should not be interpreted as a suggestion that the public is incapable of making decisions on any issues, for the public has shown in the present emergency that it has sound judgment. Gallup and Rae (8, p. 287) go farther: "The serious observer of public opinion on scores of issues cannot fail to come away with a feeling of intense admiration for the honesty and common sense with which an enormous number of ordinary people in all walks of life and at all levels of the economic scale have continued to meet their responsibilities as citizens. He will be profoundly impressed with the grasp of broad principles which voters of all types possess, and with their capacity to adjust themselves to the ever-changing movement of events."

3. *Do poll results discourage voters from going to the polls?* The argument here is that since polls reveal ahead of time what the outcome will be, voters lose interest in casting ballots. Facts do not bear out this criticism. In 1932 there were almost 40 million votes cast for President. Four years later, when both the *Digest* and the Gallup polls were widely known, there were almost 46 million votes cast. In 1940 almost 50 million went to the polls. Interest in elections seems to be on the increase, either in spite of, or because of, the polls.

4. *Do election-poll results tend to make the apparent losers give up the fight?* This indictment goes on to say that such an effect is detrimental to our democratic way of life. Closely related to the argument is the idea that there is a "bandwagon" vote—those who

are undecided as to which way to vote will be influenced by survey returns, and will want to vote with the winning side. Since these points are separate, though similar, they will be discussed separately.

There is no evidence to show that the apparent losers give up the fight. There are, as one writer (15) has shown, all sorts of factors which affect the morale of those on one side or the other of a political fence. If an effort is to be made to prevent the rank-and-file from learning any bad news at all, then they should not be told, for example, the decision of a strong union to support their opposition. Where should such a line be drawn?

There is evidence to show that the losing side does not tend to give up the fight. The Socialists have continued to nominate a presidential candidate every four years although they can be sure that they haven't a chance of electing him. In 1936 the Republicans knew before the election that their chances of winning were fairly slim. They put on a good fight despite that knowledge.

5. *Is there a rush of voters to get on the apparently winning side?* This possible "bandwagon" effect deserves more serious consideration than the preceding point. In Lewis' study among Congressmen (12), 50 per cent of our legislators sampled reported that they believed polls produced such an effect. Gallup and Rae (8) argue that there is little evidence for the bandwagon effect. They claim that if there were a bandwagon influence, it would always (p. 249) "be true that between the first pre-election poll forecasts and the actual vote on election day, a substantial rise could be logically expected." An analysis of scores of past elections on which sentiment was measured shows that in most cases there is no such rise. In an effort to get at the question experimentally, Gallup and Rae (9) asked this question on a survey: *Do you happen to know which Democratic (Republican) candidate is leading today in the polls on Presidential candidates?* Preferences of Democrats (Republicans) who knew the leader and who did not know the leader were compared, and it was found that the two groups within each party had the same distribution of preferences.

Robinson (15), using much the same election data, argues that "these examples do not prove that voters are unswayed by straw polls, because it can always be argued that the . . . trend . . . would have been more pronounced . . ." if the polls had not been made. That is to say there may be, in the cases examined, a trend for the person in the lead in the first poll gradually to have his advantage cut, but who can tell how much greater that trend might have been except for the publicizing of the polls? As Robinson concludes, however, the evidence surely argues against too easy an acceptance of the bandwagon theory.

Roslow, Hochstim, and Manheimer (*18*) have performed an interesting study which bears directly on this question of a band-wagon vote. Three questions were asked of 400 respondents imme-diately preceding the 1940 presidential election:

> Whom would you vote for today for President?
> What Presidential straw votes or polls have you heard of?
> Who is leading in (the poll or polls heard of)?

Some 79 per cent of those who had heard of a poll in which Roosevelt was leading reported that they would vote for Roosevelt. Of those who had heard of a poll in which Willkie led, only 49 per cent would vote for Willkie. It was concluded that there was a definite relation between people's voting behavior and their knowl-edge of poll results. As these writers point out, this conclusion does not necessarily prove that the poll has influenced the voters, for possibly voters look for the polls which show that their candidate is in the lead. The study does indicate that a more careful investi-gation of the bandwagon theory is necessary. There is at least a reasonable question of doubt about the glib answer that poll results do not influence voting behavior.

The whole problem is one that is still wide open for a real experimental attack. However, should a bandwagon effect be shown, this is not necessarily an argument against the opinion survey. As Allport (*1*) points out, the danger in a democracy is that propaganda may convince the ordinary citizen, in lieu of reliable evidence, that public opinion is on the side favored by the propagandists. It seems safer to permit polls, a reliable opinion indicator, to influence the voter than for him to be swayed by false propaganda.

6. *Are poll results sometimes manipulated to distort results?* An affirmative answer to this question would indicate great potential

danger to the democratic system. Legislators and the public have faith in opinion polls, and legislation is influenced by their results. The correlated argument is that the government should take over polls in order to insure their honesty.

Although it is difficult to prove or disprove this charge of manipulation, it seems safe to say that some "minor" polls probably were distorted in favor of the groups for whom they were conducted. A nation-wide poll paid for by unions would be subject to fully as much question as one sponsored by a group of wealthy industrialists. On the other hand, it seems highly unlikely that the nationally-known polls have ever intentionally distorted their results. As the director of one of these polls remarked, "You can be dishonest in this business only once and then it is curtains!" The remark assumes that there is an election upon which the survey accuracy can be checked.

There is another angle to consider here. The popularized polls are underwritten by publications. Although a *sine qua non* of the publishing business is reader confidence (hence no publication could afford to deceive its readers), at the same time almost all publications have some sort of editorial bias. Gallup states that seldom have newspapers refused to print any of his releases, even when they conflicted with editorial policy, but this is not sufficient answer. The very fact that the Gallup poll is subscribed to and paid for by newspapers means that polls have to have material generally acceptable to the newspapers, or they would never have subscribed to it in the first place. This is not a charge of distortion; it is simply pointing out the possibility that the Gallup poll material may be collected with an eye toward its ultimate newspaper publication.

Suppose that the government were to control all these surveys. In time of crisis or war it is entirely reasonable to suppose that the government might censor results it felt to be damaging. The public would then have little idea of popular reaction to many vital issues, and its entire thinking could be colored by this effort at propaganda. If politicians gained control of the polls the distortion might be worse. What would prevent political hacks from use of biased wordings, from obtaining of biased samples of respondents? Presumably, with government control, there could be no outside surveys made to check such accuracy, so there would be little occasion for the public to realize the deception.

Of course the government has already started, and surely should continue, to appraise public reaction to many of its programs, but there just doesn't seem to be any real reason why government should take over all polling work.

7. *Pre-election surveys are dangerous because they cannot predict with sufficiently high accuracy.* This charge states that the pre-election polls are likely to mis-predict, and the effect could hurt our democratic system. In 1940, it will be remembered, Gallup's last survey (conducted the Sunday preceding election Tuesday) found sentiment so evenly divided between Roosevelt and Willkie that Gallup did not venture any prediction. Then Roosevelt, in terms of electoral votes, was "overwhelmingly" re-elected. The layman naturally wanted to know how this could happen; those within the survey field raised the same question. If the opinion poll cannot predict, of what value is it?

In an effort to determine how many of 10 previous elections the opinion polls with their present degree of accuracy could have predicted, Blankenship and Manheimer (4) analyzed the state-by-state election returns for 10 previous presidential elections. In this analysis it was assumed that the "poll" made beforehand would unknowingly hit each state vote "on the nose." This would mean that whenever the state showed more than 54 per cent of its vote for one of the two major candidates, the poll would have classified the electoral votes of the state as sure for the particular candidate. Because of the 4 per cent margin of error which the polls allow themselves, however, any state returns falling between 46 and 54 per cent for a candidate would have to be classed as doubtful. The problem then became: In how many of the 10 elections could a majority of electoral votes have been predicted for one candidate? In 7 of the 10 elections there could have been a definite prediction that one of the candidates would win, while in another there was a great possibility that the poll-taker would have ventured a prediction. In only 2 of the elections was there such a large number of doubtful states that the result could not have been predicted.

The same method of analysis was applied to the 1936 and the

1940 results, and it was found that the 1936 vote could have been predicted, while the 1940 vote could not. This was the experience of the Gallup poll. If the 10 elections considered are at all typical, there seems reason to believe that 1940 was an atypical year, and that the usual presidential election would permit a prediction.

8. *Contribution of the opinion poll.* The discussion of social criticisms against the opinion poll has brought to light a number of definite contributions the polls make to our democratic way of life. There are still other ways in which the polls help our democratic system. Opinion polls are helping to educate the public. They are bringing issues to the attention of the average citizen, not merely by the questioning process, but by the reporting of the results in newspapers and other publications. There seems little doubt that the public will become more interested in such results with passage of time.

Opinion polls also help democracy by the separation of issues and men. Before advent of the polls, candidates to offices seemed to assume that the public was expressing approval for all of their present and past policies. The public opinion poll has shown that this is not true. During the time that President Roosevelt was attempting to enlarge the Supreme Court (one of the efforts he felt justified in after his 1936 re-election), all the surveys which covered the issue found that the majority of the public was opposed to the plan. In his effort to "purge" Democratic opponents from Congress the polls also found a majority opposed. Yet it should be realized that at both of these times the public was still overwhelmingly in favor of Mr. Roosevelt as President. Gallup and Rae (8) report that many polls showed public disapproval of certain New Deal measures, although the majority of respondents were still in favor of the New Deal as such. Acceptance of leaders or of a program does not mean blind acceptance of all policies under such a label.

So far all of the considered criticisms have been concerned with the public opinion poll and its effect on our democratic system. There have been relatively few attacks against the effect of the commercial survey on our social system except by those who object to our social system. These views will not be discussed here. Although most businessmen are reasonably well convinced of the contribution offered by the commercial survey, there is one charge that requires a little consideration.

9. *Are too many surveys a waste of time and money*, thus hurting our social system? A number of questionnaire surveys are a waste of time and money, and any such waste cannot be considered an asset to our social system. There are many "promotional" types of surveys which are attempting to sell goods or services. Not infrequently one sees a promotion piece sent out by an advertising medium that reports survey results which are misleading and meaningless. Many other commercial studies are a waste of effort.

This fact is probably due to two reasons: Business has probably been oversold on surveys, and many surveys are conducted by persons inexperienced in research work. Some questionnaire studies have been so startling and revealing that there is a tendency on some sides to regard the survey as a "cure-all," an end in itself. The survey is never an end in itself, but merely an agency to learn facts.

The tendency for inexperienced personnel to conduct surveys will probably disappear with time. It is hoped, at least, that this book may have pointed out so many dangers in the technique that an inexperienced reader would not attempt to conduct such a study.

Summary. There seems every reason for surveys to continue their progress. The first chapter has shown the many values of the business survey in the world of today, and the present chapter has demonstrated the many advantages of the public opinion poll. Because of the survey's contributions to democracy and business, and its probable improvements in technique, the questionnaire survey seems destined to increase in importance as a part of our way of life.

REFERENCES

(1) ALLPORT, F. H. "Polls and the Science of Public Opinion," *Public Opinion Quarterly*, 1940, 4, 249-257.
(2) AMERICAN MARKETING ASSOCIATION. *The Technique of Marketing Research*. New York: McGraw-Hill, 1937. Chapter 19.
(3) ASPLEY, J. C. (Editor) *The Sales Manager's Handbook*. New York: Dartnell, 1934. Pages 175 and 225.
(4) BLANKENSHIP, A. B., AND MANHEIMER, D. I. "Whither Public Opinion Polls?" *Journal of Psychology*, 1941, 12, 7-12.

(5) CHERINGTON, P. T. "Opinion Polls as the Voice of Democracy," *Public Opinion Quarterly*, 1940, 4, 236-238.

(6) CHICAGO ROUND TABLE DISCUSSION. Election and results. November 6, 1941.

(7) CHICAGO ROUND TABLE DISCUSSION. Testing public opinion. November 5, 1939.

(8) GALLUP, GEORGE, AND RAE, S. F. *The Pulse of Democracy*. New York: Simon and Schuster, 1940. Chapters 18, 19, 20, 21, 22, and 23.

(9) GALLUP, GEORGE, AND RAE, S. F. "Is There a Bandwagon Vote?" *Public Opinion Quarterly*, 1940, 4, 244-249.

(10) HARTWELL, D. J. "Business Asks the Public How It May Serve Best," *Nation's Business*, May, 1940, 26-28.

(11) HOVDE, H. T. "Recent Trends in the Development of Market Research," *American Marketing Journal*, 1936, 3, 3-19.

(12) LEWIS, G. F. "The Congressmen Look at the Polls," *Public Opinion Quarterly*, 1940, 4, 229-231.

(13) LYND, R. S. "Democracy in Reverse," *Public Opinion Quarterly*, 1940, 4, 218-220.

(14) McGUIRE, O. R. "The U. S. Constitution and Ten Shekels of Silver," *Public Opinion Quarterly*, 1940, 4, 232-235.

(15) ROBINSON, C. S. "Recent Developments in the Straw-Poll Field," *Public Opinion Quarterly*, 1937, July, 45-56; October, 42-52.

(16) ROBINSON, D. E. "In Agency Research, Results May Be Better if These Pet Don'ts Are Heeded," *Printers' Ink*, March 15, 1940, 61.

(17) ROPER, ELMO. "Three Weaknesses of Market Research," *Market Research*, 1938, 8, No. 6, 16-19.

(18) ROSLOW, SYDNEY, HOCHSTIM, JOSEPH, AND MANHEIMER, D. I. "Voting Behavior and Pre-election Polls." Unpublished Manuscript. 1941.

Index

ACP - 6956

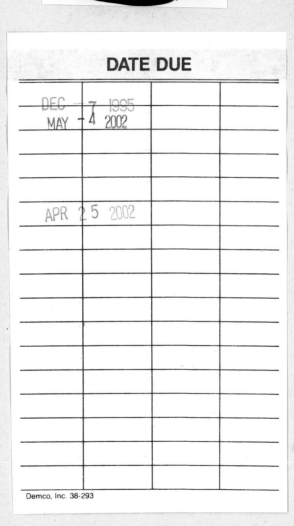

ACCURACY OBTAINED (EXPRESSED IN TWO STANDARD ERRORS) WITH VARIOUS SAMPLE SIZES AND PERCENTAGES[a]

Size of Sample	Expected or Observed Per Cent				
	10% or 90%	20% or 80%	30% or 70%	40% or 60%	50%
100	6.00	8.00	9.16	9.80	10.00
200	4.24	5.66	6.48	6.92	7.08
300	3.46	4.62	5.30	5.66	5.78
400	3.00	4.00	4.58	4.90	5.00
500	2.68	3.58	4.10	4.38	4.48
750	2.20	2.92	3.34	3.58	3.66
1000	1.90	2.52	2.90	3.10	3.16
1500	1.54	2.06	2.36	2.52	2.58
2000	1.34	1.78	2.04	2.20	2.24
2500	1.20	1.60	1.84	1.96	2.00
3000	1.10	1.46	1.68	1.78	1.82
4000	.94	1.26	1.44	1.54	1.58
5000	.84	1.14	1.30	1.38	1.42
6000	.78	1.04	1.18	1.26	1.30
7000	.72	.96	1.10	1.18	1.20
8000	.68	.90	1.02	1.10	1.12
9000	.64	.84	.96	1.04	1.06
10000	.60	.80	.92	.98	1.00
15000	.48	.66	.74	.80	.82
20000	.42	.56	.64	.70	.70
30000	.34	.46	.52	.56	.58
40000	.30	.40	.46	.50	.50

[a] Adapted and computed from H. C. Link, "How Many Interviews Are Necessary for Results of a Certain Accuracy?" *Journal of Applied Psychology*, 1937, 21, 1-17.